Value-Added
Measures in Education

Value-Added Measures in Education

What Every Educator Needs to Know

DOUGLAS N. HARRIS

HARVARD EDUCATION PRESS
CAMBRIDGE, MASSACHUSETTS

Second Printing, 2012

Library of Congress Control Number 2010942132

Paperback ISBN 978-1-61250-000-3

Library Edition ISBN 978-1-934742-06-8

Published by Harvard Education Press,
an imprint of the Harvard Education Publishing Group

Harvard Education Press
8 Story Street
Cambridge, MA 02138

Cover Design: Sarah Henderson

The typefaces used in this book are Adobe Garamond and Futura.

Contents

Foreword

All children need and deserve to be taught by good teachers. How do we achieve that crucial goal? How do we systematically and consistently help new teachers to become good teachers, good teachers to become great teachers, and struggling teachers to improve their practice or leave the profession?

In *Value-Added Measures in Education*, Doug Harris discusses one of the promising—and undoubtedly most controversial—measures of teacher effectiveness available today. It is also among the most complex and difficult to understand. I can't tell you how many times I've said to myself and others, "I really wish someone would just explain this stuff in one place." Harris's effort to bring this technical discussion out of stuffy university halls filled with statisticians and economists, to those directly responsible for improving our schools is not merely welcome, it is way overdue.

There is so much about value-added models that parents, teachers, and administrators don't understand. Scholars and other experts have explained pieces of the puzzle in various places, but before now, nobody has brought all these pieces together in one place, and the resulting picture that emerges is clear and accessible.

There is also much about what works in the classroom that only teachers understand fully. Perhaps this book's greatest achievement is that it is not only accessible, but that it explains the concept of value-added in a manner that accounts for the practical realities in the classroom. And if value-added is to fulfill its potential, it must be implemented in a manner that teachers understand, support, and can use.

In this book, Harris addresses three unifying themes for the debate around value-added that stand out as particularly important. The first is that value-added models, like any policy tool, have significant limitations. While they also have a lot of potential, they are not ready for a dispositive role in public education. Harris doesn't try to develop another list of the pros and cons of value-added, although he does a good job of explaining them. Rather, he tries to provide frontline educators, parents, and policymakers with the information they need to make informed decisions, including whether value-added estimations should be used for high-stakes decisions.

In making these decisions, the first thing we need to acknowledge is that value-added is not, in and of itself, the way to portray or really understand teacher effectiveness. Using research and common sense, Harris shows how value-added alone cannot improve instruction and underscores the need for additional information that, when combined with value-added results, can provide a more useful and accurate picture of effectiveness and how to increase it.

The second theme is that any use (or even discussion) of value-added is incomplete and misleading without an accounting for error. Those who follow politics know that pundits routinely talk about political polls but pay little or no attention to the margin of error, which tells us the range in which the "real" number is located. That might not be such a big deal on cable television talk shows, but it is a huge deal in education policy.

Harris clearly explains the various sources of imprecision, including the important idea that one of these sources is flaws in the models. For instance, models assume that students are randomly assigned to classes the way patients are assigned in a medical trial, even though all teachers know that they are not, often for good educational reasons (some teachers are better at meeting the needs of some types of students). Harris is also effective in explaining the incredibly important concept of random error, which is always a part of value-added. He describes how, due largely to the fact that classes are small, we need larger samples to create accurate estimates. The concept of error must be explicitly incorporated into the use of value-added, or we run the awful risk of labeling effective teachers ineffective, and vice versa.

At the same time, Harris presents a convincing argument that value-added's imprecision need not be a deal breaker as long as we understand where it comes from and how to account for it when these measures are used in schools. We cannot expect any measures of teacher quality—value-added or others—to be perfect.

The third theme, closely related to the second, is that using value-added in education policy is an exercise in trade-offs. More sophisticated models give better results, but they are also more difficult to understand. Additional years of data can dramatically improve accuracy, but there is an urgency to begin using every tool at our disposal immediately to address our education problems. Harris takes on these difficult choices directly and, in doing so, effectively addresses the tension between theory and practice.

Although we can never eliminate its imprecision, we can use value-added in ways that minimize it. This includes ensuring the quality and accuracy of data sets, using at least two years of data, implementing school-wide value-added (which would also promote collaboration and teamwork among teachers), and most importantly, combining value-added with other measures to provide a complete picture of teacher effectiveness.

I think most teachers are willing to accept the fact that they might not easily understand every technical detail about value-added, as long as they can know enough to be confident that it is being used responsibly, collaboratively, and for the purpose of improving instruction. However, "enough" knowledge is still a lot when it comes to having confidence in the use of value-added, and explaining the model to teachers is a difficult endeavor. This book is, in many important respects, the first that promises to achieve this goal. It is written *by* an expert, but *for* teachers and parents.

That's why I strongly encourage not only teachers, but also administrators and other school officials, to read this book closely. Just like learning, education policy is a collaborative process that builds on shared knowledge and premises; we must agree on the facts to proceed. Doug Harris has laid these out for us, along with the challenges they present. It's up to us to address them going forward.

Randi Weingarten
President, American Federation of Teachers,
AFL-CIO

Introduction

Since the early 1990s, one word has come up more often than any other in discussions about education. One word has filled the halls of schools, Congress, and state legislatures. One word has changed how schools work in ways perhaps more profound than any other in the nation's history. That word is *accountability*.

The policies that fall under the accountability banner—especially high-stakes testing—have been both a rallying cry and the target of condemnation. Educators, while generally accepting the need for accountability, have real and justifiable concerns about the details of particular policies. They want what is best for their students but believe that accountability has some, mostly unintended, negative consequences. Accountability policies like No Child Left Behind (NCLB) affect their professional lives as teachers and reduce their autonomy and opportunities for creativity.

Policy makers and the general public, on the other hand, paint with broader strokes and see accountability as a matter of more versus less. They see education and teachers' jobs as relatively simple. Many view the teaching profession from a business perspective, where accountability, as it is typically conceived, is more common. While acknowledging that businesses differ from schools, they still expect to see businesslike policies and practices. They might sympathize with educators' concerns, but their sympathy gets overshadowed by a powerful desire to see a "bottom line" and demonstrable results.

In business, accountability often emphasizes the individual worker. Following this logic, President Obama and state and local leaders have taken the NCLB focus on *school* performance a step further, to individual teachers and principals. In this view, if a teacher is not generating high test scores, the teacher needs to go. If a school is persistently failing, the principal needs to go. But educators express concern that schooling is more than the sum of the individual teachers and principals, and point in turn to interdependences in the business world—among companies' marketing, production, and engineering departments, for example—to prove their point.

It is little wonder that accountability has created so much conflict. When educators express concerns, accountability advocates hear intransigence. When advocates express support for simplistic solutions, educators hear ignorance. In this world of sound bites, none of this is very surprising, but the result is deeply problematic. By paying insufficient attention to the basic nature of education, policy makers have unwittingly put in place an accountability system that is counterproductive for students and teachers alike, and often runs counter to the deeply held beliefs and goals policy makers themselves have for education.

Value-added measures have become a key topic of contention in these accountability debates. What are these measures? The short answer is that such measures are estimated contributions to student test scores made by educators. This type of measure has gained notoriety of late because the value-added approach, in theory, provides an accurate estimate of what each *individual teacher* contributes to student learning.

Nowhere have value-added measures received greater notoriety than in Los Angeles. In August, 2010, the *Los Angeles Times* announced it had obtained student achievement data from the Los Angeles Unified School District and commissioned a researcher to estimate value-added for thousands of the district's teachers. This type of analysis was not especially new, but what was new—and disturbing—was that the newspaper published the individual teachers' value-added scores along with their names. This was an unprecedented move. Professional athletes, realtors, and a handful of other professions make individual performance measures publicly available, but for teachers—and most businesspeople—disclosing this information doesn't make much sense in general. Why? Most obviously, these measures capture only teachers' contributions to student standardized test scores, which are at best loosely related to other important outcomes like creativity and engagement. Also, there are considerable errors in value-added measures. Finally, even if the value-added reports had been accurate, placing teacher performance measures on public websites will do more to wreak havoc than help students. Value-added measures grade teachers on a bell curve, so that no matter how good the entire pool of teachers is, someone will always be at the bottom and half, by definition, will always be below average. Thus half the parents looking at the scores of their children's teachers are bound to be disappointed—and many will complain to the administration. How exactly does this help students? The *Los Angeles Times* had not thought this through beforehand or was more concerned about making headlines than improving schools.[1] Either way, this is exactly why educators distrust the ability of policy makers to design appropriate accountability policies and of the media to accurately portray school performance.

My intention in this book is to find a more productive middle ground, one that uses value-added measures as one part of a system of performance measures and accountability that improves not only test scores, but teaching and learning. Over the past several years, I have been invited to give dozens of presentations on value-added measures, most recently by educators in Los Angeles in the immediate aftermath of the unfortunate *Los Angeles Times* website release. I have found that, as the temperature has risen on value-added and accountability, so has the confusion and mistrust. The need for clarity and productive solutions will only continue to grow.

The first step is answering a basic question: How exactly are value-added measures created? Answering this question is one of my main goals for the first chapters of this book. The fact that a comprehensive explanation of value-added measures requires several chapters itself suggests that there is some genuine complexity involved. But the confusion has also been brought on by the absence of reports or books that explain the intuition and basic calculations and the practical issues that arise when using value-added measures for accountability. Instead, what we have is an academic library of hypertechnical reports that discuss value-added in excruciating statistical detail and, at the same time, ignore the many practical realities educators and policy makers face in interpreting and using the measures. Most of the topics discussed here have been discussed elsewhere, but nowhere have they been brought together in a single place in a way that is integrated, clear, and accessible to educators and policy makers.[2] My aim is to fill that void. If policy makers are going to build value-added measures (or really use student test scores at all) to evaluate teachers and schools, then they need to understand what they are dealing with, and educators need to know how they are being evaluated. I think educators today feel as though they bought a new cell phone and realized that the manufacturer sent not a user's manual, but the engineering specifications.

This book is a user's manual for value-added. I provide a balanced picture of the strengths and weaknesses of these measures. I provide concrete recommendations based on evidence and principles, and address misconceptions. I also explain how the stakes attached to a measure should be proportional to the quality of the measure. What is a quality measure? We cannot answer that question without considering one basic rule.

THE CARDINAL RULE OF ACCOUNTABILITY

The cardinal rule of accountability is to *hold people accountable for what they can control*. This might seem like common sense, but I will show that current accountability systems—particularly test-based accountability systems—generally violate this rule. By contrast, value-added performance measures are designed to hold educators accountable only for what they do control and contribute to student learning.

> **RULE 1—The cardinal rule of accountability**
> *Hold people accountable for what they can control.*

So, what do teachers control? The answer is that there is very little over which they have complete control, and those items vary by school, district, and state. Teachers control what they do to prepare for class. They control their lesson plans and the feedback they provide to students. They also control how they manage their classrooms and respond to students' individual needs.

While they have some control over what takes place in the classroom, what happens there is ultimately a negotiation between the teacher and the fifteen to forty or so other people in the room—the students. Teachers lead, prod, nudge, encourage, and occasionally punish—all in the hopes that students will respond and learn. Sometimes it works. Sometimes not. Classrooms are complicated places, and every one of them is different. All teachers have their own story about the horrible year they had because "little Johnny" was so disruptive that there was little time left for instruction—or the wonderful year when the class really "got it" for reasons unknown.

We often forget the central role in education played by the students themselves. Students' receptiveness to learning opportunities is affected not only by their individual temperaments, but by their peers and home and community factors. For this reason, as I show below, students' knowledge and skills at any given point in time are substantially determined by factors that are largely *outside* the control of educators.

Class sizes, assistance from colleagues, school and district leadership, funding for textbooks and supplies, and community support are also largely outside teachers' control. Increasingly, teachers are losing control over the curriculum as scripted curricula become more common under high-stakes accountability. Teachers control most of their own actions, but they do not control the actions of others.

Likewise, school principals have some control over how they spend their time but limited control over what happens in classrooms and in students' lives. Good principals lead, inspire, and organize the work of the school. But once the classroom door is closed, teachers maintain considerable autonomy. Principals control many important decisions, such as who gets hired and whether to suspend students. But they have little control over budgetary matters, the quality of the building, and, in many cases, even the staff they direct. We could say the same thing about control by superintendents, district staff, and just about anyone else associated with the school system.

What this means is that many people, including the children themselves, control outcomes and this makes it difficult to measure performance in a way that follows the cardinal rule. How do we hold an individual teacher accountable for students when home and community factors have such a large impact on student learning? How do we hold a student's current school accountable when the student has attended other schools—in some cases, what seems like a parade of other schools?

Yet despite the challenges, there is growing agreement that some form of accountability is necessary and that performance measures can and should play a role. Even among teachers, a group that has generally been the most skeptical about test-based accountability policies, 76 percent believed in 2009 that making it easier to dismiss ineffective teachers would improve teacher effectiveness, and 32 percent believed that tying rewards such as salary to measured performance would do the same.[3] While this is far from universal support, the fact that even this many teachers think some form of accountability might work is somewhat surprising, given

5

the acrimony of the public debate. Younger teachers, who represent the future of the profession, are even more optimistic about teacher accountability systems.[4] There is clearly an opening here to hold people accountable in ways that educators can embrace.

The question is, how do we design accountability systems in smart ways? Do we use student test scores to measure school and teacher performance? If so, how? And what exactly do we do with those measures? In designing accountability policies, how do we deal with imperfections in performance measures and the fact that some important student outcomes cannot be measured well? While educators seem open to the idea of using performance measures for accountability, the difficulties faced in answering these questions lead many to support the accountability concept while opposing many of the specific accountability policies that get proposed and adopted.

The devil is in the details, and this book addresses some of the key details. In particular, I address one fundamental problem that has been largely under the radar: the problem with test-based accountability is not only the significant limitations of the tests themselves, but that the tests do not accurately represent the contributions teachers and schools make to student achievement. As a result, we are unnecessarily misjudging school and teacher performance, which is not only unfair to educators but to the students who bear the brunt of the harm.

Value-added measures offer a potential way out of this accountability dilemma. While we can use individual student test scores to diagnose student needs, value-added allows us to go further and evaluate how well teachers and schools are addressing those needs.

PURPOSE AND PREVIEW OF WHAT'S TO COME

The purpose of this book, as the title suggests, is to clear away the fog to explain what value-added measures are and how they might be used productively to improve teaching and learning.[5] It is a user's manual, not an engineering document.

I will return to the cardinal rule of accountability again and again. The rule has two parts. The first—"Hold people accountable . . ."—acknowledges that accountability *is* important. The second—" . . . for what they can control"—means that we need to avoid the age-old critical flaw of holding educators accountable for factors outside their control.

But following the cardinal rule is more difficult than it sounds. To see why, we have to start from the beginning. In chapter 1, I place the issue of educator performance and accountability in context by discussing some examples from outside the field and summarizing the evidence and arguments that underlie the current drive for value-added measures.

In chapters 2 through 4, I expand on the short definition of value-added measures to provide a more detailed picture. Chapter 2, describes in more detail how we currently mismeasure student achievement and then misuse these measures for accountability. I use real achievement data from the "Oakville" school district to help bring to life some of the key points of this and subsequent chapters.

In chapter 3, I discuss the primary ways of measuring student growth and propose a paradigm shift away from the traditional approach of looking at "growth" across different groups of students toward focusing on the growth of *individual* students as they progress through school. Finally, in chapter 4, I cover the details of creating value-added measures. I define basic value-added as simple comparisons of average student growth between similar individual schools. Advanced value-added involves accounting for many factors outside the control of schools and relies on statistical predictions about what student achievement would have been if students had instead gone to the typical school. I highlight these approaches using figures and some numerical examples from Oakville.

These first four chapters collectively explain the potential value of value-added performance measures in their ideal form. Chapters 5 through 8 concentrate on the challenges that arise in applying value-added measures with real data and in real accountability settings. Chapter 5 focuses on the general statistical issues surrounding value-added, especially the distinction between systematic and random errors as well as type I and type II errors. We cannot properly interpret value-added measures without understanding these various ways in which the measures, and the educational decisions based on them, can go wrong.

In chapter 6, I explain the rationale for improving performance measures for individual teachers and the role that value-added might play in that process. Discussion of teacher value-added measures is critical because the federal government, as well as some state governments and school districts, are pursuing value-added as the basis for teacher merit pay and tenure decisions. The research about value-added measures discussed in chapter 7 provides a mixed story about the accuracy of value-added measures, reinforcing perceptions that, compared with snapshot measures, value-added measures have less systematic error but more random error. In chapter 8, I discuss the policy debate surrounding value-added, particularly how arguments against value-added-based accountability have been rooted in a researcher perspective that is really not appropriate for policy decisions.

The last three chapters focus on solutions to some of these challenges and clearing away some of the misconceptions that prevent the effective use of value-added measures. In chapter 9, I show how the criticisms can be partly addressed through a set of recommendations about how value-added measures should be used to improve overall performance measurement. How we plan to use value-added measures also determines how we create and report them; this is the focus of chapter 10.

As I have seen in my presentations and workshops, there are common misconceptions about value-added that will hinder their use if not addressed (see "Misconceptions About Value Added"). Therefore I conclude, in chapter 11, by explaining where these misconceptions come from. Though involving some elements of truth, they are not the most useful ways to look at value-added measures.

While I aim to objectively describe value-added and its limitations and possibilities, let me explicitly acknowledge two of my opinions, both of which I believe are widely supported and backed up by evidence. First, as I have already stated, I think we can improve the way we hold educators accountable. Moreover, I think it is possible to do so in a way that most key stakeholders—including educators—would approve of. There is simply a great deal of self-inflicted mistrust on all sides of these education and accountability debates that has made improvements difficult to accomplish.

Second, I believe value-added measures of performance can improve teaching and learning—not just increase test scores, but improve the practice of teaching and encourage the genuine learning that the vast majority of parents, students, policy makers, and educators want to see. This does

Misconceptions About Value-Added

1. We cannot evaluate educators based on value-added because:
    a. Different teachers have different students.
    b. Value-added measures have flaws.
    c. Student tests are inadequate.
    d. Teaching is complicated.
    e. Student needs are diverse.
2. Value-added is fair for teachers but not for students.
3. Value-added measures are not useful because they are summative rather than formative.
4. Because value-added measures involve comparing teachers to one another, and there are no absolute value-added standards, they are not useful for accountability.
5. Because we know so little about the effects of value-added, we cannot risk our kids' futures by experimenting with it.
6. Value-added is too complicated for educators to understand.
7. Value-added simply represents another step in the process of "industrializing" education, making it more traditional and less progressive.
8. Value-added is a magic bullet that by itself will transform education.

not mean I advocate, say, using *teacher* value-added measures for merit pay. In reality, I think the jury is still out on that particular idea. But accountability isn't just about compensation, nor is it necessarily about a focus on individual teachers. I have long advocated accountability based on *school* value-added measures. There are many reasons to think that replacing school-level snapshots with school value-added measures would produce noticeably better accountability. But it is difficult to say for sure because we are just beginning to examine the alternatives.

The temperature on value-added measures is rising because they are increasingly being used, under various names and forms, in many school districts across the country. And as greater awareness of these accountability issues has developed in policy-making circles, it is increasingly likely that value-added measures will soon be required by the federal government for evaluating whole schools. If these changes are to have any positive impact on schools, the policy makers in charge of designing accountability need to understand the tool they are working with and educators, as the subjects of that accountability, need to understand the meaning of the measures intended to capture their performance and guide their careers. Nobody will respond well to performance-based accountability if it is neither trusted nor understood. My goal is to improve understanding of value-added and, in the process, improve the design of educational accountability systems.

1

Exploring the Potential of Value-Added
Performance Measures

"Do not let what you can't do interfere with what you can do."
—John Wooden, college basketball coach

Performance measures are the foundation of accountability, but they can go badly awry, undermining the goals the accountability systems are trying to achieve. Even the most ardent supporters of educational accountability acknowledge the problems that can arise when the wrong measures are used. Some have even gone so far as to reverse their years of support for test-based accountability policies in the wake of the problems created by No Child Left Behind (NCLB).[1]

Because of the heated controversy, it is useful to preface my discussion of value-added and accountability by stepping back and discussing the relationship between performance measures and accountability in any organization. In particular, I will consider a noneducational example—accountability in some of the organizations involved in the 2008 US financial crisis.[2] Many of the policy makers and interest groups pushing for value-added have business backgrounds, so it is important to both highlight the potential usefulness of some elements of the business model while pointing out the fallacies.

I follow this with a discussion of traditional approaches to accountability in US public education. First, I'll discuss the system's heavy reliance on teacher credentials and pro forma evaluations as a way to ensure effective instruction. Second, I will describe a long-standing critical flaw of test-based accountability policies: that performance measures are based on point-in-time, or "snapshot," measures of student achievement that fail to take into account many important factors that are outside the control of educators.

POSITIVE ROLES OF PERFORMANCE MEASURES AND ACCOUNTABILITY

Accurately measuring performance is important to any organization—for banks, other businesses, governments, charities, and, yes, schools. Accountability is one reason. Good performance should be rewarded and bad performance penalized. It's not that people are lazy (though some are), but that when faced with choices between serving their individual needs and those of the organization, they tend to opt for the former: No one will really notice if I do this, right? I'm not really sure that the extra effort will help, so why bother? It doesn't *really* affect the organization that much, does it? These questions highlight what is sometime called the *free-rider* problem; that is, when only group performance is measured, some individual workers ride free on the backs of those putting in greater effort. A well-designed accountability system discourages this "me first" behavior by aligning individual and organizational goals and encouraging people to work together toward common goals. The free-rider problem is what business leaders and others seem to have in mind when they express concern about low performance in education. This is partly because the private sector generally has much greater control over individual employment relationships than the public sector. While the accountability in the private sector is not as strong as it is often claimed to be, private-sector employees do work "at will" and can be fired for performance reasons at any time.

But discouraging free riding may not be the main benefit of well-designed accountability systems in the education sector; instead, three other factors—personal accountability, mission, and messages—come to the fore (see figure 1-1). Even when group-level accountability induces educators to hold themselves accountable, they cannot do this if they do not know how well they are performing. Teachers usually have some sense about whether they are doing well or not, but these perceptions might not perfectly reflect reality. As a college-level teacher, I receive detailed

FIGURE 1-1 Roles and importance of performance measures

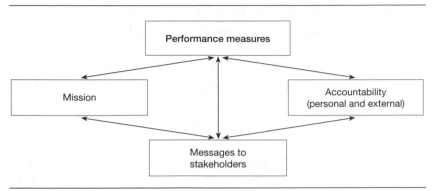

student evaluations each year. I read them as soon as I get them and re-read them before I teach the same course again. I also compare myself to my colleagues and seek out advice from those who get the highest ratings to learn how I can improve. This has helped my teaching immeasurably.[3] In this way, external accountability can help facilitate *personal accountability*.

Performance measures also help to define a clear *mission*. Without one, schools and other organizations are no more than the sum of their disjointed parts. Almost every major organizational guru—from Peter Drucker to Stephen Covey—talks about mission. And any list of the characteristics of "effective schools" mentions it as well.[4] An effective school—one with a clear mission—is greater than the sum of its parts.

Clear missions and sound accountability systems also help schools send *messages* to stakeholders outside the school. First, they send messages about what the schools are trying to accomplish to parents and voters who are crucial to any school's success. Second, performance measures, and the ways in which they are used, send messages that help attract the right kind of new teaching talent. One study found that half the benefit of performance incentives in one company came from attracting more ambitious and hardworking people.[5] Since even in good schools, teachers and administrators come and go, the right measures of accountability not only induce people to work harder, but attract new hires who are a good fit for the school's mission. In one of my own studies, I asked school principals what they look for when hiring teachers. One of the most common answers was they wanted teachers to "fit in" or "match" the cultures of their schools.[6] But match what culture exactly? A missionless school will attract missionless teachers.

Other studies have documented the increasing difficulties we face in attracting the best and brightest young people to become teachers.[7] While there are many factors contributing to this, the messages being sent about the profession and resulting perceptions of it may be one factor. Teaching is often seen by outsiders, including prospective teachers, as an easy and comfortable job—off work at 3:30 p.m. during the school year, summers off, great job security, and health and pension benefits. One of my own relatives once asked me about going into teaching and described it just this way. Needless to say, I suggested he try something else. "Easy" is hardly the message we want to send to prospective teachers, nor is it the reality of professional life for our best teachers.

What do missions, messages, and accountability have to do with performance measurement? Everything. The process of defining performance measures forces stakeholders to think carefully about what the school is trying to accomplish. The resulting performance measures in turn help to define that mission in concrete terms. "Every student will be successful" might sound like a strong mission but it is a meaningless platitude if the school fails to define and reward success.

A CASE STUDY IN ACCOUNTABILITY FAILURE:
THE 2008 US FINANCIAL CRISIS

The financial crisis of 2008 may seem far away—and unrelated to education—but in fact, it offers a useful and universal example of what happens when incentives go awry. I will return to it frequently throughout this book as I introduce new concepts.

In August of 2008, the chairman of the Federal Reserve Bank called an emergency meeting with then-President George W. Bush to inform him that the entire financial system was melting down. Bush, shocked, responded by asking, "How did we get here?"[8]

Good question. The United States faced one of the greatest financial crises in its history. While the full explanation is complex, one factor was that the performance of investment bank executives and their employees was poorly measured and created the wrong incentives. Compensation was (and as of this writing still is) based on short-term profits rather than long-term success. Moreover, investment bankers are rewarded for large profits but not punished commensurately for losses; that is, if investments pay off, bonuses can be enormous. However, if bankers lose money, they receive a reduced bonus, but they do not have to compensate the bank for losses.

The disastrous results of this compensation scheme are well documented in books like Michael Lewis's *The Big Short*.[9] Investment bankers placed large bets on risky assets promised large returns, and therefore large bonuses. By investing in home mortgages granted to people with low credit ratings—a very risky asset—investment bankers helped drive up housing values, worsening the already growing housing bubble. Unrealistically high housing values made the mortgages even riskier. Most investment bankers knew housing prices would begin to drop eventually, but the bubble burst seemed far away. Once housing values dropped, many homeowners would owe more than their homes were worth and default on their mortgages. Increasing default rates would further erode housing prices, making matters still worse. And get worse they did. The 2008 crisis and ensuing recession was the worst since the Great Depression.

The resulting damage to the economy and social fabric was far-reaching, and the aftershocks are still being felt. Five of the largest and oldest investment banks no longer exist, and the remnants of those banks have fallen under unwanted government regulation.[10] People from all walks of life lost their jobs. Government revenue declined and, with it, funding for many key government services, including education.

The banks made a choice. They did not have to design their compensation incentives to encourage risky behavior focused on short-term gains. A number of companies, Apple Inc. among them, have instead adopted a "pay for success" compensation system.[11] The system follows certain basic principles: incentives are not paid for below-average performance; performance targets are challenging; incentives are based on long-term performance rather than short-term profits or fluctuations in stock prices; some incentives are companywide, and the system used to compensate the CEO is similar to the one for lower-level managers (though compensation *levels* between the CEO and managers obviously vary). One business writer recently lamented that the investment banks that were the prime movers in the 2008 financial crisis had not followed Apple's lead.[12]

So, back to President Bush's question, "How did we get here?" Part of the answer is that the system was designed to fail. Naturally, the banks did not *want* to fail. They did not *want* the economy to fall apart. But these results were nevertheless natural outgrowths of the choices they made about measuring and rewarding performance. Investment banks failed to hold their employees accountable for key decisions that were well within their control.

CREDENTIALING AS A SUBSTITUTE FOR EDUCATIONAL ACCOUNTABILITY

Unlikely as it may seem, the same general kinds of mistakes made by the banking industry leading up to the financial crisis have long been repeated in our schools. Do our schools do any better in aligning the needs of their key personnel—teachers and administrators—with the needs of their schools and students? Do schools focus more on long-term success? In both cases, critics make a strong case that the answer is no.

Public schools have long been criticized for focusing too much on inputs, rules, and compliance. Education debates from the 1960s through the 1980s focused heavily on school finance and how much schools spent. In addition, federal, state, and district policy makers seemed to be in a competition to see who could construct the most complex rules and regulations.

The Four Elements of the Credentialing Strategy

This focus on inputs and rule compliance is nowhere more evident than with the strategy we use to ensure teacher effectiveness, which I'll call the credentialing strategy. Briefly put, the strategy has four elements: tenure, the single-salary schedule, low-stakes evaluations, and certification. Unlike the private sector, in which job security and compensation depend on evidence of performance, the credentialing strategy focuses on almost everything except what happens on the job, making it a poor substitute for accountability. Let's start by looking at tenure.

Teachers are usually granted tenure after two to five years on the job. The terminology may differ—for example, teachers may be granted "continuing contracts"—but the idea is the same: Before a teacher achieves this status, school districts have considerable latitude to dismiss teachers for poor performance; the burden of proof is on the teacher to show that a dismissal is unfair. After a teacher has been granted tenure, the burden of proof shifts so that teachers cannot be fired unless the district provides clear and convincing evidence of poor performance. This makes the tenure decision quite important because once teachers receive tenure, they are likely to continue for many years to come.

In addition to tenure, almost 90 percent of school districts in the United States operate on a single-salary schedule under which compensation is determined by years of experience and academic degrees.[13] This means that teachers get raises regardless of how they perform, which might make sense if these factors were closely related with performance. Tim Sass and I recently reviewed evidence about how closely teacher performance was related to experience and degrees. While teachers do improve noticeably in their ability to raise student achievement over their first five years on the job, and some even up to ten years, not much improvement occurs over the remaining twenty years—the majority of a teacher's career.[14] The linkage between teacher performance and their academic degrees is even more tenuous. Teachers with master's degrees are, on average, no more effective than other teachers (after accounting for experience).

In theory, the single-salary schedule could be eliminated and staffing and salary decisions based on the teacher evaluations of actual classroom practice that are now fairly standard in most school districts. But teacher evaluations have their own problems. While many indicators suggest that there is a wide distribution of teacher effectiveness, in districts that use simple satisfactory-unsatisfactory evaluation ratings, the evaluation system places 99 percent of teachers in the satisfactory category.[15] The very fact that the top category is often called "satisfactory" is a problem in itself and suggests that true excellence is not really expected.

Mary Kennedy, a widely respected scholar of teacher evaluation, recently commented that school evaluation systems "lack attention to the very things that constitute the intellectual core of teaching: classroom discussions and learning activities."[16] Moreover, she writes that teacher evaluators "are rarely asked to evaluate the accuracy, importance, coherence, or relevance of the content that is actually taught or the clarity with which it is taught."[17] This is a scathing critique—how could we possibly evaluate teachers without paying attention to those activities related to student learning or to coherence and relevance of content? The news gets arguably even worse if the examination turns to what teacher evaluations *do* focus on. As Kennedy further notes, typical teacher evaluations boil down to "a couple of dozen items on a list: 'Is presentably dressed,' 'Starts on time,' 'Room is safe,' 'The lesson occupies students.' . . . In most instances, it's nothing more than marking 'satisfactory' or 'unsatisfactory.'"[18] And for veteran teachers, even this simplistic evaluation is administered only once every two years.[19]

These evaluations inaccurately assess teacher performance and fail to provide any useful guidance for improvement for even the most motivated teachers. In one study, 73 percent of teachers said their most recent evaluation did not identify areas for improvement and, even when such areas were identified, fewer than half of the respondents reported receiving any support to facilitate improvement.[20] Teacher unions, which are often seen as hostile toward change, also agree that teacher evaluations need to be improved. Randi Weingarten, president of the American Federation of Teachers, noted in a recent speech that "our system of evaluating teachers has never been adequate. For too long and too often, teacher evaluation—in both design and implementation—has failed to achieve what must be our goal: continuously improving and informing teaching so as to better educate all students."[21] A recent report from the National Education Association indicates that "The inadequacy of this [teacher evaluation] approach is apparent, as evidenced by studies showing that over 90 percent of teachers are classified as top performers and only a tiny percentage are denied tenure or dismissed due to evaluation results."[22]

The problems with tenure, single-salary schedules, and evaluations might not be so serious if the teachers coming in the door were well-prepared. Teacher certification is intended to help ensure that teachers come in with basic subject matter knowledge and pedagogical skill. The vast majority of teachers are certified through state-sponsored, college-based teacher education programs and by passing paper-and-pencil tests of skills and knowledge. Unfortunately, while the evidence on certification is harder to interpret, certified teachers seem to perform about as well as other teachers, or sometimes a little better.[23] The National Board for Professional Teaching Standards (NBPTS) provides a more elaborate and improved form of certification, but even this qualification tells us fairly little about how effective teachers will be in the future.[24]

The Rationale Behind the Strategy

I refer to this group of approaches—tenure, single-salary schedule, checklist evaluations, and certification—as the *credentialing strategy* of teacher effectiveness because it focuses on the pieces of paper teachers hold—mostly before they enter the classroom—rather than their demonstrated performance. I include the checklist evaluations as part of the group as well because, although they are *supposed* to be based on classroom performance, they fail on that count, and so become just another piece of paper.

The fact that the crendentialing strategy seems to have little research support is unsurprising, given the complexity of the work. Teaching is in the top-third of all jobs in terms of job complexity.[25] While this suggests that a great deal of skill and training is required, supporting the idea of credentials, part of what makes the job complicated is that fact that it is so context-specific. Student needs vary considerably from school to school, and even class to class, as do the textbooks and other resources that teachers work with to address those needs. It is unrealistic to expect standardized credentials to be good indicators of performance when the work itself is anything but standardized.

While each of the elements in the credentialing strategy is individually problematic, collectively the situation looks worse. At no point in the current system does a teacher have to show that he or she is improving student outcomes—not during the tenure process, not in compensation decisions, not through the annual evaluation, and not through certification.

The belief that the credentialing strategy is ineffective is widely held, even by teachers themselves. I've never met a teacher who said she thought the credentialing strategy worked well. One recent survey found that "78% [of teachers] say their school has at least a few teachers who are simply going through the motions, and just 14% say it is easy to remove incompetent teachers."[26] In another survey, teachers reported that their district was not doing enough to recognize and retain the most effective teachers.[27] Most alumni of colleges of education (62 percent) do not believe those programs prepare their graduates to cope with classroom realities.[28]

Administrators believe even more strongly that there are too many ineffective teachers and that too little is being done about it. For example, administrators in private schools, where tenure and single-salary schedules are less common, report greater satisfaction with their teachers than public school administrators, who work in settings where the credentialing strategy is more predominant.[29]

So, why do we use the credentialing strategy? The single-salary schedule and tenure policies developed a half-century ago as ways of taking the politics out of school staffing decisions. School and district officials were prone to hire friends and relatives and fire others for reasons unrelated to anything like real performance. Also, women were generally paid much lower salaries than men, and the single-salary schedule helped fix this inequity. Certification, for its part, may play a useful role in screening out clearly unqualified or inappropriate candidates (though it probably also screens out effective teachers, too).

There are also several broader rationales for credentials. One is that the autonomy that goes along with the credentialing strategy helps ensure teacher "professionalism," but this term is used in a somewhat distinctive way in teaching. Law and medicine are considered professions partly because they have a core set of standards of practice and at least some form of professional accountability for their members. But professional standards and accountability are largely absent in teaching. Teachers should be treated more as professionals, but relying on credentials as a substitute for accountability falls short as a strategy for doing so.

It is important to note that, as with other professions, accountability does not preclude a considerable degree of teacher autonomy. Teaching is complicated and context specific, and it would be impossible to prescribe exactly how teachers should act in every conceivable situation. They have to use their own judgment. While it has gotten lost in the debate, one of the original rationales for test-based accountability was that it would free teachers to find the best approach to produce results. Analogously, we expect doctors to follow a core set of standards of practice while also exercising their judgment regarding the best course of treatment for each individual patient. The problem is that policy makers haven't followed through and have instead specified what students must achieve *and* how teachers should go about it. This is clearly not a recipe for success.

The overarching rationale behind the credentialing strategy is this: if teachers are well prepared (as suggested by certification) and caring (indicated in interviews during the hiring process), and if there are financial incentives for teachers to stay in the profession and to continue their formal training (pay based on experience and graduate degrees), then teacher will use their autonomy to do what is in the best interests of children. Further, because student needs and outcomes are many and hard to measure, it is best to leave decisions up to the experts—the teachers—and trust that the results will be positive.

In the private sector, they might start with trust, but they finish by verifying. Investment banks, for example, rely little on credentials and heavily on financial incentives. This is because the goal of investment banks—making a profit—is fairly simple and the industry's high compensation draws people who are motivated by money. The roles of credentials and financial incentives are reversed in education, and this makes sense. Educators are trying to achieve many goals and to prepare students for their future roles as workers, voters, citizens, and community members—all simultaneously. This makes it harder to measure performance. Also, teachers and administrators are not paid especially well, so they are obviously not in it for the money. They want to help children. Trying to measure performance and hold teachers accountable based on student outcomes is therefore seen as unnecessary, creating unintended consequences without any of the intended benefits. The potential consequences are easy to see in the investment banking example, as well as in education.

My contention is not that the rationale underlying the credentialing strategy is wrong, but that it falls short. Basic certification has a role to play in ensuring that unfit candidates never enter a classroom and for making sure teachers have a certain up-front level of commitment to the job. More advanced certifications like NBPTS also play a part in identifying master teachers and teacher leaders. Finally, given the importance of teacher experience over the first several years and the fact that experience also plays an important role in private-sector compensation, paying teachers partly on the basis of experience makes some sense.

Do we really think that this is enough? Can we justify relying exclusively on a system that measures almost everything about teachers *except* what they do in the classroom?

The Central Importance of Teachers

One of the primary reasons there is so much criticism of the credentialing strategy today, and so much interest in teacher accountability, is that there seem to be such large differences in effectiveness between the most and least effective teachers—not differences in the shallow checklist evaluations, but differences in *real performance*. Tim Sass and I found that school principals' confidential assessments of teachers varied much more widely than the formal evaluations do.[30] Other studies, based on student test scores, draw similar conclusions (discussed in more detail in chapter 7).

One study discusses the potential benefits of firing or denying tenure to the bottom 25 percent of teachers as step toward eliminating the student achievement gap.[31] I show later that the benefits of such policies are exaggerated, and for that and other reasons would oppose using value-added measures as the main basis for such a policy. Nevertheless, the importance of teachers cannot be denied and therefore the current focus on teacher policies like certification, compensation, tenure, and evaluation is well placed. To get better instruction, we need to evaluate and hold educators accountable for instruction.

The Importance of Student Achievement—and Other Educational Goals

One might reasonably argue that autonomy is so valuable that it trumps strict accountability, or believe that the unintended negative consequences of test-based accountability are just too great to allow such measures to be introduced. But there is another major problem with lack of accountability that is not so easy to reason away. At least since the report *A Nation at Risk* was published in 1983, the fact that the United States is only about average on international comparisons of test scores—and well behind economic competitors in Asia—has raised concern about the nation's economic competitiveness.[32] While *A Nation at Risk* and some recent studies greatly exaggerate how much test scores really drive worker productivity and national economic success, there is a real and important link.[33] In the knowledge and information economy, students really do need academic skills to excel. And countries that develop these skills in their youth are at a distinct economic advantage.

In addition to our poor international standing, progress in student scores on our own National Assessment of Educational Progress (NAEP) has been slow. Elementary students have made significant progress in both reading and math, but these successes have ultimately not shown up where it matters—trends in high school NAEP scores have been almost completely flat for decades.[34] In short, we do not fare well compared with other countries and we don't seem to be improving.

We cannot lay our mediocre performance at the feet of teachers, or entirely blame the credentialing strategy. Again, policy makers have created problems themselves by maintaining outmoded rules and bureaucracy. This backwardness is partly attributed to school boards elected by only 5 percent of voters and influenced heavily by interest groups such as labor unions, PTAs, and chambers of commerce.[35] Some also argue that parents should have a greater say in public education, although market-oriented policies like charter schools and vouchers have generally not had the effects their advocates expected and have been accompanied by consequences such as the resegregation of schools.[36] There is also a general lack of capacity and support for school improvement. I return to these problems later because they are intertwined with my arguments about value-added accountability. It is important not to lose sight of the larger educational reform effort when looking at accountability as one piece of the puzzle.

Emphasis on student test scores must also be revisited. The scores are imperfect measures of student learning, and there are important outcomes like creativity that tests don't even try to measure. While the United States races to expand high-stakes testing, most of the rest of the world is moving in the opposite direction, focusing less on standardized academic skills and testing and more on creativity.

We can clearly build a better accountability system. The system of credentials doesn't make sense to anyone and, by almost any measure, it is not generating good results. If the problem is low test scores, then shifting the focus from inputs to outputs and demanding higher test scores seems like a sensible strategy. But student test scores have been used for accountability about as badly as investment banks used bonuses to reward their employees. To move forward toward something better, we need to consider the ways in which traditional accountability systems fail.

MEASURING PERFORMANCE: THE CHALLENGE OF STARTING-GATE INEQUALITIES

The substitution of credentialing for accountability means we measure performance and reward poorly. But credentialing is not the only problem. Accountability based on student test results has been in place since the early 1990s and greatly expanded with NCLB. So, rather than a substitute, credentialing is now layered on top of accountability. The problem is that the performance measures are still so inaccurate that they do little to improve accountability, mission, or messages.

Back in the 1800s, teachers and schools held spelling bees to show the public what students were learning. Of course, schools were apt to put their best students forward, and spelling constituted a fairly narrow slice of what students were supposed to learn. This approach made it difficult to compare schools with one another or to accurately gauge student or school performance. But this did not stop parents from running teachers out of town if they thought their children were not learning enough. This naturally placed a lot of pressure on teachers. Indeed—and admittedly it's an extreme example—a teacher in England during the 1800s noted, "When one of my backward boys died of bronchitis a few weeks back I felt a measure of relief; for his death would make one failure less."[37]

To improve on spelling bees and other local student assessments and provide a more objective basis for measuring student knowledge, some standardized testing for students was adopted by school districts as early as the 1840s, and their use really took off during the 1920s. Not coincidentally, the 1920s represented the peak of the "scientific management" movement, which attempted to standardize practice and improve efficiency in all types of organizations and work, not just education. One of the key tools of scientific management was psychological testing of knowledge and thinking skills.

Another major shift occurred in the 1990s. Before that time, standardized tests were used primarily to hold students accountable for their own success with graduation exams. The tide began to turn in the 1980s with the publication of *A Nation at Risk*. The report emphasized the importance of content standards and formed the basis for the expansion of testing that followed its publication. In the 1990s, the federal government completed the shift to the "new accountability" by requiring school report cards with average student test scores. Of course, the most recent and significant increase in testing, and in high-stakes accountability for schools, came with the adoption of NCLB.

But accountability for student results has suffered from the same critical flaws since the horse-and-buggy days. Knowledge and skill accumulate over a person's life. What adults know depends on what they experienced as school-aged students, which in turn depends on experiences before school, all the way back to birth. There is now wide agreement among psychologists and social scientists that children's early years are the most important and formative in our lives.[38] And the fact is that there are vast inequalities in early life experiences across the United States. Research is clear that students start kindergarten at vastly different levels of academic skill. These *starting-gate inequalities* are obviously not the fault of the schools—many students have not even set foot in a classroom before kindergarten—at least not in the public schools that are now the targets of accountability. One study finds that at the very beginning of kindergarten, high-income children have average test scores that are 60 percent higher than low-income children.[39]

Figure 1-2 reinforces this point using data from nearly 15,000 schools across the country. It shows student achievement on state standardized tests at a point in time in schools with different percentages of students eligible for free- or reduced-price lunch ("low-income"). The pattern is unmistakable. Achievement drops steadily as the number of low-income students rises. The same data also show that high-income schools were twenty-two times more likely than low-income schools to be high-performing on state tests—further evidence of income-related disparities in achievement.[40]

Now, one could question whether this figure alone proves that low achievement is the result of poverty and other social and economic disadvantages. Some education reform advocates say there should be "no

FIGURE 1-2 Student test scores are lower in low-income schools

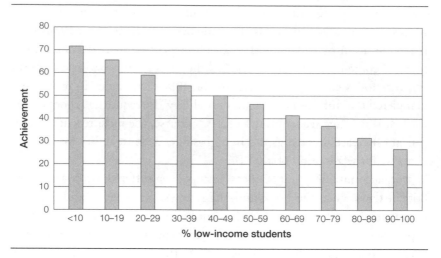

excuses" and that these widely divergent outcomes are really generated by the schools themselves, pointing to evidence that the "achievement gap" between low- and high-income students widens as students pass through school. This is true. The gap does widen, but the vast majority of the gap is present the first day students enter kindergarten.[41] So there is little question that factors outside of school control have a dramatic effect on student outcomes before schooling even begins.

It might seem like this problem should go away in later grades. Students' home lives might matter a lot at the beginning, but surely the schools eventually take over and control student outcomes by sixth grade or eighth grade, right? Unfortunately not. The gaps at kindergarten are so large that it is difficult for schools to overcome them. And doing so is all the harder because the same factors influencing child development in the early years continue to influence children as they progress through school. The parent who doesn't read to his toddler son generally doesn't read to him at age six either. The libraries that are absent when children could start to look at picture books are still missing as students get older and want to read. Crime-ridden neighborhoods and limited access to health care and other services do not go away either.

The fact that the home environment influences students even after they enter school is perhaps clearest in the research about *summer learning loss*, which shows that low-income students either learn nothing or actually regress during the summer in terms of their reading skills, while higher-income students continue to move forward.[42] (Importantly, these same studies find that student learning *during* the school year is largely unrelated to income, which suggests that schools are indeed helping disadvantaged students. I return to this later.)

Low income per se is not responsible for less learning. In reality, income and race/ethnicity are proxies for the environments these groups of students tend to grow up in. Consider a different example: People with blond hair tend to have lighter skin, and people with lighter skin are more prone to sunburn. This means that people with blond hair are more prone to sunburn even though having blond hair does not in any way cause skin to burn. Having blond hair is a proxy for the likelihood of sunburn in the same sense that being minority or low-income is a proxy for achievement. This is not a perfect analogy. Limited income does, for example, make it harder for parents to buy books for their children to read when they are young. Also, minorities are sometimes discriminated against in a way that causes lower achievement. The key point is that these groups of students are not inherently less able to learn, but that they are, in very real ways, hampered by their environments

On top of starting-gate inequalities and the influences of home and community is the issue of movement from one school to another. Most students attend more than one school in the course of their education— elementary, middle, and high school. Each school builds on the successes (and failures) of the previous ones. Some students switch schools even more frequently because, for example, their parents move to a new address—sometimes multiple times during the same school year. For these and other reasons, each school's students start off each school year at a different level of achievement, and if we fail to account for that, then the student's current school will be punished (or rewarded) for achievement differences that are outside its control, violating the cardinal rule.

THE SNAPSHOT PROBLEM

In his book *Outliers*, Malcolm Gladwell looked at the other end of the achievement spectrum. Bill Gates, the founder of Microsoft and one of the wealthiest people in the world, got his big break by obtaining almost unlimited access to mainframe computers provided by a local college while he was still a high school student, at a time when even the most educated workers hardly ever saw a computer. He did this on his own without the help of high school staff.[43] Should we give complete credit to Bill Gates' high school for his success? Of course not. Nor should we place all the blame on schools when students growing up in poverty—without library books, adequate health care, safe neighborhoods, or parents to prod and help them along—end up with low test scores.

Yet this is exactly what we have been doing for more than a century with local, state, and now federal accountability systems that look only at point-in-time test scores and fail to account for where students start when they enter a particular school. Given the rapid expansion of testing, one might think that the necessary information is available and being utilized well, but that has not happened. NCLB required a lot more testing, but then essentially told schools to consider only the same old student "snapshots" of achievement. In other words, federal accountability policy encourages schools to look at achievement at a single point in time.

Focusing on snapshots, as I will discuss in chapter 2, creates a wide range of perverse incentives that are bad not only for schools but also for students—especially for the disadvantaged students the law is intended to help. It also doesn't make much sense. Think about your favorite movie for a moment. (I happen to like old movies, so I'll pick Orson Welles's *Citizen Kane*.) Imagine that instead of watching the movie we cut up the film into a bunch of snapshots and then pick just one to try and understand what the movie is about. The movie ends with the scene of a wooden sled with the word *Rosebud* painted on it. Without knowing what came before that snapshot, how would we know what this scene really meant? We wouldn't, yet this is what we do now with achievement scores. The school's story is lost.

The focus on snapshot measures was not the intent of NCLB's originators. When he was running for president, George W. Bush chose Sandy

Kress, a school board member from the Dallas Public Schools, as one of his key education advisers.[44] Owing partly to Kress, Dallas had been one of the earliest innovators in going beyond snapshots of school performance to value-added measures. But when Kress brought the idea to Washington, it was unfamiliar and misunderstood.[45]

Unfortunately, just as we have done since the spelling bees of the 1800s, we still focus overwhelmingly on snapshot measures of student achievement and therefore violate the cardinal rule of accountability. Federal Adequate Yearly Progress (AYP) does not measure school contributions to student learning any more than spelling bees measured how much teachers helped students improve their spelling a century ago. Snapshots largely reflect starting-gate inequalities, and these are obviously not under the control of schools. Using these misleading measures of performance is a critical flaw in current accountability systems.

This is why I am skeptical when I hear people talk, for example, about finding better approaches to turning around failing schools. Of course we should do what we can to improve or get rid of failing schools and teachers, but first things first. Right now, the performance measures in use cannot even tell us which schools are truly failing. This is like wandering through the woods guided by a broken compass. We may want to head north, but if the compass says that north is east, then we will just wander aimlessly.

The core of any well-designed accountability system—and the place to start—is with improved performance measures. With better measures, we can do better than the investment banks, and do something that is, historically, almost unprecedented: We can have effective accountability, a clear mission centered on teaching and learning, and messages that convey that mission to key stakeholders. We need to fix our educational compass.

2

Using—and Misusing—Achievement Tests

"Everybody gets so much information all day long that they lose their common sense."

—*Gertrude Stein,* Reflection on the Atomic Bomb (1973)

Tests. Tests. Tests. If you work in public schools, you spend a lot of time preparing for and administering them and then become awash in test data, sliced and diced every which way. Data on individual students, racial and ethnic subgroups, and whole grade levels. Math, reading, and other subjects. Diagnostic tests and state standardized tests. Scores reported by scale scores and percentiles and performance standards. But what does it all mean? One of the biggest problems with test-based accountability is that educators do not have the time, resources, or training to interpret and use test data to improve teaching and learning. But since performance of schools and teachers is being measured by those student scores—and these scores are the raw materials for value-added—it is important to carefully consider what they tell us. We have to figure out how to turn the raw data into real information that is useful for decision making.

Consider the 2008 financial crisis again. Investment banks measure success based on profits but, like student test scores, profits are just snapshots in time. They can be distorted by accounting gimmicks and do not reflect investment risk or the long-term prospects for the banks' success. There is a phrase for data like this: garbage in, garbage out. For the purpose of measuring investment bankers' contributions to the banks, the information about their contributions to profit was garbage and this led to bad decisions—more garbage. The same is true when measuring school performance, except that the problem is not whether the value of assets reflects risk, but whether student outcome measures might inaccurately capture students' knowledge and skills and therefore produce unhelpful responses by educators.

Since the value-added approach is most commonly applied to student test results, as opposed to other student outcomes, it is important to start there. Standardized tests are widely criticized for being "dumbed down" to low academic standards, for failing to capture deep understanding of concepts over mechanical processes and memorization, for not being culturally relevant, and for ignoring skills such as creativity and problem solving that are hard to test or expensive to score. There are also concerns about the curriculum and standards underlying the tests—in particular, the fact that in some schools the test is becoming the curriculum.

These are all valid criticisms, and no statistical tool, including value-added, can fix them. Standardized tests do need to be improved, and policy makers and researchers are working toward making that happen.[1] Connecticut, New York, and Vermont are among the states have taken some steps toward richer assessments. The federal government is currently investing $350 million in the development of new student assessment systems that states could decide to adopt. These efforts are important for all types of test-based accountability, not just ones that use value-added.

In the meantime, it is important to understand how to interpret student test scores. Excellent books and articles by scholars such as Daniel Koretz and Robert Linn do just that.[2] Rather than repeat what others have said, I focus below on the issues of testing that arise when using standardized testing to measure growth and value-added.

STANDARDIZED TESTING AND VALUE-ADDED

Measures of student achievement or other student outcomes are just that—measures. The numbers they produce do not tell us the truth about what we want to know. When we use a ruler and find that a pencil is 7 inches long, the true length is probably more like 6.99 or 7.01 inches. Likewise, the true amount of student knowledge and skill for any given student is never really known. There is the truth, and then there is our measure of the truth. It is better to think of standardized tests as indicators or approximations in each domain or subject (reading, math, etc.).[3]

If student test scores are to be used to compare educator performance, then the tests must be standardized across students to make the comparisons possible. This means, for example, that the classroom assessments that individual teachers design and utilize cannot be used for accountability. Classroom assessments, by definition, vary from teacher to teacher, and this makes it impossible to know whether the higher scores of students in one class reflect easier questions or students' greater knowledge and skill. For this reason, one of the earliest widespread uses of standardized tests was the college entrance exam. Colleges wanted to decide which applicants were the best students, but they could not base that decision on high school course grades and GPA because high schools used different grading standards.

The sections below discuss three main distinctions among standardized tests:

- The way the tests are designed (norm- versus criterion-referenced)
- The way the results are reported (proficiency, scale scores, etc.)
- The way the test results are used (low-stakes versus high-stakes)

These issues turn out to be closely interconnected.

TEST DESIGN: NORM- VERSUS CRITERION-REFERENCED

The appropriate design of a standardized test naturally depends on what one hopes to learn about student knowledge and skill. If the goal is to learn how students compare with each other, then a norm-referenced test is in order. The results of norm-referenced tests are reported in terms of percentiles; that is, the percent of students in the population who are below a particular score. A student at the fiftieth percentile is at the median (and near the average).

Most states have turned away from norm-referenced tests because of federal requirements and the growing popularity of content standards. Content standards represented one of the primary recommendations of 1983's *A Nation at Risk,* and have long been popular with the general public as well as—to the surprise of many—teacher unions.[4] For some, the logical next step was to design standardized tests measuring student success according to those standards. Such tests are considered *criterion-referenced* because they measure knowledge and skill on specific content, or criteria, instead of relative to a norm. Criterion-referenced tests are the right ones for holding educators accountable because they require the government to specify what schools are expected to teach and therefore what schools will be evaluated on. This is consistent with the cardinal rule: holding people accountable for what they can control requires telling people what they will be held accountable for.

The results of criterion-referenced tests are usually reported as raw scores, scale scores, or percentage of students passing particular performance standards. Since federal rules now require states to use criterion-referenced tests, and there are reasons to think these will be more useful than norm-referenced tests for value-added purposes, I focus most of my attention below on criterion-referenced test design.

TEST REPORTING: SCALE SCORES, PERCENTILES, AND NORMAL CURVE EQUIVALENTS

Unfortunately, measuring knowledge and skills, even along specific content standards, is more difficult than measuring the length of a pencil—there is simply no clear unit of measure. An inch is an inch when we measure a pencil. But there is no "inch" of knowledge and skill. What is the ruler? Answering this question is one of the main—and most difficult—challenges for test designers and there are many different possibilities (see table 2-1 for a summary of test-reporting methods).

One problem is that every test question has a different level of difficulty. Suppose that there are three questions on a test measuring knowledge of arithmetic—one easy, one medium, and one hard. Then suppose that two students, Norah and Dawson, each get two of the three questions (67 percent) correct, but Norah gets the medium and hard ones correct, while Dawson gets the easy and medium ones correct. Though they have the same percentage correct—that is, the same *raw score*—it is obviously misleading to say these students have the same true achievement. Norah performed better because she got the hard question right. Raw scores therefore are not very useful for measuring student achievement.

TABLE 2-1
Summary of test-reporting methods

Raw score:	The number of items a student got correct on a test.
Scale score:	Adjusted score that weighs correct answers on more difficult questions more than correct answers on easy questions.
Developmental scale score:	A type of scale score that can be compared across grades. However, a 10-point increase in test scores does not necessarily mean exactly the same thing across grades (see discussion of interval scales).
Normal curve equivalent (NCE):	Raw scores, scale scores, and development scale scores can be converted to percentile rankings to show how students compare with one another. Percentiles can be converted into NCEs.

For this reason, testing companies now commonly estimate *scale scores*, which take into account the test's level of difficulty. If a student gets a hard question correct, the scale score increases more than it does when a student gets an easy question right. But getting beyond the simple categories of easy, medium, and hard and assigning specific, numeric levels of difficulty to each item is a challenge. Test designers use a technique called *item response theory* (IRT) to try to quantify item difficulty, but there is considerable controversy about how well this approach really creates an accurate scale.[5]

Depending on the specific IRT method chosen, the scale accounts for difficulty in one of two ways. In the example above, the scaling procedure accounts for the difficulty of each item within each test. But current practice is not this sophisticated. The companies that design and scale most state tests typically use a simpler method that accounts only for the overall level of difficulty within grades across years (e.g., third-grade tests in 2010 versus third-grade tests in 2009). Without additional scaling, Norah and Dawson could be compared if they took the test in the same grade. If Norah were younger than Dawson, they would be taking tests in different grades each year and their results would be hard to compare without additional scaling procedures.

Any college basketball fan can get an intuitive grasp of scale scores and difficulty levels by considering the *Ratings Percentage Index* (RPI). Each team's RPI rating is based on the team's winning percentage, the winning percentage of opponents, and the winning percentage of the opponents of the opponents. These last two statistics are intended to capture the level of difficulty of beating the team. Beating a really good team (with a high winning percentage) counts for more because the level of difficulty is higher. This is why some teams from very weak conferences with high winning percentages still don't get invited to the "March Madness" national basketball tournament; they never play the more difficult teams—or answer the hard questions correctly.

One reason to care about the difference between raw and scale scores is that it would be useful to know whether each student learned more this year compared with last year. If a student gained 50 points on the scale last year, but only 30 points this year, we might wonder what went wrong this year and try to correct it. But drawing this type of conclusion—specifically, making comparisons *across* grades—demands even more of the tests. *Developmental* scale scores compare achievement growth across grades, at least in principle. To improve this type of comparability, test designers include some items, called *linking items*, from each test in multiple grades. So, for example, in the 2003 Colorado state assessment, roughly one-third of the items on the third-grade test also showed up as linking items in the fourth-grade test for that same year.[6] These linking items provide an anchor or point of reference for comparing the difficulty of items on the fourth-grade test with those on the third-grade test.

In principle, developmental scale scores based on linking items can be *interval-scaled*, meaning that a 10-point increase means the same thing no matter where you start on the scale—even across grades. This allows educators to track the growth of students over long periods of time and, as the example suggests, to figure out what went wrong for the student whose growth has slowed down. Because value-added measures are based on individual student growth, it is easy to see how useful it is to have an interval-scaled test. Unfortunately, creating an interval scale is hard. For example, the level of difficulty of an open-ended math question may be based not only on math knowledge, but also, because it is a word problem, on reading skills. While the test item may be called a "math" question, pulling out the math part is like trying to take the eggs out of the cookie dough after they have been mixed with the flour and sugar. Test designers refer to this as the problem of *multidimensionality*. This means that math scores might rise because reading skills improved, calling into question the meaning of "math growth." I return to this issue again in chapter 7 because the absence of an interval scale is one of the principle criticisms of value-added measures. The interval scale is not absolutely required for value-added, but it is helpful. For this reason, I simply refer to *scale scores* throughout much of the rest of the book and omit the word *developmental*.

Once scale scores have been established, imperfections and all, they can be reported and adjusted in various ways. Many researchers standardize scale scores by assuming that the overall distribution of achievement should be the same across grades and years.[7] Others assume that true performance always follows a bell curve and convert the scale score to a percentile, then convert the percentile into *normal curve equivalents* (NCEs). The advantage of the NCE is that, in contrast to percentiles, a one-point difference at two parts of the scale does mean the same thing for all students, no matter where they start off on the test. As with scale scores, there are additional assumptions that have to hold before NCEs can be considered interval-scaled, and there is not yet agreement among researchers about which of these two approaches is best for value-added purposes.

Norm-referenced tests are also sometimes reported as *grade-level equivalents* (GLEs) so that 6.0 refers to the achievement of the student starting the sixth grade at the fiftieth percentile, 6.1 refers to the fiftieth percentile at the end of the first month of sixth grade, and so on up to 6.10 for the tenth month, with similar designations for other grade levels. However, from the standpoint of growth, this is the same as reporting the percentiles themselves, so I do not consider this further, and do not include them in the summary of test reporting methods in table 2-1.

PERFORMANCE STANDARDS AND PROFICIENCY

Up to now, I have focused on scale scores and NCEs because those are most relevant to value-added, but it is important to compare these test reporting methods with what is by far the most common way of measuring achievement—the performance standard, which places students into categories by setting bars or cutoffs. The most common performance standard is proficiency, which played a prominent role under No Child Left Behind, but most states also designate other performance levels, such as basic and advanced. If Dawson has a score of 70, he might be above the cutoff for basic, but below the bar for proficient.

To make it easier to place students in specific performance categories, criterion-referenced tests are usually designed to be more accurate near the performance bars. While this seems sensible at first, an important implication is that the range of knowledge covered by criterion-referenced tests is often not as broad as the knowledge and skills across all students. This means that some students' abilities will be captured better than others, which creates problems in all high-stakes uses of student scores, including, as I show later, for value-added measures.

How are performance standards set? In some cases, there are very elaborate processes for making these judgments, including going through tests item by item and categorizing each based on a detailed set of criteria. The lowest standard is established based on the percentage of the easiest questions students get right, and so on for higher standards and harder questions. The less-sophisticated methods amount to little more than eyeballing the distribution of student scores and deciding what percentage of students passing a standard seems reasonable. But no matter how much effort is put into them, these performance standards are still arbitrary. In one study, researchers found that one approach to setting standards resulted in 50 percent more students being judged as failing compared with a second, but equally reasonable, method for defining proficiency.[8]

Another sign of the arbitrary nature of performance standards is the fact that state definitions of proficiency vary dramatically. A study by the Education Trust reports that 21 percent of students in Louisiana were proficient on state reading tests in 2005, compared with 89 percent in Mississippi.[9] This would seem to suggest that students in Mississippi have far higher achievement than those in Louisiana. But the results from the National Assessment of Education Progress (NAEP), a federally sponsored test taken by representative samples of students in every state, tell an entirely different story. When the two states are put on this even playing field, scores show that *fewer* students in Mississippi were proficient than those in Louisiana for the same year and subject (20 percent of Louisiana students were proficient on NAEP, compared with only 18 percent of Mississippi students). Clearly, Mississippi's definition of proficiency is much more lenient than Louisiana's. Such large differences are not unusual—other states see wide swings in percentage of proficient students, depending on the test, and the same patterns also emerge with tests in other subjects and grades.

While there are many reasons behind these discrepancies, one is clearly that there is no set-in-stone definition of proficiency. Is there a single score that shows that a formerly failing reader can now read at a basic level? Is there a specific point at which students' academic skills become sufficient for carrying out some task when they enter the workplace? No. Clearly, the choice about where to draw the line is always going to be somewhat arbitrary.

Performance standards also throw out a lot of very useful information. Suppose there are two schools in which 75 percent of fourth-graders are at the basic level for math. Is achievement the same in these schools? It's impossible to tell. School A might have most of its students barely above the basic hurdle while school B might have students far above it (but still slightly below the advanced standard). Achievement in school B is clearly higher, but this information gets lost when the measure is percentage passing performance standards

Suppose that car manufacturers decided to stop installing speedometers and instead just put in a warning light to indicate when the car was traveling above the speed limit (easy to do with GPS technology). Imagine driving in such a car. The warning light would be off most of the time, but at some point it would go on. Without a speedometer, you have no idea how much to slow down, so you might hit the brakes too hard, annoying and possibly endangering the person behind you. Or suppose you happen to be a fast driver: the light would be on all the time, and you would just learn to ignore it. But you might end up doing 80 in a 25-mile-per-hour zone. There are good reasons that speedometers have been standard on cars since almost the very beginning. We need speedometers on our test scores for the same reasons—so that we can see exactly how fast we are going.

The arbitrariness and crudeness of performance standards does not mean that proficiency measures have no place in the education system. Indeed, some decisions are inherently up-or-down decisions and there is little choice but to set some type of performance standard. When minimum competency testing was becoming more common in the 1970s, policy makers set a minimum bar to provide a standard that all students could shoot for. For graduation exams or tests used to end social promotion, the performance standard is really the only approach that makes sense.

Part of the motivation for using proficiency standards is to ensure that teachers and schools do not set lower expectations for disadvantaged groups. In 2001, President Bush proposed NCLB, citing the "soft bigotry of low expectations" and set a goal of 100 percent student proficiency by 2014. While this was a worthy goal, the problem with NCLB was that it confused the broader goal with the purpose of performance measures. We all want world peace, for example, but this doesn't mean we necessarily punish military leaders when war breaks out. Likewise, 100 percent proficiency is something we should all aspire to, but punishing schools that fail to reach 100 percent proficiency is not the best way to reach the goal. Accountability is a means to an end—a way of moving toward the aspiration. So I say "Peace, love, and 100 percent proficiency"—but don't confuse those aspirations with performance measures and accountability. I will show later the unintended consequences of failing to follow this rule.

TEST USE: LOW- VERSUS HIGH-STAKES

Finally, there is the question of how to use test results appropriately. The growing trend toward using student tests to hold teachers and schools accountable is one of the main reasons I am writing this book. At present, each state in the country has its own test for at least grades 3 through 8, as well as for one high school grade. These tests are now essentially required under federal law, and the penalties for failure are severe, including closing schools that fail to make AYP in the percentage of students who are proficient. In other words, the state tests are high-stakes.

There are many examples of low-stakes tests as well. For example, although the federal NAEP scores receive national attention, they do not directly affect anyone's job (except perhaps the state superintendent or governor). Also, some states administer a low-stakes test in addition to their high-stakes test, partly because of concern that, to avoid penalties, schools will manipulate the high-stakes tests to make their performance look better than it is.

Because the results of almost any test are publicly reported in some fashion, there aren't any "no stakes" tests, but the stakes do increase as we drill down to smaller and smaller units—say, from schools to teachers—and extend the use of tests to determine decisions such as tenure and compensation.

Real Data Example: Introduction to Oakville

To put the ideas in this book into action, I will occasionally report, discuss, and analyze data from the city of "Oakville" (to maintain anonymity, I have disguised the name and changed the location and demographics). The Oakville example will help bring the ideas of this book to life, so let's start by getting to know the city and its people a little better.

Oakville is a generally middle-class city with a mix of manufacturing plant workers, medical professionals, and other white-collar workers. But a rising share of people in Oakville live in poverty. Because of robotics and overseas competition, the local car plant has fewer and fewer workers. Some buildings on Main St. are boarded up. There are more "For Sale" signs, but still plenty of diehard residents.

What about the schools in Oakville? Table 2-2 below shows the snapshot results of high-stakes state tests, reported in various ways, for thirteen schools that are representative of the whole district. The schools are also given pseudonyms, using names to the first thirteen US presidents.[10] To keep this simple, I report only the end-of-year scores for the last grade in each school (5, 8, and 10 respectively). I limit the table to math scores, though all the patterns discussed below and throughout the book also apply to reading.

Table 2-2 also reports scores in three different ways: percentiles, scale scores, and percent proficient. Schools are listed in order from high to low on percentiles and average scale scores. Reporting percentiles might seem to contradict my earlier argument against percentiles. But here I am using them in a very different way: rather than calculating the average of the percentiles, which is a bad idea statistically because of the lack of interval scale, I report the statewide

TABLE 2-2
Oakville schools—Math achievement snapshots

		Achievement		
School	% Low-income*	Statewide percentile	Scale score	% Proficient
Elementary (fifth grade)				
Quincy	7%	99	159	98%
Monroe	7%	86	148	93%
Madison	39%	56	140	84%
Jefferson	71%	33	136	69%
Adams	90%	30	135	82%
Washington	94%	14	131	69%
Middle (eighth grade)				
Tyler	7%	95	168	90%
Harrison	14%	84	164	87%
Van Buren	54%	48	158	67%
Jackson	81%	9	151	53%
High (tenth grade)				
Fillmore	4%	97	176	97%
Taylor	17%	87	172	93%
Polk	60%	39	165	93%

*Eligible for free or reduced-price lunch.

percentile of the school average. One reason for doing this is to demonstrate that this small group of schools covers a wide range of achievement levels.

Not coincidentally, the percentiles and scale scores move in tandem because the percentiles are based on the scale scores. For example, Washington Elementary is at the fourteenth percentile, which means that 14 percent of the elementary schools in the state have scale scores below 131. The percentiles and scale scores are also related to percent proficient, but not as closely. As I showed earlier, proficiency lumps students into broad categories. Students who are just above the proficiency cutoff are put in the same achievement group as those at the very top. Look at Jefferson Elementary, for example: the school is in the middle of the elementary school pack in terms of average scale score, but the percent proficient is the lowest among the elementary schools. This means that there are many students in Jefferson who are far above the proficiency cutoff (increasing the average scale scores) and many still below it.

Can we conclude anything about the performance of these schools by looking at table 2-2? No, all three achievement measures represent student snapshots rather than growth. Unfortunately, this does not stop the local *Oakville Gazette* from publishing a table very much like this one each year. Year in and year out, Quincy, Tyler, and Fillmore are at the top, while Washington, Jackson, and Polk are at the bottom. And these rankings play a big role in determining where parents buy their houses.

Notice also the relationship between achievement scores and the percentage of students who are eligible for free- or reduced-price lunch, labeled *low-income*. The pattern is nearly perfect. If we were to rank schools based on income rather than math scores, we would get exactly the same ranking in this case. As I showed in chapter 1, this is typical of the nation as a whole.

THE UNINTENDED CONSEQUENCES OF MEASURING SCHOOL PERFORMANCE WITH TEST SCORE SNAPSHOTS

The Oakville example illustrates the unfortunate reality that snapshot data is driven to a significant degree by family and community factors that are outside the control of schools. Using tables like this one to evaluate schools violates the cardinal rule because schools are being held accountable for things they do not control.

All of the previously mentioned ways of reporting scores—scale scores, performance standards, and percentiles—are potentially useful. But using only a *snapshot* of any one of them to judge school performance creates significant problems. Snapshots of any of these measures have a common flaw: they fail to take into account students' starting points and therefore fail to measure what schools actually contribute. This violates the cardinal rule and induces educators to do things that are inconsistent with their missions. Consider the following examples of unintended consequences of using snapshot measures.

Excluding Students. In Florida, research shows that schools are more likely to suspend students for longer periods when the test date is near and when the students in question had lower test scores the previous year.[11] In Texas, teachers went out of their way to find ways to move students into special education so that low-scoring (i.e., low-snapshot) students would be excluded from testing and therefore not counted as part of the school's accountability rating.[12]

Pushing Good Teachers Out. In North Carolina, research shows that teachers were more likely to leave schools that had low accountability scores, even among schools with similar student demographics.[13] This is unsurprising—teachers care a lot about how the outside world views their success. The idea that accountability would drive teachers out is especially ironic since test-based accountability has arisen partly from research showing that teachers are the most important school resources.[14]

Spinning Wheels in Low-Scoring Schools. The current system provides incentives for schools to change curricula, personnel, and policies when schools fail to meet accountability standards. That would be a sensible response—if the schools, programs, and policies were actually failing. This is part of the story that Frederick Hess tells in his book about urban school districts, Spinning Wheels.[15] His metaphor aptly reflects the continuous cycle of symbolic "reform" that urban school districts pursue, like a school bus spinning its wheels in the mud. The only way for school superintendents to maintain community and school board support is for them to show some success. But the starting-gate inequalities make it very difficult for the school system to show large and measureable progress on snapshot measures. This leaves superintendents in a quandary—they cannot keep their jobs without showing success but they cannot show success because they are judged based on snapshot measures of student achievement that incorrectly assess their performance. The obvious superintendent response is to start changing things—anything—and buy some time in the hopes that test scores will go up, if only by chance. But changing "anything" can mean things that are working well already. In one Massachusetts district, a new superintendent introduced reforms that actually undermined what was seen by many as an effective district organization. It took years for the next superintendent to undo the damage. This is a particular problem for urban school districts that fall on the wrong end of the starting-gate inequalities and are always under the microscopes of local newspapers and state officials.

Constant cyclical change is characteristic not only of particular districts but also of particular reform strategies. Teacher merit pay has gone through at least four waves of previous interest, adoption, and abandonment—in the 1920s, 1950s, 1980s, and today (in fact, it would appear that there is some type of unwritten law that merit pay has to be reconsidered every thirty years!). We know these waves did not last long, but we do not know whether the focus on snapshots had anything to do with that. It could be that teacher merit pay just cannot work, no matter how well we measure performance. But these earlier waves measured teacher performance in the same bad way that the *Oakville Gazette* measures the performance of Oakville schools—based on student snapshots—and this almost certainly contributed to the problems with prior merit pay waves.

Allowing Complacency in High-Scoring Schools. The same problem occurs in reverse in high-scoring schools. Rather than spinning their wheels, these schools can coast along on cruise control. The tests only capture low-level skills that most of their students would achieve rather easily no matter what the schools actually does. It is probably no coincidence that students who started off above the ninetieth percentile on the national NAEP test made minimal gains after NCLB was introduced; similar patterns emerged in the state accountability systems of the 1990s.[16] For such schools, more-involved parents probably make up for this lack of test-based accountability pressure by placing their own pressure on schools to succeed, but this does not mean accountability based on measureable student outcomes is unnecessary.[17]

Creating Unnecessary Frustration and Reduced Motivation. Given all of the above problems, it should come as little surprise that educators are frustrated by the current system. Consider this report by Thomas Toch about Marcus Elementary, a school that produces high test scores despite serving a heavily disadvantaged population of students in Dallas, Texas: "The sense that Texas' NCLB ratings are unfair has demoralized the staff at schools like Marcus. Several of [the school's] veteran teachers have left in frustration for wealthy suburban school districts where they felt their achievements would be more fairly recognized, staff members at Marcus say. Keeping good teachers is always a struggle for inner-city schools, and in many cases, NCLB has made things worse."[18]

Also, a recent survey found that much teacher frustration with accountability had less to do with incentives or student testing per se, but rather with being held accountable for factors like student behavior, over which they have little control.[19] The fact that typical accountability systems tend to drive teachers out of low-scoring schools is therefore a predictable result.

This frustration can in turn reduce motivation. In one study of schools on probation for low achievement, teacher motivation increased in the schools that got off probation—that is, when their efforts were recognized—but decreased in the schools that stayed on probation.[20] This is somewhat ironic, given that one goal of accountability is to induce additional motivation.

The same type of problem arises when we shift from evaluating individuals to evaluating programs. Even when reforms are effective, they seem to increase scores only modestly. This leads to still more frustration, especially for teachers who have been around for many years and seen the never-ending cycle of reform. Why change anything if it will not show up in higher performance measures or please administrators and the public? In Hess's study, only 13 percent of districts reported positive effects of reform on student achievement.[21] Lack of accurate information on the effects of particular reforms may be partly responsible for this dismal cycle. If we knew which schools were truly successful, then schools could do a better job of keeping what works and making changes when it's really necessary.

These are not the only problems that arise with test-based accountability (see, for example Rothstein and colleagues' *Grading Schools* for others[22]) but, as I will show, these are important ones that value-added measures can help to address.

This chapter's introduction to student achievement tests is important because the tests are the raw materials that go into value-added measures. These measures can be no better than the tests themselves—garbage in, garbage out.

There are many ways to design, report, and use standardized tests. Throughout this book, I will be mainly dealing with criterion-referenced tests reported as scale scores and NCEs. This is not to say that the other types of tests and reporting methods have no use, but measuring educator performance is not one of them.

Unfortunately, to paraphrase Gertrude Stein, educators get so much achievement information all day long (and with so many strings attached) that they begin to lose their common sense. They receive student achievement data of every size and shape, reported in every which way, for every student group imaginable. We need to do a better job of separating the wheat from the chaff. Scale scores and NCEs from any one point in time aren't really any more useful than performance standards. Viewing snapshots measures as indicators of educator performance is perilous and creates significant unintended consequences.

But the overarching questions remains: How can we transform these measures of performance into something that really follows the cardinal rule? To do this, we have to shift away from snapshots to a new way of looking at achievement data that just so happens to be the first step in creating value-added measures.

3

Measuring Student Growth

"The purpose of learning is growth, and our minds, unlike our bodies, can continue growing as long as we live."

—Mortimer Adler

A century ago, the US economy was dominated by manufacturing and the factory came to symbolize the nation's greatness. Henry Ford was the Bill Gates of his time and "high-tech" meant an assembly line where the car parts moved to the workers instead of the other way around. The whole system was driven by the 1920s "scientific management" craze in which tasks were broken down into small steps and organized in the most efficient way possible. The factory model therefore became the metaphor of choice for people wanting to make schools work more like businesses.

The factory model is important here for two reasons. First, many who criticize test-based accountability in education do so because they think it represents an inappropriate extension of the factory model to education. In a factory, it is easy to determine who has made a mistake because the lines of responsibility are clear. As I already showed, education is more complicated, in how difficult it is to isolate individual contributions and in the number and complexity of its goals. But this argument is also a bit of a straw man because, while accountability designs can and should vary, accountability is important in any organization.

The factory analogy is also useful because it clearly shows where the concept of value-added came from: the value-added is the difference in the total costs of the inputs (labor and raw material) that goes into the plant and the dollar value of the final product that comes out. In the car manufacturing example, if the materials and labor cost $6 million and the cars are sold in showrooms for a total of $10 million, then the value-added is $4 million. Value is determined by what consumers are willing to pay for these items, or market prices. Plant managers and company executives are held accountable for how much value the plant has added. The plant manager can control the price by making a quality product that consumers really want or by reducing costs: negotiating lower prices from suppliers, getting workers to work harder and smarter with what they have, or buying new equipment to help workers do their jobs better. More value-added means more profit.[1]

But the fact that the factory model has worked well in manufacturing (and could work better in investment banking) does not mean that it works everywhere. As we will see, it is not easy to measure value-added in professions such as education where the outputs (goals) are hard to define and even harder to measure. This means we have to think differently about both performance measures and accountability systems in the educational context.[2]

The Oakville Hospital Example

Let's return to the town of Oakville.

Down the road from the Oakville car plant is Hanna Hospital, which cares for area residents. Hanna, like all other organizations, has inputs and outputs, but they are quite different from those in the auto plant. People walk in the hospital door with sicknesses that are hard to identify and far less standardized than the wires and metal that go into the manufacturing plant. The people coming through its doors are different every day, and different from those walking in the doors of hospitals in nearby cities.

The inputs for Hanna Hospital are people, and so are the outputs. This means that neither can be measured in dollar terms. In theory, we could rely solely on the market to supply health care and use market prices to measure the value of output, but we do not do so for a variety of reasons, including a widespread belief that everyone should have at least basic health care, regardless of income. This means that the price of health care does not signify value in the same way that it does in manufacturing or investment banking. Hospital value-added can still be measured, it just has to be done differently—specifically, value-added to health is the difference between the health of people when they come into the hospital and their health when they leave it (or several years later).

But for many years Hanna hospital had a snapshot accountability problem (as described in chapter 2). The state government, like thirty-nine others around the country, rated hospitals based on outcomes such as mortality.[3] But, given Oakville's growing low-income population and above-average crime rates, Hanna sees more than its share of patients who eat unhealthy food and fall victim to violent crime. Many also lack health insurance so that they do not seek medical care until problems become severe. As a result, by just looking at health snapshot measures, it would look as though Hanna Hospital were performing poorly.

But this conclusion would be inaccurate. The measures do not account for the health of patients at intake. In reality, Hanna has outstanding doctors and nurses, and its patients give it high marks. People in neighboring cities often chose Hanna over their local hospitals because of its reputation for quality care—but, because of the (inaccurate) state quality measures, they have stopped doing so. While many hospital leaders and policy makers are aware of this problem, and despite a wealth of data and research showing that actual hospital performance differs from what the performance measures imply, the state has not changed its measures. To combat its low performance ratings, the hospital increasingly refers patients with the most severe illnesses to other facilities, which saves money and increases performance measures, but does nothing to improve health care.[4]

Schools face the same problem as Hanna Hospital did. Instead of focusing on students' growth, education policy makers focus on student snapshots from standardized assessments and rates of high school graduation and college entrance. And in the same way that the hospital's overseers failed to account for patients' baseline health, education policy makers fail to take into account initial student achievement. To satisfy the cardinal rule—to hold people accountable for what they can control—it is far more appropriate to apply the concept of value-added to hospitals and schools.

The good news is that policy makers have made substantial progress toward improving hospital performance measures in recent years (see chapter 10). The bad news is that the same cannot be said for education performance measures.

PERFORMANCE AND GROWTH

Defining the terms is the first step toward being able to measure performance. My definition of performance comes directly from the cardinal rule: performance is what each school and teacher contributes to student outcomes.[5] The key to turning that definition into an accurate measure of performance is making the best and fairest comparisons between schools and between teachers.

As I explained in chapter 1, one of the main difficulties in using student test scores to evaluate educators is that students vary a great deal in what they bring with them to the classroom. But it is reasonable to think that the baggage some students bring is already reflected in the scores they had in the previous year. If they have few role models, then this was probably reflected in lower scores last year. If their parents do not pay much attention to their schoolwork, then this too should be reflected in last year's scores. If they had a low-performing teacher, then they received lower scores last year as a result of learning less in that year.

This suggests an easy way to measure performance: identify a group of schools whose students had similar scores one year, put these schools in the same imaginary bucket, and then compare each school's scores the following year to the other schools within each bucket. For example, there might be three buckets based on third-grade scores: low-, medium-, and high-scoring schools. The schools in each bucket can then be more reasonably compared—the ones with higher fourth-grade scores next year would be contributing the most to achievement. But fourth-grade achievement in the low bucket would not be compared with that in the high bucket because students in each bucket started at very different achievement levels in third grade.

FIGURE 3-1   Using a growth approach to performance measurement

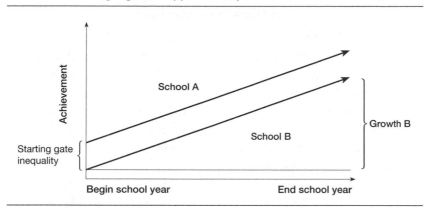

The logical extension and more fine-grained version of this approach is to simply subtract the third-grade score from the fourth-grade score for each student to calculate *growth*. This is illustrated in figure 3-1. Each arrow represents the achievement growth of students over time in two schools. The differences in initial achievement—the starting-gate inequality—are indicated by the bracket in the lower-left-hand corner. The students at school A have walked in the door in a stronger position than those in the school B, and thus their relative positions are outside the control of schools. Once we account for starting-gate inequality, schools A and B are adding exactly the same achievement to students each year, whereas a snapshot would indicate that school A is superior. Given that the starting-gate inequalities are outside of school control, a growth view provides a much fairer comparison (but, as we will see later, still an imperfect one) relative to snapshot measures. We don't want a snapshot but a full-length movie. In *Citizen Kane*, we want to know that *Rosebud* didn't show up only at the end of the movie, but in the opening scene as well, with a mysterious whisper of that same word. Knowing where the movie started, it is much easier to see that the ending reference symbolizes a brief, happy period in the lead character's childhood that he longs for throughout his life. Movies, like school years, have a beginning, end, and much in between.

Oakville Data Example: Comparing Snapshot and Growth Approaches

In chapter 2, I showed the snapshot achievement of Oakville schools and the close relationship between student income and snapshots. Table 3-1 shows test results for the exact same schools, but instead reports achievement *growth* (fourth- to fifth-grade growth in elementary, seventh- to eighth-grade growth in middle, and ninth- to tenth-grade growth in high school). This table also reorders the schools based on growth.

A major change in the story is immediately evident. Washington Elementary, ranked last in the snapshot measure and with the highest percentage of low-income students, is now the third *highest* in terms of growth, ranked ahead of the school with the highest snapshot measure—Quincy. A similar reshuffling of the performance deck occurs in the middle and high schools.

TABLE 3-1
Achievement growth in Oakville

School	Snapshots		Growth	
	Percentile	*Scale score*	*Percentile*	*Scale score*
Elementary				
Jefferson	33	136	71	12
Adams	30	135	69	12
Washington	14	131	46	10
Monroe	86	148	19	7
Quincy	99	159	14	7
Madison	56	140	9	5
Middle				
Jackson	9	151	82	8
Harrison	84	164	33	6
Van Buren	48	158	15	5
Tyler	95	168	6	4
High				
Polk	39	165	46	3
Fillmore	97	176	22	3
Taylor	87	172	13	2

Table 3-1 shows clearly that if we were to measure performance based on growth, we would make very different judgments about who is doing well—and different decisions about who deserves rewards and praise. The table also demonstrates that, unlike the link between snapshot and student income, which is very close, the link between growth and student income is a loose one. (Note that, as in chapter 2, the statewide percentiles are not necessary in this table to show the disjoint between snapshots and growth, but I have included them in the table to demonstrate that this small group of schools covers a wide range of achievement levels.)

MEASURES OF GROWTH: WHICH TEST REPORTS TO USE?

While it seems simple enough to say that value-added measures are rooted in student growth, it turns out that there are many ways to define and calculate growth and each has its own meaning. Table 3-2 summarizes these choices

TABLE 3-2

Summary of different types of growth calculations and their limitations

| Type of growth | Test Reporting Method | | |
	Scale scores	Normal curve equivalents	Performance standards
Student growth	• Best approach for measuring school performance if scaling procedure is trustworthy	• Best approach for measuring school performance if scaling procedure is questionable	• Wastes information
Cohort-to-cohort growth	• Captures irrelevant changes in student cohorts	• Captures irrelevant changes in student cohorts	• Captures irrelevant changes in student cohorts • Wastes information
Growth-to-proficiency	• Holds schools accountable for factors outside their control	• Holds schools accountable for factors outside their control	• Holds schools accountable for factors outside their control • Wastes information

Percentiles and Performance Standards

I have already asserted that scale scores and NCEs are best for measuring student growth and making other important distinctions among the various measurement approaches. Assuming that there is an interval scale—so that an inch of learning is really an inch—it's the same basic arithmetic I used in figure 3-1. But life is more complicated if performance standards and percentiles are used as tools to measure growth. Recall the speedometer problem—throwing out the nuances of car speed (achievement) in favor of a blinking light indicating whether the car is over the speed limit (proficiency).

To see how this creates problems for school performance measures, consider the students who started third grade in school A in 2007. As depicted in figure 3-2, there are three performance standards, ranging from below basic to proficient. A significant number of students improved from the below basic (left vertical bar) to basic level (middle vertical bar) between third and fourth grade.

Now, suppose that the government, as under the federal NCLB policy, has decided that only the percent proficient (right vertical bar) really matters for the sake of accountability. This means that the improvement in

FIGURE 3-2 How performance standards hide real achievement growth

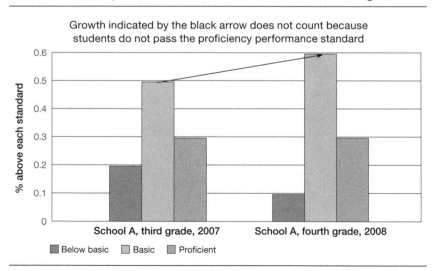

school A from below basic to basic will not count from the standpoint of the performance measures. The percent proficient is exactly the same for this group of students in both years. The change in percent proficient is therefore zero—the same as it would be for schools that did not generate growth from below basic to basic (the arrow).

What this example shows is that, by setting an arbitrary proficiency standard, we throw out a lot of useful information—we assign the same score of proficiency to students whom we know have very different levels of knowledge and skill. Making matters worse, some schools and teachers have more students who are near the cutoff—the *bubble kids*—and they will always have a greater opportunity to show improvement on proficiency. Not surprisingly, when high-stakes decisions have been attached to the percentage of students meeting a performance standard, schools have tended to focus their attention on the bubble kids.

Consider again the case of mortgages and investment banks. One piece of information that lenders use to judge creditworthiness is the potential homeowners' credit score, which is reported as a continuous measure—like speed on the speedometer. In the United States, the credit score (sometimes called the FICO) is on a scale of 350–850. Suppose that instead of reporting specific scores on this scale, credit agencies only told the banks whether the potential homeowner is rated low risk or high risk. This would throw out a lot of useful information. If the cutoff is 600, then a score of 599 gets the same high-risk label as a score of 350. A lender would much rather see the actual score to provide a more nuanced picture of the borrower's situation.

Recall that, as well as discarding potentially valuable information, performance standards are highly arbitrary. Thus, these changes in percentages tell us little about how much students are really learning. They are even more arbitrary when we track students across grades. A student who shifts from nonproficient one year to proficient the next year might have learned a great deal or nothing at all. This uncertainty can be partly addressed by comparing growth in percent proficient of each school with others. Nevertheless, the above examples demonstrate how questionable it is to rely on performance standards for growth calculations.

Growth in percentile rankings is also problematic, but for different reasons. Going from the fiftieth to the fifty-first percentile implies much less improvement than going from the eightieth to the eighty-first percentile.[6] This is because in the typical bell curve, there are far more students near the fiftieth percentile, which makes it easier to leap over other students *with a small changes in learning*. Continuing the FICO score example, suppose you are at the fiftieth percentile with a score of 600 and that the vast majority of people have scores in the 550–650 range. In that case, if you increase your score by 50 points, you will surpass large numbers of people. But if you had a FICO of 700, you would have fewer people with scores near yours, so raising your score another 50 points, wouldn't increase your percentile as much. The fact that you can move past large number of people more easily at the fiftieth percentile might make it seem like it is easier to make gains from that point, but the opposite is true. Lenders don't care how the borrower ranks relative to other borrowers, but about the probability of default, which is very similar between the fiftieth and fifty-first percentile. In short, the percentile for any given person depends on everyone else's probability of default, or how those probabilities are distributed—if it is a bell curve, they mean one thing, but with a relatively flat distribution, more like a box then a bell, the percentiles would mean something else. This problem with percentiles is another example of the importance of interval scale discussed in chapter 2—an inch of skill is not an inch and a percentile point is not a percentile point.

As I explained in chapter 2, percentiles can be converted to normal curve equivalents (NCEs) that are in a sense interval-scaled. NCEs are used in one of the most prominent value-added models, the SAS-EVAAS model created by Bill Sanders. So, let's consider this approach in more detail. An NCE is created as follows: start with the scale score (or raw score), convert to percentile, assume there is a bell curve in students' actual knowledge and skill, then adjust the percentiles to create NCEs so that 10-point NCE improvements refer to the same change in knowledge and skill regardless of the student's initial score. Similar to percentiles, NCEs are scaled so that the average is 50 and they range from 1 to 99.

Notice that this process starts with the scale score. This begs the question, if we already have the scale score, which we've established we can use to measure growth, then why convert the scales score into NCEs? The answer depends on how well scaled we think the test is. I noted in chapter

2 that scaling is difficult because "an inch is not an inch." If the scaling procedure doesn't work very well, and if there is good reason to think that true student achievement really does look like a bell curve, then converting to NCEs might correct problems with the scaling procedure. On the other hand, if the scaling procedure works well, then converting scale scores to NCEs throws out valuable information. The right approach may depend on the particular achievement test being used, and there is no universal agreement about which approach is best, either in general or in specific circumstances.

Student Growth Versus Cohort-to-Cohort Growth

The issues with creating growth measures go beyond how the test scores are reported. When I use the term student growth, I mean individual student growth tracked over time. Unfortunately, student scores are often used in ways that measure growth that are unrelated to individual students, and these pseudo-growth measures are often misinterpreted.

For many years, accountability systems focused on the percentage of students proficient in each grade—for example, how third-grade scores evolve from the year 2000 to 2005. There are two significant problems with this *cohort-to-cohort* approach. First, as mentioned earlier, using growth in the percentage of students passing proficiency standards is a crude indicator that throws out a lot of useful information and fails to recognize growth for most students.

The second problem is that cohort-to-cohort growth is not growth of individual students, but of different groups of students in the same grade over time. This is not useful for assessing educator performance because each third-grade class comprises a different group of students— and I've already shown that students themselves contribute a great deal to their own achievement. An upward trend in this cohort-to-cohort growth could mean that the school is getting better. But it could just as easily mean that the students are entering third grade better prepared for reasons that have nothing to do with school performance (the local library might have created a new reading enrichment program, for example).

To see the difference between student growth and cohort-to-cohort growth, consider the growth (in scale scores) in elementary school A in table 3-2. This table shows both types of growth. The far right-hand column shows the difference in end-of-year scale scores for the 2007 third-grade cohort minus the end-of-year scale scores for the 2008 cohort. The scale scores dropped, so the number is negative—specifically, −10 points. Scores dropped by 5 points in fourth-grade across the two years. The last row indicates student growth based on the same data. The 2007 cohort of students saw achievement growth of +20 points, while the 2008 cohort saw even greater growth of +25 points.

Think about this for a minute. If we are trying to understand the performance of school A, which of these two growth measures should we be most interested in?

The answer is student growth. If we looked at cohort-to-cohort growth, as is typically done in accountability systems, we would be worried that school A is going downhill. The scale scores declined from 2007 to 2008 in both of the grades shown. But the downward trend could derive from factors that have nothing to do with school performance: The students who entered third grade in 2007 might have been better prepared academically than those students who entered third grade in 2008.

In contrast, the student growth measures have a simpler interpretation. Reading down, an observer would actually draw the opposite conclusion from the table about school A. Achievement gains increased between the 2007 cohort (+20) and the 2008 cohort (+25). Cohort-to-cohort growth tells us something very different, and nothing very useful about school performance.

The issue here is more than hypothetical because cohort-to-cohort growth was the basis not only for NCLB but also for state accountability systems like that used in California for many years. The problem was even

TABLE 3-3

Why student growth is more informative than cohort-to-cohort growth: The case of School A

	2007 cohort	2008 cohort	Cohort-to-cohort growth
Third grade	50	40	−10
Fourth grade	70	65	−5
Student growth	+20	+25	

worse under NCLB because that system used cohort-to-cohort growth based on performance standards rather than scale scores.

Focusing on individual student growth is a better approach and sends the right message to educators. I once made a presentation on value-added to a group of educators and said that growth provides the right way of thinking because it suggests that schools should accept students wherever they start when they walk in the door and the school's mission should be to help students learn as much as possible from that starting point. Someone responded by asking, "But isn't that what education is all about?" Yes—exactly.

Student Growth Versus Growth-to-Proficiency

Growth-to-proficiency models have also garnered considerable attention in recent years as a result of a federal Growth Model Pilot program adopted in 2005 that now includes fifteen states.[7] Growth-to-proficiency does focus on individual student growth, which is a positive, but in this model, schools are judged by whether their students are "on track" to become proficient within a certain period of time (say, three years). On the face of it, this approach is intended to acknowledge the starting-gate inequalities and give schools with low initial test scores a chance to get students caught up.

The basic idea is highlighted in figure 3-3 below. It is similar to figure 3-1, but there is now a line at the top indicating the proficiency cutoff that all students are expected to reach. Because students in school B start with lower achievement—the starting-gate inequality again—the educators in that school have to generate faster achievement growth to reach the standard, compared with school A.

The first problem with this approach is that, as I explained earlier, proficiency and other performance standards are completely arbitrary. Growth-to-proficiency doesn't change that. Second, given that the factors causing the starting-gate inequality—family, neighborhood, and community—are still in play, expecting these schools to generate even faster learning than other schools is questionable at best. In fact, it amounts to the very same thing as ignoring the starting-gate inequalities altogether, which I have already established is a bad idea. It is therefore unsurprising that a study by Michael Weiss shows that school performance measured

FIGURE 3-3 School performance measurement under growth-to-proficiency

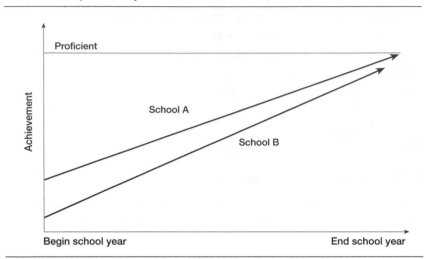

based on growth-to-proficiency look almost exactly the same as with proficiency snapshot measures.[8]

Growth-to-proficiency, while it includes the word "growth," is just a fancy way of coming to the same false conclusion as snapshot measures. Once again, this violates the cardinal rule of accountability—that we should hold people accountable for what they can control.

GROWTH AND TEST EQUATING

While I have argued that focusing on individual student growth based on scale scores is the best approach to measuring school performance, there are some complications that I have not yet raised.

In the example discussed in table 3-2, I argued that student growth increased between the 2007 and 2008 cohorts (from +20 to +25). While this measure is clearly more useful than cohort-to-cohort growth, the interpretation is not perfectly straightforward because the tests change from one year to the next. Such changes are made in part so that teachers do not simply drill students on test items from the previous year. But the fact that the test changes also means that the interpretation of the test scores can change, too. Test designers do their best to equate the tests from year to year to improve comparability, but this process is imperfect. A change in the test that makes it harder to attain a particular score, might give the false appearance that cohort-to-cohort growth is declining when, in fact, the change in scores simply reflects the change in the test itself. In other words, in addition to changes in the students entering third grade, the test might have been imperfectly equated and produced different scores even for students who have the same knowledge and skills. This problem does not change the basic conclusion of table 3-2 that individual student growth and cohort-to-cohort growth can yield very different answers, but it does mean we should be somewhat cautious about concluding the 2007 and 2008 student cohorts learned different amounts.

The test-equating problem should sound similar to the test-scaling problem, and in some ways it is. But there is also a difference: test equating is about ensuring comparability within grades over time and test scaling is about ensuring comparability across grades.[9] Equating is therefore somewhat less of an issue than test scaling when it comes to individual student growth—because individual students don't usually take the same grade-level test more than once. Let me show this more concretely. Suppose that the state changes standards and/or the standardized test in third grade one year. This means that it may be difficult to compare third-grade scores this year to third-grade scores last year. But, for growth purposes, this doesn't really matter because last year's third-graders would be taking the fourth-grade test this year. Even if the fourth-grade standards and assessments also changed, this applies to all the schools similarly. Because a change in the standards and assessments could affect only certain parts of the scale, and therefore only certain types of schools, there is an additional step that can be taken: comparing schools whose students start at similar points on the test scale (i.e., placing them in buckets again, this time based on prior scores). This way, even if the change does affect some schools more than others, the basis for value-added calculations reduces the problem by comparing the affected schools only to one another.

The bottom line here is that cohort-to-cohort growth depends on accurate equating across years within grades, while individual student growth based on scale scores relies on scaling across years and across grades.

(Chapter 4 shows how more sophisticated value-added measures further complicate the issues.)

Oakville Data Example: Comparing Individual Student Growth with Less Preferable Approaches

In table 3-1, I showed how the story of school performance in Oakville changed considerably when the measures were changed from snapshots to growth. But then I also explained how the term *growth* is used to mean many different things. These differences are far from trivial.

Figure 3-4 compares the statewide percentiles for the six elementary schools based on each of the three growth calculations discussed above. For each school, the left-hand bar shows the statewide percentile using the method I am recommending—individual student growth based on scale scores. This is followed by growth in percent proficient and cohort-to-cohort growth.

For some schools, like Monroe and Adams, the method of calculation does not seem to matter much, but for the others, the differences are dramatic. If we were to give equal credibility to these measures, Madison would be either doing so well that it deserves an award or so poorly that a major intervention might be warranted.

FIGURE 3-4 Comparing different types of growth

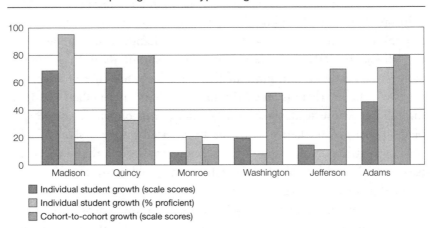

- Individual student growth (scale scores)
- Individual student growth (% proficient)
- Cohort-to-cohort growth (scale scores)

One pattern is that high student growth often means low cohort-to-cohort growth. This makes sense because if a school has high snapshot one year for a particular grade, it really has nowhere to go but down in that same subject and grade the following year. Likewise, very low-scoring schools have nowhere to go but up. Look at Washington and Jefferson, for example. Each has very low student growth (on both scale scores and proficiency), but much higher cohort-to-cohort growth. (Quincy is the only real exception. This could be because the school had a large number of students just below the proficiency bar in the prior year.)

Again, these various measures are not equally credible. For the purpose of measuring school performance, student growth based on scale scores or NCEs is the best approach.

HOW VALUE-ADDED BASED ON STUDENT GROWTH
HELPS AVOID THE UNINTENDED CONSEQUENCES

The above discussion and examples show that I am not splitting hairs when I talk about the differences between snapshot and growth measures. Using individual student growth also avoids some of the consequences of snapshot measures that I discussed in chapter 2:

Excluding Students. With value-added measures, there would be little incentive to exclude students. This could only happen if educators could predict how much students are going to learn the following year. This is harder than it looks. We know we can predict students' point-in-time test score (snapshots) based on their previous year's score. This is why the value-added approach is such a powerful way of measuring performance. But this is different, and easier, than predicting who is going to learn more after accounting for factors outside of teachers' control, and after comparing growth with students in other schools.

Pushing Good Teachers Out. The value-added approach takes into account where students start. If students start off far behind and teachers help them catch up then teachers will be rewarded accordingly. In other words, with value-added, performance measures would be less likely to induce teachers to leave schools serving low-snapshot students.

Spinning Wheels in Low-Scoring Schools. With value-added, there would be no incentive for low-scoring schools to continue the endless cycle of reform in curricula, policies, and personnel. If a program is working—really working in the sense of value-added—then the incentive would be to keep the program and try to improve by changing other less successful programs and practices.

Allowing Complacency in High-Scoring Schools. With value-added, high-scoring schools would be unable to continue resting on the questionable laurels of high snapshot scores. If they are really doing a good job and producing high value-added, then the performance measures would not change much. But it is equally likely that many of these schools are not as effective as they have long appeared and need to improve at least as much as schools we now call failing.

Creating Unnecessary Frustration and Reduced Motivation. Since value-added addresses so many of the problems with current accountability systems focused on snapshots, it could reasonably be expected to reduce the frustration many teachers feel with performance measures. In chapter 1, I quoted a study by Tom Toch about how educators in Dallas saw snapshot measures as unfair.[10] Another study in Pennsylvania found that 80 percent of administrators thought value-added measures were accurate assessments of their performance, compared with fewer than half who said the same thing about the federal AYP, a snapshot measure.[11] Accurate performance measurement won't necessarily drive frustration away, but it certainly should help.

CONCLUSIONS: THE VALUE OF GROWTH

Whether in manufacturing, investment banking, health care, or any other type of organization, value-added measures are important because they represent the only approach that measures and rewards performance in ways consistent with the cardinal rule. Yet, the specific way in which performance is measured in areas like schooling and health care is a complex matter, because the inputs and outputs are people and thus their value cannot readily be measured in dollars or other fixed terms.

To the degree that educator performance measures are based on student achievement, they should be based on individual student growth in either scale scores or NCEs—not on cohort-to-cohort growth, growth in performance standards, or growth-to-proficiency (or any other performance standard). Individual student growth is most consistent with the cardinal rule because it accounts for where students start when they walk into the classroom—for the influences and learning outside the control of the present teacher or school. Using this approach helps to avoid the unintended consequences that arise with snapshot measures.

The data on Oakville schools shows that the specific approach to measuring growth matters. School performance measures based on snapshots are quite different from growth—and quite wrong. Growth measures are better, but not just any growth measures will do. Cohort-to-cohort growth tells us much more about changes in testing instruments and cohorts of students than it does about school performance. Yet, the cohort-to-cohort method was, and to this point remains, the basis for federal accountability. In addition to NCLB cohort-to-cohort growth, some states are using growth-to-proficiency measures, but these are equally misleading as true pictures of school performance. We need to be measuring growth in individual students in either scale scores or NCEs.

When I conduct hands-on workshops about value-added with district officials, they usually get excited about the idea of measuring growth in individual students, and express frustration about how the current system subverts efforts to focus on how each student learns and grows over time. Except in places already using value-added, state and district achievement reports invariably present the data in ways that tell us almost nothing about school performance. I spend hours in these workshops helping educators track down the information they need from different reports so that they learn how well they are really doing. Some get angry because they feel they have been misled all these years, being pressured to focus on performance standards and cohort-to-cohort growth that not only distorted the performance measures but prevented from using student growth for diagnostic purposes, to help individual students.

But this anger is tempered by hope that we can develop an accountability system that more accurately assesses school performance, and one that can be broadly embraced by the educators and administrators who are being evaluated. They have long believed that taking students where they start and helping them learn as much as possible is what education is all about. Everyone has the potential for growth. But our current accountability system often pushes educators *not* to think that way. By this point in the workshop, and this point in the book, it has become clear that taking all students as far as they can go is also what value-added is all about.

4

—

Creating Value-Added Measures

"We think in generalities, but we live in detail."

—Alfred North Whitehead

When it comes to creating specific value-added measures, the details matter. I wrote in chapter 3 that growth should be defined not in terms of changes over time within grades (cohort-to-cohort gains), but for individual students over time based on scale scores or NCEs. This approach sends the right message to schools—that they should take students from wherever they start and move them forward as far as they can. It also yields a more accurate assessment of school contributions to student outcomes.

Since we "live in detail," this chapter goes beyond the generalities of chapter 3 to show exactly why growth is a stepping stone to value-added measures and describe the other steps that follow. I begin with the simplest possible approaches—what I call *basic value-added*—and then describe the limitations of the basic approach and how those limitations can be addressed through *advanced value-added*, which takes into account measureable factors that are outside the control of educators, predicting what achievement students would obtain if they were in a typical school with similar student and school resources, then comparing this prediction to what actually happens. While I write in terms of school value-added in this chapter, the discussion here is also necessary for understanding value-added for individual teachers (a topic discussed at greater length in chapter 6).

FROM GROWTH TO BASIC VALUE-ADDED

Figure 4-1 compares the achievement growth for a single group of elementary students in a single school as they progress through grades 3–6 with the average growth of students throughout the entire state. Since every school has many groups of students, average growth trajectories can be added across groups in the school to get the average school growth. For this elementary school example, the third- to fourth-grade growth, fourth- to fifth-grade growth, and fifth- to sixth-grade growth in a given year are added together to get a measure of school growth. (This might seem like cohort-to-cohort growth, but it's not; it is just adding up the individual student growth across cohorts to get a measure of school success.) Then, the same is done for the whole state and school growth. If statewide growth is lower than a school's growth (as it is in figure 4-1) then the school's value-added is higher than average, and vice versa. Doing this for every elementary school gives a value-added measure for each school that shows not just whether it is above or below the state average, but by how much, so it is possible to compare all schools. The larger the distance between statewide and school growth indicated by the bracket in figure 4-1), the larger the value-added.

FIGURE 4-1 Illustration of basic value-added using growth

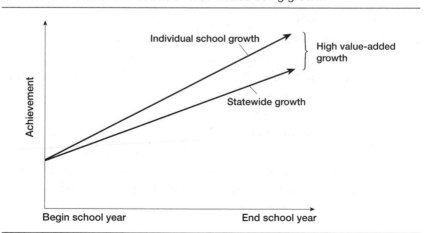

Comparing school growth to state growth, however, rests on a questionable assumption—that accounting for prior achievement alone places schools on a level playing field. But as I have shown, the factors that create the starting-gate inequality also significantly affect subsequent growth.

One alternative value-added approach would be to compare each school with similar schools, which indirectly takes into account the differences in nonschool factors. But what does *similar* mean? Similarity in *initial snapshot* is one reasonable approach. This alternative approach does not change the picture in figure 4-1 at all. It just requires changing the word *statewide* in the legend to similar schools.

The similar-schools approach also has the advantage of addressing limitations in the test scale. I showed in chapter 2 that even scale scores are imperfect and that a 10-point gain can mean different things depending on where the student starts. Comparing schools with similar initial scores means that the students are starting at about the same place and growth around that initial score can be meaningfully compared even if the scale is wrong—because the problems with the scale affect each school's score similarly. From this point on, I will refer to this figure 4-1 comparison of simple growth measures across similar schools as *basic value-added.*

MOVING FROM BASIC TO ADVANCED VALUE-ADDED

If there were an infinite number of schools—and therefore an infinite number of comparisons—basic value-added would be enough to provide accurate comparisons of school progress. Many similar schools and teachers could be placed into buckets and comparisons made within those buckets or groups. Unfortunately, even in the largest states, the number of reasonable comparisons is far from infinite, so applying basic value-added in such circumstances can be problematic. Relying on the bucketing approach would require either that we cut down the number of buckets and make less fine-grained distinctions among schools or create many buckets with fine-grained distinctions, but with so few schools within each bucket that we could not conclude anything with statistical confidence.

To illustrate these problems, and to find a solution, it is necessary to first dig deeper into the issue of student growth. I show below that the idea of making a good comparison group of schools is essentially the same as making a good *prediction*. That is, the point of developing a good comparison is to make a good prediction of what student outcomes would have been if the students had been in the typical similar school, which can be then compared to actual outcomes.

From Comparison to Prediction

At the beginning of each season, television sportscasters predict how our local teams will do. They do this partly by looking at what happened previously. A sports team that finished in last place in the previous season is unlikely to finish in first place the next year. Off-season trades, draft picks, and player retirements might all influence a sportscaster's prediction. The goal of this kind of prediction, of course, is to be as accurate as possible. We want the sportscaster to tell us who will win the Super Bowl or the college basketball tournament, so that we can win bragging rights (and maybe a little cash) in the annual office pool.

The purpose of prediction in performance measurement is a bit different, however. Suppose we are trying to determine who should be the coach of the year. One logical approach would be to look for sports teams that perform better than predicted, indicating that they overachieved. For example, in 1998, Michigan State University Coach Tom Izzo was named national Coach of the Year by the Associated Press. The team won the Big Ten Championship and made the "sweet 16" in the national NCAA tournament, despite losing 12 of 29 games and finishing only fifth in its own conference the prior year. No one expected the team to do so well, and its unexpected success was reasonably attributed (at least partly) to Coach Izzo. So, the *point of the prediction when measuring performance is not accuracy per se, but providing a basis of comparison for judging performance.*

The same is true of performance measures in education. We want a prediction that is as close as possible to the achievement students would have had in the typical school with similar students. If students would have learned less in the average school, then the school has high value-added. We never actually see what the students would have learned in another school, but taking into account all the relevant factors that are outside school control makes it possible to achieve a fairly close prediction of what would have happened. The focus on student growth is critical to making accurate predictions because prior achievement is a strong predictor of future success.

Figure 4-2 is nearly identical to 4-1, but the terminology and the comparison groups have been changed. The statewide or similar schools growth line from basic value-added is now called *predicted achievement* (and the thick line is now dashed to emphasize the difference). This highlights the fact that basic value-added offers one of many possible predictions. The difference between the actual and predicted achievement (indicated again by the bracket) is the school's value-added. In this particular case, the actual achievement is higher than predicted, and therefore the school has above-average value-added.

Up to this point of the discussion, I have only reformulated the basic value-added approach—the pictures are the same, but figure was reframed as prediction. Now, we also need to change the picture. Simple growth measures are a good starting point because prior achievement provides a good prediction of future achievement, but it is not the only important factor.

In fact, the reason for talking about value-added in terms of prediction is that there might be factors we want to take into account but cannot because there are too few schools that are similar. Instead, making

FIGURE 4-2 Value-added from a prediction perspective

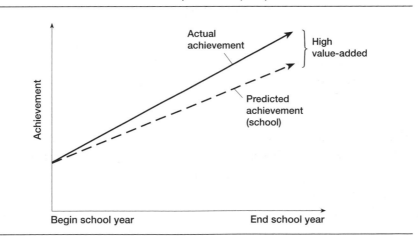

predictions that use statistical techniques takes into account the influence of other factors on achievement for each student. This idea of accounting for multiple factors outside the control of schools in making the achievement prediction is what defines *advanced value-added*.

Accounting for Demographic Factors

Should value-added models take into account student race, income, and other student factors when estimating value-added? On the one hand, the answer to this question seems simple. We should follow the cardinal rule and account for anything that is outside schools' control. And minority and low-income students do still learn at slower rates. One study finds that while most of the gap in achievement between lower and higher income families exists in first grade, it grows by about 30 percent between first and fifth grade.[1] Almost all of the widening of the achievement gap occurs not in the school year, but during the summer vacation—the summer learning loss. This is most likely because the same factors creating the starting gate inequalities also affect learning retention/growth over the summer. Because standardized tests are administered only once per year, the summer learning loss is embedded within the student growth measures each year.

Student factors, including summer learning loss, are outside schools' control, so we should account for them in predicting achievement, right? The answer is a firm maybe. One concern with accounting for these factors is that it gives the impression that the learning rates are lower for these groups *because* of their racial/ethnic minorities or low-income demographic, when in fact these factors are just proxies for home and community environments that have a dramatic effect on learning.[2] (Recall the blond hair and sunburn example in chapter 1.)

A second concern is that the apparent relationship between student background and achievement growth may partially reflect the fact that disadvantaged students are more likely to end up in ineffective schools. While research shows that students tend to learn about the same amount while they are in school, and that summer learning loss is the main culprit explaining why low-scoring students fall further behind, it is possible that schools themselves *really are* contributing to the apparent relationship between student background and race. If this is the case, then accounting for student demographic in the predictions would mask real differences in educator performance.

A third concern is that some see accounting for race and income as reducing expectations for these students. However, "lower expectations" may mean two entirely different things. On the one hand, it could mean that accounting for race and income allows schools to put in less effort to raise achievement for disadvantaged students. Value-added measures that account for race and income do *not* lower expectations in this sense. In fact, the whole point of value-added is to create an even playing field and provide incentives for schools to help all students, including disadvantaged ones.

Alternatively, some interpret "lower expectations" to mean that schools serving disadvantaged students will have the same performance measures as schools serving advantaged students while generating *less* student learning. In this case, there is indeed basis for concern. Value-added models that adjust predictions based on student race and income do require schools to produce less learning for disadvantaged students to reach any given value-added score, since they reflect the rationale that schools should not be held accountable for factors outside their control—in this case students' home and community.

There is some potential middle ground on this issue. For example, when statisticians estimate value-added, they also end up estimating the statistical correlation between student race and income and student achievement growth. If this exercise shows that disadvantaged students growth at slower rates, as it almost certainly would based on the research evidence, then districts could use the measured relationship between student disadvantage and learning as an indicator of how well the district is doing to overcome racial and income achievement gaps.[3] Since social and economic disadvantages are commonly associated with lower growth, this might motivate districts to try even harder to help disadvantaged students. That is, rather than lowering expectations, accounting for student demographic factors would drive greater effort and higher expectations.[4]

It is also worth recalling that value-added measures can help reduce the problem of driving out teachers of low-scoring schools, which also tend to have disproportionate shares of disadvantaged students. To the degree that student race and income are associated with their achievement growth, accounting for those factors will reduce the odds of teacher flight from low-income schools.

The debate about whether to account for student demographics appears to have only modest practical significance for the actual value-added measures of specific schools. As I suggested earlier, student background characteristics are much more closely related to snapshots than growth. If student demographics are associated with achievement in every grade, then the association should largely cancel out when one score is subtracted from the other (as discussed in chapter 3). Here is a simple concrete example to highlight this: Suppose that a student scored 60 points in one year and 80 points in the next year and grade, for growth of 20 points. Now, suppose that one factor explaining these scores is that fact that the students' parents do not make sure the child does her homework each night (in all years). This might reduce the student's score by 5 points in each year from what it would have been. So, the student would have scored 65 and 85 (instead of 60 and 80) if the student had done her homework. Notice that the growth is exactly the same in both cases—20 points. To the degree that the influence on student scores is constant over time, the influence on scores should cancel out in this way. Summer learning loss remains a prime example of a situation in which this is not the case and where the influences generally do not cancel out.

Reasonable people can disagree on whether to account for student demographics. How, and how much, schools try to reduce achievement gaps almost certainly depends much more on how they use value-added measures than it does on whether and how they accounted for student background characteristics in creating those measures.

Oakville Data Example: The Diminished Role of Student Disadvantage in Growth Versus Snapshot

Since the decision about whether to account for student race/ethnicity and income is so central, it is important to explore the issue further in Oakville. I had already shown in chapter 2, using a large national sample of schools, that students' family income was closely linked to test score snapshot. Figure 4-3 below shows this more explicitly and, this time, for a larger group of elementary schools in Oakville (more than the six schools I have shown so far). The two measures line up

FIGURE 4-3 The strong relationship between student income and math
snapshot

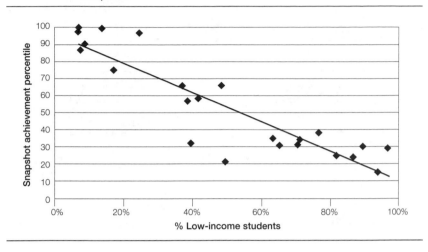

closely—as the number of student eligible for free or reduced price lunch goes up, math scores go down. The line is steep and the dots are close to the line, indicating a strong relationship.

The picture changes quite a bit when advanced value-added rather than snapshot is applied. In figure 4-4, line indicating the general relationship between the two measures is much flatter, and the dots tend to be further away from it, indicating only a loose relationship. Consider the school with the lowest growth among the higher-income schools (an arrow points to this school). There are three schools with greater than 80 percent low-income students (in the oval) that have higher value-added than the high-income school. (Figure 4-7 details exactly how I estimate advanced value-added.)

What is really important about figure 4-4 is that the value-added measure does *not* explicitly account for student race or income (i.e., does not bucket based on these factors). In fact, we see very much the same pattern when using simple growth measures that do not account for anything at all. Similar patterns emerge when we go through the same exercise using student race. This doesn't mean that deciding whether to account for student demographics is unimportant, but it

FIGURE 4-4 Relationship between student income and advanced value-added

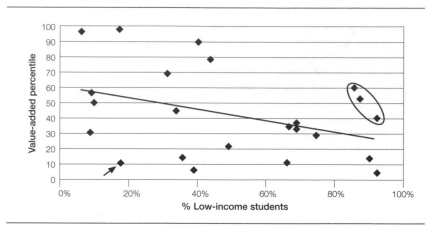

does mean that the decision has less of an impact on the performance measures than might be supposed.[5]

It is also important to note that, in making the above calculations, I have averaged grade-level growth across grades to get school value-added. Specifically, since these are all elementary schools, I averaged third-to-fourth-grade growth with fourth-to-fifth-grade growth. This is one example of how we gradually build up to reporting and analyzing school value-added measures.

Accounting for Uncontrollable School Resources

So far, I have focused on adjusting predictions based on student characteristics, but there are also school factors over which teachers and schools have very little control, and many over which they have almost no control at all. Moreover, most of the factors that are outside of teacher and school control cannot be measured or accounted for in value-added measures. Nevertheless, the general rule is that performance measures should try to account for as many of those uncontrollable factors as possible.

In the basic value-added approach, for example, comparisons could be limited to schools that have similar class sizes and so on. Advanced value-added measures would do this in a more sophisticated and nuanced way, by essentially giving small "bonus" points to schools that are at disadvantage because they have fewer uncontrollable resources.[6]

Figure 4-5 provides an example, using class size as the uncontrollable factor. Research shows that having large classes reduces achievement slightly, at least in elementary schools.[7] The figure shows two different prediction lines, one for small classes and one for large classes. The correct prediction line depends on the specific classrooms to be compared. The figure depicts the actual achievement and value-added for a school with small classes, so the correct prediction line is the one for schools with small classes—the middle line. If this school really had larger classes, then the bottom prediction line would be the right one for comparison and value-added would be even higher. (In reality, the techniques used to create value-added measures make these adjustments in more fine-grained ways than "small" and "large." If a school has an average class size of 17, it gets a slightly smaller achievement bonus then one with an average of 18, which gets a slightly smaller bonus than a school with an average of 19, and so on.)

It is important to emphasize that the difference in the prediction lines is based on what the data actually say about the roles of class size and other factors. When I compare the performance between schools in the

FIGURE 4-5 Value-added with adjustments for uncontrollable school factors

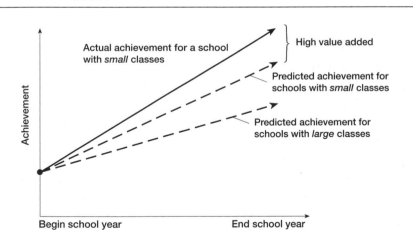

Oakville School District, then the difference in the prediction lines will be determined by the role that class size seems to play in that district, not on what research tells us happens in other districts or in general. Also, note that using bonus points in this way also means that we are once again comparing schools across buckets, but we are doing it in an apparently fair way—by taking into account the effects of the factors on student learning that led us to think about putting them in separate buckets to begin with.

Consider again the case of the FICO credit rating scores that banks use to assess creditworthiness. Banks use statistical models like value-added to predict the likelihood of loan repayment and the FICO score is one of the factors they use to make this prediction. Data might show, for example, that every 50 points on the FICO scale increases the predicted probability of full repayment by 5 percent. The banks can then give a "bonus" of sorts to loan applicants with high FICO scores by charging them lower interest rates.

Class size is one of the easier examples of uncontrollable resources because this is largely outside of the control of the vast majority of schools and teachers. But as table 4-1 shows, a increasingly large number of variables are measured in state and district databases. I have placed these in two categories: *uncontrollable* and *partly uncontrollable* resources. The uncontrollable category is then split into measured and unmeasured factors. It should be clear that any factor that cannot be measured cannot be accounted for, but the complete picture must show what is being excluded. (Notice that I have placed a question mark next to student race/income, reflecting the earlier discussion and debate on this issue.)

Funding and staff positions (other than teachers) are two factors that, like class size, are measured and can therefore be accounted for. They are generally controlled at the district level or by other government agencies and therefore might be relevant for holding those agencies accountable, but not individual schools.

Among the more intangible factors is one that I will broadly define as *district leadership*, which includes everything from inspiring staff and defining a mission to more nuts-and-bolts management issues like coordinating across schools levels (elementary, middle, and high); procurement of supplies; payroll; and communicating with the media, parents, and other stakeholders. District leadership is hard to measure and account for; therefore, some aspects of district performance are (unfairly) credited to the school value-added measures.

Finally, there are the partly controllable factors. Teachers decide, for example, what credentials to obtain and school leaders decide which teachers to hire, including what credentials to look for. Of course, as I showed in chapter 1, credentials do not seem very important, so whether we account for them is unlikely to have much impact on school value-added measures.

There are also partly controllable student factors. Schools have some, though not much, control over *student absences*. Someone in the school (usually not the teacher) is typically responsible for contacting the parents, guardians, and/or, in extreme cases of sustained truancy, calling the local social services office. But these activities play only a small role in whether absences occur, so control here is modest. *Student mobility* refers to students who switch schools, beyond the predictable moves from elementary to middle and middle to high school. Research shows that such moves have a clear negative impact on student achievement, yet whether students come to a school is determined almost entirely by family circumstances, not school or teacher performance. Student mobility is almost entirely outside the control of schools, being driven by external factors. Student mobility is a big issue, especially in low-income areas where children often bounce around between different homes and relatives.

As the cardinal rule suggests, uncontrollable factors should if possible be accounted for in the same way that I showed with class size in figure 4-1. The partly controllable factors should generally not be accounted for, since the effects of these factors are part of the performance that is being measured.

To this point, I have discussed the cardinal rule in somewhat black-and-white terms, but the discussion of different types of schools and student factors suggests that a little more nuance is in order. Specifically, the partly controllable category comprises factors that are controlled by multiple individuals and groups. Rule #2 therefore amends the cardinal rule to reflect this more complex reality. People must be held accountable even for factors only partly within their control. Otherwise, performance measures are likely to create perverse incentives for educators to limit action

TABLE 4-1

Factors to consider accounting for in creating school value-added measures

	Uncontrollable		Partly controllable
	Measured (Maybe account for)	Unmeasured (May want to account for but cannot)	Measured (Shouldn't account for)
School Resources			
	Class size	District leadership	Teacher credentials
	Funding	District funding	Teacher experience
	Staff positions	District policies	
		Collaboration among schools	
Student Factors			
	Prior test scores		Student absences
	Race/income		Program participation (e.g., special education, gifted)
	Mobility		
	Variation in snapshot achievement		

in areas in which they might be able to make positive change. For example, taking teacher experience into account might induce schools to hire younger teachers in order to raise their value-added scores, even though we know that more experienced teachers are generally more effective.

RULE 2

Hold people at least partly accountable for important factors they partly control.

Some More Realistic Cases: Year-to-Year Bounces

When I make presentations about value-added, many educators at about this stage make a comment that goes like this: "But you're assuming that students follow this nice linear path. My students bounce around all over." That is exactly right. There are four main reasons why scores bounce around. The first, somewhat obvious, reason is that school performance varies across grades and over time. Schools should be held accountable for this. But there are three other reasons (discussed in detail in chapters 5 and 6) all of which are outside of school control: (1) changes in (uncontrollable) nonschool resources; (2) changes in (uncontrollable) school resources; and (3) statistical errors.

In figure 4-6, I have added actual and predicted achievement for each grade. The prediction line is still the same, but the actual achievement scores (shown as usual with a solid line) no longer line up. (I could have drawn jagged lines within each school in the earlier figure to reflect this "bouncing," but I did not want to unnecessarily complicate the initial picture.) Notice that in grades 4 and 6, actual achievement is above the predicted line, and in grade 5, it is below. In fact, if we look at the two actual scores for fourth and fifth grade, it looks like students learned almost nothing in fifth grade. But the fourth-grade teachers, and especially the sixth-grade teachers, in this school seem to have made up for it so that the overall school value-added is still above average. This highlights the fact that value-added can be used to learn about the performance of groups and individuals within each school, such as the teachers in a particular grade. I take up this question in chapter 6 but continue to focus for now on school-level value-added examples.

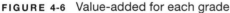

FIGURE 4-6 Value-added for each grade

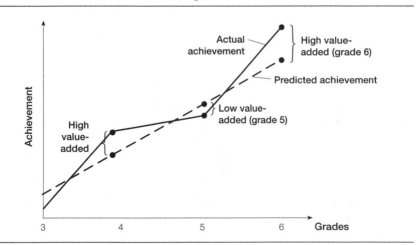

The key point here is that scores bounce around because of factors within school control—what I am calling *school performance*—and factors outside their control, and it is important to distinguish between them.

Oakville Data Example: Basic Versus Advanced Value-Added

The main purpose of this chapter is to explain basic value-added (growth) and advanced value-added. So, in figure 4-7, I show how the two measures compare with one another in Oakville. The basic value-added measures are based on simple comparisons between growth in each school and others in the state, without accounting for any unmeasurable characteristics of schools to students. The advanced value-added measures account for the factors described in table 4-1 as uncontrollable but measured: prior student achievement, student-teacher ratio (similar to class size), staff positions; student mobility; and variation in snapshot achievement.[8] To be consistent with the earlier figures, I also excluded race and income. Funding is excluded because no measure is available in these data. This same approach to advanced value-added is used throughout the remainder of the book.

Note that this is the first time I have reported value-added measures in terms of standardized scale scores rather than percentiles. One implication is that the vertical axis in figure 4-7 shows negative values for

FIGURE 4-7 Basic and advanced value-added usually yield similar results

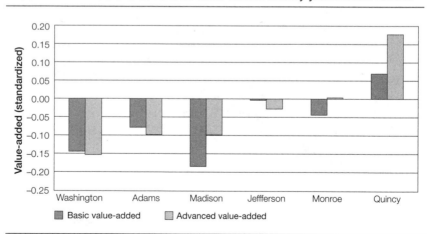

some schools. This means only that the value-added in these schools is lower than the average school. If you prefer, you can think of zero as being roughly the fiftieth percentile of school performance. Measures are often reported this way and I follow this approach throughout the remainder of the book. (The other value-added estimates earlier in this chapter were also based on standardized scale score, but I chose to report them more simply at first.)

Value-added doesn't seem to change very much when uncontrollable factors are accounted for (again, see figure 4-7). This doesn't mean they shouldn't be accounted for—every effort should be made to improve the measures. It also doesn't mean that that uncontrollable factors aren't important; indeed, much of what really matters about schools, even the uncontrollable parts, is hard to measure. What it does mean is that accounting for commonly measured factors does not usually change the results very much. This is different from the analysis in chapter 3, where I showed that individual student growth measures are *quite* different from snapshot measures, cohort-to-cohort growth and so on. Decisions about the specific approaches to value-added therefore matter less than the decision to use value-added at all.

ARE THERE ABSOLUTE STANDARDS OF PERFORMANCE ON VALUE-ADDED MEASURES?

The discussion of standardized scale scores (with average value-added equal to zero) highlights an important property of all value-added measures—they are based on comparisons between individual schools and typical schools. Critics express concern that, when such measures are used, some teachers and schools will always be in the lowest category and some always in the highest. It might seem preferable to make a comparison with an absolute standard against which everyone has a chance to excel. If, for example, all schools that average 10 points in (scale score) growth are classified as high-value-added, then this would be an absolute comparison. But establishing such a standard would create serious problems.

First, a condition for making absolute comparisons across schools would be the ability to make absolute comparisons in test scores between individual students. This is most obvious when using the one test reporting method that is clearly relative: NCEs, which are derived from percentile rankings. If school A has an average score at the fiftieth percentile in third grade in one year and the fifty-second percentile the next year in fourth grade, then school A has above-average value-added. But if students in other schools improve more, then school A's percentile would drop, even if growth for school A was unchanged from the prior year. So the percentile—and therefore the NCE—for each student obviously depends on how other students do, making the comparisons of schools relative as well.

Scale scores, as I have already discussed, seem like a plausible alternative to NCEs that might allow us to make absolute judgments about students and therefore about schools. A student either makes 10 points of growth or not, regardless of whether other students do so. This is exactly like the situation when value-added in manufacturing or investment banking is measured. A dollar is a dollar, so it is possible to make absolute comparisons. A company makes a million-dollar profit or it does not, regardless of what others do.

But scale scores are also imperfect—10 points might mean something similar at each point on the scale, but not the exactly same thing. And attempting to work around this problem by establishing different absolute standards for different groups of students would again call into question the idea that any standard is really absolute.

A second reason that absolute comparisons are difficult is that shifting to student growth accounts for much of what affects student learning in any given year—but not everything. Different teachers have different class sizes and different schools have different (uncontrollable) resources that contribute to student learning. The only way to figure out how much these other factors contribute to student learning is to estimate how much each factor contributes to student learning in the *typical* school (and assign bonus points accordingly). The fact that these adjustments are based on the typical school means that each school's performance depends on what happens in the other schools—again, relative.

While some prefer absolute standards, it is not clear that the relative nature of value-added measures really creates a problem. If school A is excellent but school B is even better, parents will choose school B regardless of whether either school passes any absolute standard. An "absolute" standard in this case morphs into a relative one. Here is a related example: Suppose there was a state policy where schools were taken over by the state if they fell below a particular absolute threshold, and suppose we believed that the absolute standard was based on sound performance measures. Further suppose that the policy worked well so that all schools eventually reached the absolute standard. If the goal is to improve schools, and all schools have reached that bar, then it makes sense to raise the bar again. So, as a practical matter the concern with relative measures is really present with absolute measures anyway. There is no getting around the fact that the educational world is driven by relative comparisons, though some efforts have been made to try and combine the two approaches and build in some absolute component.[9]

SUMMARY

This chapter explains how basic and advanced value-added measures are created, using growth as a basic building block. In basic value-added, we compare similar schools on the basis of simple growth, where "similar" means schools whose students have the same range of initial achievement. Growth is also the basis for advanced value-added, except that value-added comparisons—or, really, the predictions—also account for factors like student demographics and class size. This is very much like grouping similar schools ("bucketing"), except that when there are many factors for which adjustments are necessary, there will almost never be any schools that are similar on all the factors. Thus it is more accurate to adjust predicted achievement for each (uncontrollable) factor based on what the data show about how those factors influence student achievement. If the data on these schools show that, after accounting for all other differences among the schools, schools with smaller class sizes have higher achievement, then the measures can be adjusted for that by building in bonus points for schools with larger classes to offset their disadvantage. Because advanced value-added takes into account more factors that are outside of school control, it provides a more accurate indication of school performance.

As a general rule, any factor that affects student achievement and is outside the control of the school should be used in making the prediction.

Some factors such as class size are fairly uncontroversial, though the appropriate list is somewhat context specific. School-level control of particular factors varies across districts and states, making different adjustments necessary according to contexts. The most controversial factors outside school control are student race and income. While I have presented evidence that minority students have lower achievement growth, it is unclear how much of this is caused by the schools themselves versus the students' environments and preparedness. On the one hand, if prior student achievement insufficiently accounts for student background, then accounting for race and income in predicting achievement makes some sense. On the other hand, accounting for these factors means that schools serving these students can reach the same value-added as schools serving advantaged students, even while generating lower achievement growth—potentially institutionalizing low expectations for minority and low-income students. I will discuss this issue in greater length in chapter 9 when making specific recommendations about how to design and use value-added measures. But, for those who might understandably be concerned about this issue, let me emphasize here that accounting for demographics is not a necessary part of value-added measures and that doing so can actually serve as a tool for helping these students if used appropriately.

By now, you probably have a grasp of the basics of value-added measures. But stopping at this point could give you an overly rosy view of their potential. This and the previous chapters emphasize what is right about value-added. It is important to get a complete picture to really understand what value-added can—and cannot—do for teaching and learning. Thus, the next three chapters are about what can go wrong.

5

—

Understanding Statistical Errors
in Value-Added

"We made too many wrong mistakes."

—Yogi Berra, baseball coach

Whether in business, government, or education, people make mistakes all the time. In the 2008 financial crisis, investment banks systematically underestimated the risk of the mortgages they were buying, but other statistical errors in the crisis were random. Even if bankers had been evaluated according to sophisticated long-term performance measures, and even if they had access to and used good information about investment risk, they still would have made errors by chance alone. In this chapter, I discuss these statistical errors—systematic and random errors—in detail.

The real problems arise when the statistical errors are allowed to become *decision errors*. Investment banks did not incorporate risk taking into their performance pay system. They paid bankers the same bonuses whether they took big risks or small ones, as long as they made a short-term profit. Statistical errors—or what we might call *information errors*—are sometimes hard to avoid, but there is less of an excuse for decision errors. If investment bankers had been more careful with the information they were working with, they could have avoided these problems. Their carelessness was encouraged by the compensation system.

In the education field as well, value-added performance measures will include statistical errors, which makes errors in decisions more likely. In showing that statistical errors distort value-added measures, I begin to show the dangers of using the measures, especially that they entail a trade-off of reduced systematic error in exchange for increased random error. Hence the quotation that opens the chapter: we will inevitably make some mistakes and we have to decide which ones are the "wrong" ones.

INTRODUCTION TO SYSTEMATIC VERSUS RANDOM ERRORS

I'll start by considering how systematic and random errors might arise in education performance measures. As I pointed out in chapters 1 and 2, snapshot measures of school performance understate the performance of schools serving disadvantaged students. In other words, traditional accountability systems make systematic errors that are unfair to specific groups of schools and teachers. Snapshot measures put certain types of schools at a systematic disadvantage, and this in turn leads to a range of unintended negative consequences.

With nonsystematic or *random error* there is no real pattern. They occur by chance. Suppose we want to know whether a coin was rigged so that it was more likely to come up heads or tails. To test this, we could flip the coin 100 times and we would expect 50 heads and 50 tails. However, by chance, the actual distribution would be more like 49–51 or 52–48. This is not because the coin is rigged. It is just luck.

The coin toss example also highlights the distinction between systematic and random error. Suppose two coin flippers carry out the above test and one of them starts each coin toss with the heads side of the coin face up and flips the coin almost exactly the same way each time. This would likely lead to a disproportionate number of heads or tails, leading to splits of 55–45 or even 60–40. In that case, the results for this coin flipper might imply that even fair coins are rigged—and this is a systematic error because other coin flippers using different flipping techniques are likely to come to systematically different conclusions. So, systematic and random errors are both possible even in the simple case of a coin flip.

Note that *systematic* doesn't necessarily mean *deliberate*. The coin flipper might not even realize what is happening.

RANDOM ERRORS

There are two main sources of random error in value-added measures: measurement error in student test scores and sampling error, which I discuss below in turn.

Measurement Error in Student Scores

Some random error in school performance measures is due to the student achievement tests themselves. Suppose a student scores 1,200 on the SAT exam. The student's "true" knowledge is almost certainly not 1,200 exactly, but it is almost certainly within a reasonable range of, say, 1,100 to 1,300. There are three specific types of measurement error that prevent the score from being regarded as true: choice of test questions, subjectivity in grading open-ended questions, and influences on students while taking the test.

The first is measurement error relating to the choice of test questions. Test publishers report this as the degree of test *reliability*. With complete reliability (reported as 1.0), a student who takes the test over and over again, under the same test conditions, will receive exactly the same score. Reliability of 0.8 or higher is typically considered the minimum, and test companies typically report values above 0.9. As a practical matter, reliability is less than complete because only a limited number of test items can be included on the test to measure any given domain or skill. Reliability is also influenced by the similarity and quality of questions in the test pool, from which the actual test items are chosen.

While multiple choice tests remain the norm, there is considerable interest in more sophisticated testing that includes open-ended (constructed response) questions, and even portfolios, graded by trained scorers. These tests have great advantages in that they can capture a wider range of skills than multiple-choice tests. But the fact that there is not one clear "right answer" means that there is also an element of *subjectivity*, no matter how well trained the scorers are and this reduces reliability. So, there is a trade-off between the goal of capturing all the skills we consider important and the goal of capturing those skills reliably.

Measurement error arises not only from the tests themselves but the students who are taking them. If Lyndsey gets sick on test day, then her score will probably not capture her true knowledge and skills. Measurement error also occurs at the school level. If Lyndsey got sick because there is a flu outbreak going around the whole school, then this will affect not only her score, but her schoolmates' scores, while not affecting the scores of similar schools that did not experience the flu outbreak. Or there might be a loud and distracting road construction project outside on test day in Lyndsey's school.

There are also some ways to reduce measurement error. Test designers can include more test questions or use computer-adaptive testing; that is, a computer chooses questions based on the answers to prior questions. When, for example, a very good student gets the first ten questions right, the computer can move on to harder questions to more precisely establish the student's level of knowledge and skill. These approaches obviously come with some disadvantages—the test design and development become more expensive, and not all schools have enough computers to make computer adaptive testing practical. Nevertheless, reducing measurement errors in each student's score would in turn reduce the random error in value-added measures.

An important consequence of measurement error is that student scores that are far away from the mean—that is, very low or very high scores—tend to return toward the mean in future years. The reason is simple: if a student obtains an extremely high score, the odds are that this success is partly due to random chance. So it's likely that the error will be smaller and the student's score will be lower in the next testing period. This is called *regression to the mean*. Of course, there are real differences in students' knowledge and skill, and students who have truly low or high skills will not regress all the way back to the mean. The point is that those real differences can get confused with illusory differences.

I'll use a sports example to illustrate how this works. At the beginning of every baseball season, a few players inevitably start on a record-breaking pace, batting above .450 or hitting a home run in every game—something that no player has ever accomplished over an entire season. Inevitably, as the season wears on, these players come back down to earth and finish the season with numbers similar to their career averages. In some cases, the players really do improve, but real and dramatic changes are unusual. Similar regression to the mean patterns are seen with students who have very low test scores, and can easily be misinterpreted as genuine achievement changes.

Understanding measurement error in individual student scores is important for this discussion because it is one key factor contributing to random error in school and teacher performance measures. Any problem that arises in measuring an individual student's performance creates problems in measuring educators' performance—again, garbage in, garbage out.

Sampling Errors in School Performance Measures

Measurement error is not the only source of random error in school performance measures. The coin toss I described earlier represents exemplifies not only random error, but is also an example of a sampling error.

Statisticians distinguish between *populations* and *samples* taken from those populations. Every ten years, the United States government conducts a census that is supposed to include every individual residing in the country—the entire US population. This endeavor is very expensive, which is partly why it is done only every ten years. Government agencies regularly carry out demographic studies—of unemployment, business investment, education, health, to give a few examples—based on small samples from larger populations. Political polls also rely on small samples of likely voters.

It turns out that, as long as samples are carefully—and *randomly*—selected so that they are representative of the population, the conclusions drawn from them are extremely close to the conclusions that would have been drawn from a census of the entire population. While political polls often represent only a tiny fraction of the population, they are typically very accurate indicators of later voting patterns. But there is always some degree of sampling error because the sample varies, by chance, from the larger population. Consider the coin toss example. You can think of each set of one hundred tosses as a sample from a larger population of possible tosses. We could toss the coin a thousand times, greatly reducing the sampling error, so that the average number of heads would be extremely close to 50 percent. Other things being equal, the larger the sample, the smaller the error.

Every public school in the country is now required to test essentially every student, with the result that we have data on almost the entire population of students—a near census. Why spend so much time and money when we could just test a sample instead? For one thing, the goal of accountability is to measure the performance of the individual school and/or teacher, not just the state or national averages.[1] Taking samples within classrooms would yield significant random errors because even the largest class is still a very small sample. The national NAEP test, discussed earlier, does use a sampling design, but NAEP's purpose is not to hold individual students and educators accountable for test results, but to provide a general picture of national achievement patterns and trends.

Even though we have test data on essentially the entire population of students, it is still useful to think of the data for each school (usually two hundred to one thousand students) as being a sample from much larger state and national populations. Students do not end up in schools by chance, in the way that pollsters randomly select survey respondents from among likely voters, but there is some element of chance. The students who live in a particular neighborhood at a particular time are essentially random, a small fraction of those similar students who could have lived there. We can ask, Why does Norah go to Madison School? The answer might be that her parents got good jobs nearby, or she grew up there, or the bus line happens to go there. Again, none of these things are completely random, but they are largely so for the purpose of measuring school performance. So, even though we have data on the whole population, the goal is to draw conclusions about each individual school and, from the school's standpoint, its students are still just a sample and therefore subject to sampling error.

Since sampling error is outside the control of schools, it must be taken into account to meet the cardinal rule. To that end, the degree of sampling error involved must be clearly communicated along with test results. Political polls usually report that their results are accurate to "±3.5 percent. This is called the *confidence interval* because it indicates confidence that the polling result for the entire population is within this range (interval). Suppose that a political poll reports that one candidate has support from 52 percent of the sample, with a confidence interval of ±3.5. This means there is a 95 percent chance that the level of support for the candidate among the relevant population is within the range of 48.5 to 55.5 percent. The poll indicates that the candidate is winning, but there is a small chance that support is less than the 50 percent necessary to win. Increasing the sample would narrow the confidence interval and our confidence would continue to grow.

The larger the sample, the smaller the sampling error. The larger the number of questions on the test, the lower the test-measurement error (and the higher the reliability). The larger the sample of test items and students, the lower the random error in the educator performance measures that are based on student tests.

Random Errors in Growth and Value-Added Measures

Unfortunately, moving from snapshot measures to growth increases random errors. To see why, let us look at student growth in school A. Suppose the school's average test score in one year is 1,300, with a confidence interval of ±100, meaning there is a 95 chance the true score is in the 1,200–1,400 range. Further suppose that the following year the same students take the test again and achieve a score of 1,400 and the confidence interval is 1,300–1,500. This is shown in figure 5-1.

The confidence interval of each score is the same, ±100, but the confidence interval around the *change* in score is larger. The school's score increases from 1,100 to 1,400 (indicated by dots), for growth of 300 points.

FIGURE 5-1 Why random error is larger in growth and value-added measures

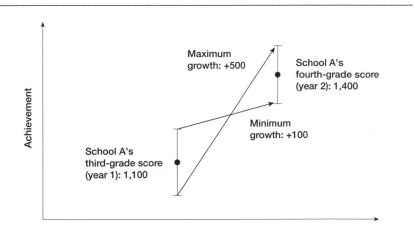

But the confidence interval (indicated by the vertical lines) applies to *both* scores. With a confidence interval of ±100, the school's initial score might have been as low as 1,000 and the second score as high as 1,500, for growth of 500 points. Alternatively, the student's score might have increased by only 100 points—there's no way to know based on the usual standards of statistical confidence. So, while it's clear that random error increases, the precise amount cannot be determined without a more sophisticated analysis.[2]

One implication of this lower reliability is that growth measures can bounce around over time in unpredictable ways, which undermines their usefulness. Given its randomness, the influence of error is likely to change from one time period to the next. If reported growth for this group of students from third to fourth grade was +300, the reported growth for the next group might be only +100, even if actual student learning in these schools is unchanged. Again, because random error is more prevalent in growth measures, the tendency to bounce around randomly is also greater compared with snapshot measures.

Random errors would be an even greater problem in any attempt to measure growth using performance standards such as proficiency. The reason is that the scores of the bubble kids near the proficiency bar could easily go up or down by random chance, and those random fluctuations could push students above or below the bar. In addition to the highly arbitrary nature of the proficiency cutoffs, this is yet another reason to avoid using performance standards.

Oakville Data Example: Random Error in Snapshot Versus Growth

The above discussion explains what random error is and why it gets worse when measures shift from snapshot to growth. Figure 5-2 illustrates this problem by showing snapshot measures for six Oakville elementary schools along with their confidence intervals. If the confidence intervals do not overlap, then we can be sure the snapshot of one school is different from the other. The bottom of the Quincy confidence interval, at about .08, is above the top of the other confidence intervals, clearly demonstrating that Quincy has higher snapshot than the other schools. Only Adams and Jefferson are not clearly distinguishable.

FIGURE 5-2 Random error in achievement snapshot is small

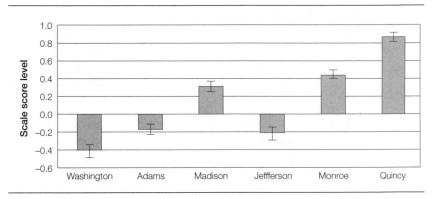

Confidence intervals widen when the measure shifts from snapshot to growth (see figure 5-3). Moreover, average growth rates are much more similar across schools than are snapshots—so much so that, to show the differences in growth, I had to magnify the scale so that the minimum and maximum values are only −0.3 and +0.3 instead of −0.6 and +1.0 as in figure 5-2. This again reflects the way snapshots are driven by factors associated with student income that vary across schools, but income differences largely cancel out when reporting growth. In other words, after subtracting one achievement measure

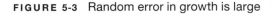

FIGURE 5-3 Random error in growth is large

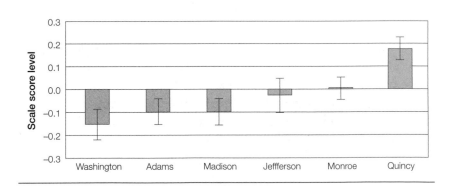

from the other, what remains are (small) differences in student growth and school performance.

As a result, it is now clearly harder to distinguish performance between these schools with statistical confidence. Quincy clearly has the highest value-added of this group, and Monroe is better than Washington, but it is impossible to distinguish Washington, Adams, Madison, or Jefferson from one another.

Differences in growth between schools are harder to distinguish for two reasons. First, the confidence intervals grow larger and, second, differences in growth are simply smaller than differences in snapshot measures. I return to this issue later because it highlights an important misunderstanding about our ability to measure the value-added of schools versus teachers.

Confidence in educator performance measures increases when there are more students, which is why value-added experts always suggest using multiple years of data. To show how this plays out in practice, I have taken a larger sample of schools from the state Oakville is located in and plotted the advanced value-added measure from chapter 4 along with the number of students in each school. As you can see from figure 5-4, extreme values for the value-added measures are most likely to arise with smaller schools. To make this pattern even clearer, I have drawn in arrows connecting the extreme values. This creates a "funnel" shape, meaning that the range of value-added scores becomes smaller as we increase the number of students. In other words, the range of value-added measures is larger on the left-hand side, where the number of students is small and random error is large. As we look to the right-hand side of the picture, the range decreases as the number of fourth-graders increases.

Since smaller schools are most subject to random error, they are most likely to show up with extreme performance measures. This is problematic because, in the context of accountability, it means that smaller schools are more likely to be subject to rewards and punishments—in ways unrelated to their actual performance. Therefore, once they have the student scores—errors and all—researchers also often adjust value-added measures based on the size of the confidence

FIGURE 5-4 Relationship between random error and number of students

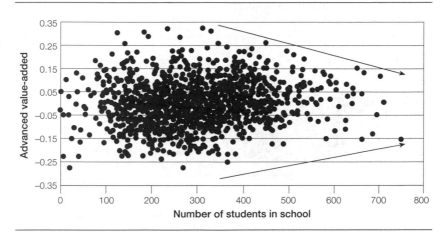

intervals. If a teacher has only a small number of students, then the un-adjusted value-added measure is "pulled back" toward the average teacher value added. To take an extreme example, suppose a teacher had only five students and all five performed poorly and had little achievement growth. This should cause concern about what's happening in the classroom, but there is simply not enough information in that case to draw a conclusion with confidence. In this case, statisticians would assume the teacher is close to the average unless proven otherwise. Such assumptions are sometimes referred to as *shrunken estimates* or *estimates adjusted for measurement error* (see figure 5-5).[3] There is wide agreement among statisticians who study value-added that these corrections should be applied, especially when estimating the value-added of individual teachers whose student enrollments in a given subject vary widely.[4]

The bottom line is that although moving from snapshots to growth reduces systematic error, the problem of random error gets worse. The problem can be reduced by creating value-added measures only for teachers who have a large number of students and/or shrinking value-added measures based on statistical confidence in the measures, but the role of random error cannot be eliminated.

FIGURE 5-5 The reduced range of value-added scores for small schools after shrinkage adjustments

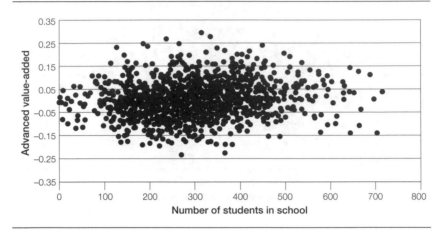

SYSTEMATIC ERRORS AND GROWTH AND VALUE-ADDED MEASURES

The good news is that, while random errors get worse in growth measures, the likelihood of systematic errors is reduced. This is part of the reason why growth and value-added measures are potentially useful. I showed this with the Oakville example in chapter 3. Again, when we measure growth, we can take into account the significant differences in student achievement when students walk in the door—the starting-gate inequality—and therefore avoid systematically punishing schools that serve low-scoring students.

But there are other, less obvious ways in which value-added measures reduce systematic error. Some students get anxious, forget things they know, and fill in the wrong bubbles by accident. For these students, test scores will systematically understate their actual achievement. However, if that particular student is a consistently poor test-taker from year to year, systematic errors in student growth roughly cancel out.

Other errors do not cancel out in measuring individual student growth but do cancel out when educator performance measures are created because they average out across students. For example, one of the first concerns teachers often express when I discuss value-added is the case of a student who has especially significant family problems, such as an abusive parent. Given the importance of family factors, this could reduce achievement, which in turn would influence the performance measures for that student's teachers and schools. In this case, the problem is not measurement error itself—the student really is learning less and the lower scores reflect this—but it does introduce measurement error in the educator performance measures, since they are now failing to eliminate the influence of a factor outside educators' control. But to the degree that all schools have students with these difficult home situations, the errors again cancel out.

Another example is *stereotype threat*. Research shows that minority and female students tend to score lower on tests when they see these tests as reinforcing stereotypes that other students like them are not very good academically.[5] For girls, this is mainly an issue in specific subjects, namely math and science.[6] While this is an unfortunate reality and does call into question some types of conclusions that might be drawn from test scores, there is little reason to expect this pattern would introduce error in growth and value-added measures. Just as the effects of being a poor test taker will tend to cancel out in growth measures, so too would the influence of stereotype threat if it is constant over time. Even if it does not cancel out for individual students, the gender stereotype threat should be fairly evenly distributed across classrooms. Except in all-girls and all-boys schools, the proportion of male and female students in reading and math courses doesn't vary much across schools. Anything that affects all teachers and schools equally cancels out in performance measures. (I could also argue that reducing the stereotype threat is part of the school's job because it involves ensuring that girls feel confident in their ability to do science.)

The potential effects of systematic and random error in student test scores on educator performance measures are summarized in figure 5-6, along with other potential sources of error.

Systematic error in educator performance errors can be introduced not only because of errors in student test scores, but because of *real achievement differences across students*. One of the main advantages of value-added is that prior achievement helps account for important differences in students, reflected in starting-gate inequalities. This means that a third rule should be added to those shown in figure 5-6 (see figure 5-7). And, as noted earlier, even when there are no systematic errors in educator performance measures, we still have to worry about sampling error.

FIGURE 5-6   How errors in individual student test scores affect value-added performance measures for educators

(1) Random error in an individual student's score:
   (a) Increases random error in educator value-added performance measures, but
   (b) Does *not* increase systematic error in educator value-added measures (except with test-based tracking).

(2) Systematic error in an individual student's score does *not* introduce systematic error into value-added performance measures if:
   (a) Systematic error is constant across years for individual students and therefore cancels out for those students (the test anxiety example); or
   (b) Systematic error in student scores is evenly distributed across classrooms and schools (stereotype threat with girls and their math and science scores).

One cannot assume that all potential problems fall into one of these convenient categories. But the rules do highlight the advantages of value-added measures. Rule (2a) does not work with snapshot measures. That is, systematic errors in individual student scores and real differences in students' readiness to learn *do* introduce systematic error in snapshot-based performance measures even when the systematic error and differences are constant across years. Given the reality of starting gate inequalities, this is a major flaw.

FIGURE 5-7   How real differences in individual student achievement affect value-added performance measures for educators: the third rule

(3) Real differences in prior student knowledge and skill do not introduce systematic error into educator value-added performance measures if:
   (a) They are fairly constant across years for individual students (the income example); or
   (b) The real differences in student achievement are evenly distributed across classrooms (the abusive parent example).

It is now possible recast some of the problems identified in chapter 3 with regard to growth based on performance standards and percentiles, as well as cohort-to-cohort growth and growth-to-proficiency. Performance standards throw out useful information by giving the same score (basic, proficient, etc.) to students who have been established as having very different levels of knowledge and skill. Percentiles are not interval-scaled. Both approaches introduce unnecessary random error at best and may introduce systematic error as well. Using any of these test-reporting approaches (including scale scores) with cohort-to-cohort or growth-to-proficiency also adds systematic error.

The various types of errors and key points discussed about them are summarized in figure 5-8.

"SIGNIFICANCE" AND THE BURDEN OF PROOF

To this point, I have focused on errors that can be made in measuring things like performance. But this is just the first step, because the real issue is avoiding errors in decisions when using value-added measures to judge school performance. When measures are used to make decisions, the statistical errors in the measures can result in decision errors and, just as with statistical errors, decision errors can be random or systematic. That is, certain decision errors may systematically favor some teachers and schools over others (a systematic decision error) or the decision errors might be sporadic and follow no clear pattern (random decision errors).

Take the decisions made by judges and juries in the American judicial system. "Innocent until proven guilty" is one of the system's basic

FIGURE 5-8 Sources of statistical errors in value-added

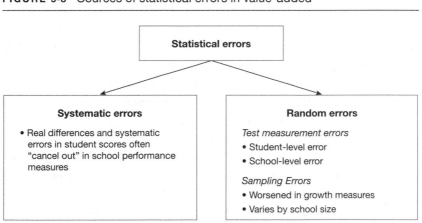

principles and it means that the burden of proof is on the accuser. In criminal cases, prosecutors must show that the accused are guilty "beyond a reasonable doubt." But as anyone who has ever seen a TV crime drama or movie knows this approach sometimes lets the guilty go free—one very significant type of decision error. The "Innocent until proven guilty" principle is much like the approach schools use with teachers. Once tenured, teachers are considered effective enough to retain their jobs unless the school or district can prove otherwise.

In statistics, researchers usually take the same approach as the legal system. We do not say there is a difference between two numbers—for example, in the performance measures of two schools—unless there is close to zero possibility that sampling error is making them look different when they are really the same.

I have used the term *confidence* to describe the possibility of sampling error, but many other statisticians refer to this as *statistical significance*. Significance is a somewhat unfortunate term because the word has a very different meaning in everyday language. Earlier, I discussed the significant problems that low-income students have at home, by which I meant that home and community environments have an educationally *meaningful* impact on students. School performance measures for two schools can be different in ways that are educationally meaningful—that is, one school might actually be doing a much better job than another—but this difference might not be statistically significant in the sense that we might not be statistically confident that the difference is as large as it appears. Conversely, in other cases we might be statistically confident that one school is better than another, but the difference might not be practically meaningful. To avoid confusion, I will continue to use the word *confidence* when referring to the effect of sampling error. Without data on the entire population, there can never be 100 percent statistical confidence about how different groups (in this case, schools) are performing. There is always some uncertainty because of sampling error.

Statistical confidence can also be defined in terms of the probability of making a *type I* error. To say that we are 95 percent confident that the numbers are different is the same as saying the probability of type I error is 5 percent (100 − 95 = 5). This term refers specifically to the likelihood of deciding two numbers are different due to sampling error when in fact the true values (for the population) are the same. Researchers focus most of their attention on type I errors and tend to be very conservative to avoid making them.

But researchers typically give little attention to *type II* errors.[7] Such errors concern the opposite problem—concluding that two numbers are the same when they are really different. To see the difference, consider the tenure process again. Because the burden of proof is on the school system to show teacher ineffectiveness, the system will tend to allow low-performing teachers to stay on the job, minimizing type I errors. Unfortunately, this means some genuinely incompetent teachers will retain their positions, an example of a type II error.

For another example, turn back to political polling. Our candidate has 52 percent support with a confidence interval of ±3.5 percent. This means there is a 5 percent chance that that a sampling error is large enough that the true level of support is really less than 48.5 or greater than 55.5.[8] So, using the usual research standards, we could conclude that we are unsure whether the polling figure is different from 50 percent. But being highly confident of avoiding a type I error also means increasing the chance of a type II error—in this case, the probability of concluding that the poll number is no different from 50 percent when it is really higher, and sufficient for victory on election day. If you conclude that the poll number is indistinguishable from 50 percent and decide to campaign for the candidate to help ensure victory, but the candidate ends up winning comfortably, then this constitutes a type II error. This error also comes at some cost—you spent time helping a candidate who was going to win anyway.

So, there is a trade-off. Setting standards to reduce type I errors simultaneously increases the likelihood of type II errors and vice versa. Both types of errors can be reduced by increasing sample sizes and reducing test measurement error, but neither can be completely eliminated. I will discuss in chapter 8 how confusion over the roles of these two types of errors introduces further confusion into the debate about value-added measures.

Again, the focus of this discussion is whether and how statistical errors result in decision errors. The causes and types of decision errors are summarized in figure 5-9. As I described above, random errors produce both type I and type II statistical errors. These in turn can lead to errors in decisions if no other information is used to make decisions. It is important

FIGURE 5-9 Causes and types of decision errors

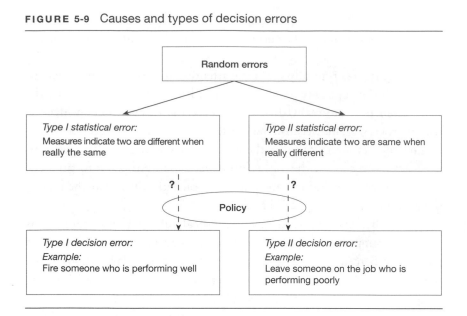

to emphasize, however, that statistical errors do *not necessarily* lead to decision errors, which is why the lines are dashed and the question marks included.

People, not numbers, make decisions. And people make those decisions, especially in education, through policies (shown in the middle oval). I return to this topic in chapters 9 and 10, in which I describe ways of using value-added measures in ways that minimize decision errors.

Systematic errors also contribute to decision errors, though I have excluded them from the figure since the focus here is on random error—and systematic errors are not usually part of the conversation about type I and type II errors. This is an important distinction because it means, in cases like snapshot measures, that we can say we are "statistically confident" that two measures are different when in fact substantial systematic error has not yet been accounted for. Statistical confidence in this sense is only one aspect of the overall confidence desired in any statistical analysis.

So, which error should be of more concern—type I or type II? It depends on what type of conclusion needs to be drawn, as well as the judgment of the decision maker. While avoiding type I errors is arguably the correct target of researchers for the types of decisions they are trying to make, these decisions are very different from the those school systems need to make. For policy makers, type I and type II errors are both very important—punishing a good teacher is a problem, but so is rewarding a bad teacher. Of course, educators and policy makers would rather measure performance perfectly, but since that is impossible they have to make some hard choices.

SUMMARY

The material presented in this chapter forms the basis for a more comprehensive discussion of the strengths and weaknesses of value-added measures in chapters 6 and 7. Several key points are worth emphasizing:

1. *Systematic errors are reduced in value-added measures, compared with snapshot models.* This is important because traditional accountability systems have used snapshot and therefore introduced considerable systematic errors, unfairly punishing schools that serve students who enter school less ready to learn.

2. *Random errors—both measurement and sampling—worsen when shifting from snapshot to growth measures such as value-added.* This is a problem for stakeholders using performance measures to make decisions because it means the measures will bounce around from year to year, giving misleading impressions of actual performance. In addition, this could lead educators to lose confidence in the measures and ignore them, undermining accountability systems that are based on the measures.

3. *Random error is lower with scale score growth and NCEs compared with performance standards.* In the case of performance standards, this is because placing students into broad categories like proficiency throws out a lot of useful information and therefore introduces a form of measurement error.

4. *Random errors produce type I and type II statistical errors.* Both types of errors can be reduced by increasing sample sizes and improving test reliability. But for a given sample size and test, there is a trade-off between type I and type II errors.

5. *Statistical errors can, but do not necessarily, lead to decision errors.* Decision errors can be avoided by combining different measures and by exercising judgment.

The more errors there are in performance measures, the more likely it is that they will lead to decision errors that have real consequences. On one level, it doesn't matter whether the errors are systematic or random, type I or type II. Wrong is wrong. But the distinctions among the errors also matter. First, it matters for interpreting patterns in the data, such as why performance measures bounce around. As we will see later, it also might matter in the inevitable court challenges, and in the court of public opinion, whether certain types of schools and teachers are at a systematic disadvantage.

Anyone can make poor decisions. But in the case of performance measurement, mistakes can be minimized if the decision makers have a clear understanding of the errors that may lead them astray.

6

Shifting from School to Teacher Value-Added

"The whole is more than the sum of its parts."

—*Aristotle, Metaphysics*

The history of accountability is mainly a history of school accountability. We produce school report cards, identify schools failing to help students, and threaten to sanction schools that fail to improve. This level of accountability has a certain logic, because most of the relationships affecting student outcomes—between teachers and students and among teachers, school staff, and school administrators—are based within schools. No Child Left Behind took this same school-level approach, and research suggests that has indeed led teachers and school administrators to change how they teach and lead. Teachers increased instructional time on reading and math by 40 percent, sought to improve their instructional practices in these tested subjects, and increased use of test results to guide instruction.[1]

Teacher response to NCLB is noteworthy because the law includes little direct accountability for teachers.[2] The hope was that the goal of accountability would filter down indirectly to individual teachers through communications, the behest of school and district administrators, and professional pride. While they did not always respond in the precise ways policymakers and parents would have liked, there is no doubt that teachers did respond. More striking is that teachers responded despite being deeply ambivalent about the law's provisions.

While the response to NCLB suggests that school-level accountability can change instructional practice, teacher performance still varies considerably, suggesting that it might be worthwhile to take accountability a step further and hold individual teachers more directly accountable for their performance. But how can we do that? How can we measure the performance of individual teachers and hold them accountable in ways that actually improve teaching and learning? Also, can value-added measures help create missions and messages that attract, develop, and retain teachers who are both caring and highly skilled?

Until very recently, these questions have been irrelevant. Testing was so infrequent that student outcomes could not be used to evaluate teachers, and no other evaluation methods were considered accurate and fair. The rapid expansion of standardized testing, with individual student scores linked to specific teachers over time, has opened up a world of evaluation possibilities, including value-added measures. Even so, good answers to the above questions remain hard to come by. Chapter 5 helps to explain why—performance measures often include substantial systematic and random errors. Errors make it more difficult to make accurate judgments about performance and therefore call into question the accountability decisions we might use the measures for—decisions about professional development, tenure, compensation, and more.

This chapter explains why errors are likely to be magnified with teacher value-added compared with school value-added. I extend the chapter 4 discussion of school value-added and illustrate how teacher value-added measures are created, identifying sources of systematic error that are distinctive to such measures and explaining why random error may be greater than with school value-added. I also discuss how teacher value-added measures vary across school levels (elementary, middle, and high) and which (uncontrollable) factors should be taken into account when creating these teacher measures. Finally, I discuss a middle ground between teacher and school value-added—team value-added.

But first, I need to tell a short story to put things in perspective.

THE CASE OF MS. BLOOM

If you are or have been a teacher, you might be coming into this chapter thinking that teacher value-added is highly problematic. And you might think that, since I've described some potential advantages to teacher value-added, that I am unsympathetic to those concerns. So, I want to give you a better sense of my own perspective and why I care about this.

Like most people, I've been lucky to benefit from many excellent teachers over the years. For me, one who stands out the most is my sixth-grade teacher, Ms. Bloom. I don't recall much about her teaching style and had certainly never heard the word *pedagogy* when I was eleven years old. But what I do remember is a class project in which groups were assigned to lead their own made-up country. Each country had its own set of resources, and we had to decide how to use them. Each day, Ms. Bloom presented us with a change in world events that we had to respond to—natural disasters, changes in the economy, war. How she pulled this off, I do not know. (Or perhaps I've just forgotten what I knew then—summer learning loss for the middle-aged!)

I cannot say whether it was this project or not, but I do give her some credit for my love of education and public service. As I consider accountability policies, I always have in the back of my mind the idea that our performance measures and accountability systems should give awards to the many teachers out there like Ms. Bloom who not only motivated me but taught me skills not covered on any multiple-choice test.

CREATING TEACHER VALUE-ADDED MEASURES

So how exactly could value-added be used to evaluate Ms. Bloom? I'll set aside the problems with today's standardized tests for a moment and just explain the basic mechanics of teacher value-added.

Extending the chapter 4 discussion of how the measures are created is a good place to start. Rather than moving in a nice smooth line, I showed how learning is jagged across grades. At first blush, the situation is not all that more complicated even in schools that have more than one teacher per grade. Figure 6-1 depicts an elementary school with exactly two teachers in each grade 4–6. Ms. Erickson, Ms. Stuart, and Mr. Hacker are above the line, indicating that they are producing above-average value-added, and Ms. Williams, Mr. Brown, and Ms. Smith are below the line. (The dots are not connected by a line as in previous figures because students switch classrooms as they progress through school, so student growth is no longer as clear visually.)

FIGURE 6-1   Illustration of teacher value added within a school

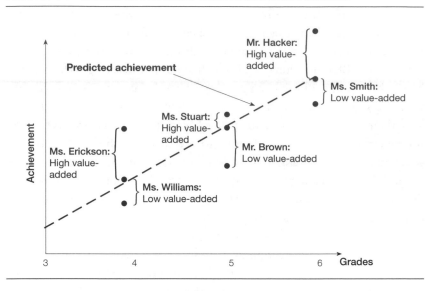

I have deliberately drawn the picture this way because it reflects the general consensus among researchers that teacher effectiveness varies considerably even within schools. This is one reason why there is so much interest in teacher value-added. If it were possible to identify teachers below the line and help them improve—and hire and retain only the most effective teachers—the entire curve could be raised and the education system improved.

The situation is more complex than this simple figure suggests, however. Most of the general sources of complexity have been introduced in other chapters, but they apply somewhat differently to teachers versus schools.

STUDENT TRACKING AS A SYSTEMATIC ERROR IN TEACHER VALUE-ADDED

Recall that one of the main advantages of value-added measures is that they take into account where students start, which is important because classrooms and schools vary widely in this regard. This is partly because students are tracked into different classrooms based on their prior academic success and other factors. Value-added reduces the role of tracking by accounting for prior achievement, but it doesn't appear to be perfect on this count. Whether tracking introduces systematic error depends on how exactly the tracking system works—if it is based on test scores or hard-to-measure student characteristics like motivation, then value-added measures do not completely solve the tracking problem. This is a particularly important issue in middle and high schools where tracking is most pervasive.

Figure 6-2 illustrates the problem. The actual scores of the students are exactly the same as in figure 6-1, but now there are two predicted achievement lines because tracking means that each grade-level pair of classes (Erickson and Williams in fourth grade, etc.) has different predicted achievement. But tracking appears to change the value-added measures considerably. Ms. Smith was low-value-added in figure 6-1, but is now actually above average. It is highly unlikely that teacher value-added measures are influenced quite this much by tracking, but figure 6-2 does illustrate the potential problem.

Notice that I have not indicated in figure 6-2 whether track 1 or 2 is the higher track. The ranking is counterintuitive. It might seem reasonable to expect that the higher-track teachers are at an advantage because

FIGURE 6-2 Illustration of teacher value added with student tracking

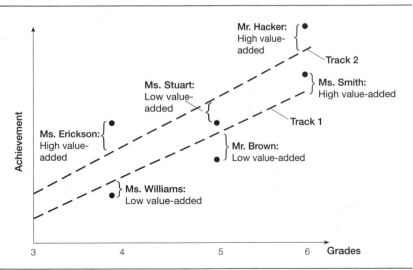

they have higher-scoring students (because of lower summer learning loss, for example). But it's really not clear whether higher-track students have higher predicted achievement after we have accounted for their already high previous (snapshot) scores.

Regression to the mean (discussed in chapter 5) explains this interpretation. If students are assigned to classes based on their prior year's test scores, then some students assigned to the higher track will be there by chance—a lucky break owing to random error. Their gains will most likely be lower than expected because that lucky break is likely to be a one-time event. This in turn can give the false appearance that the higher-track teacher is doing a poor job. Because random error is worse for individual teachers (because they have fewer students than whole schools), the regression to the mean problem is also worse than it was for school-level value-added measures.

DIFFERENCES IN TEACHER VALUE-ADDED IN ELEMENTARY, MIDDLE, AND HIGH SCHOOLS

The problems of systematic and random error with teacher value-added are fairly different depending on the grade levels covered. In elementary schools, there is typically little tracking across classes (though teachers do track within classes). This helps reduce systematic error at the elementary level, but on the other hand elementary school teachers have the fewest students because they have smaller classes and typically instruct only one class per year. This makes random error a particular problem.

In middle school, tracking is more common; and in high school, it is almost universal. But this disadvantage is offset by the fact that middle and high school teachers are responsible for very large numbers of students. If the average teacher in these schools teaches five classes per day, performance evaluations will be based on five times as many student test scores—or more, because class sizes are usually larger in middle and high schools than in elementary schools. This means that the in middle and schools the confidence intervals are narrower.

Another difference across grade levels is that some states administer end-of-course exams in high school that are tightly aligned with course content. The tighter the alignment of tests with course content, the more instructionally sensitive the results will be and the easier it is to measure teacher performance on the basis of test results. On the other hand, high schools typically do not test in every grade and end-of-course exams are more specialized, complicating analysis of growth. The ability to create valid value-added measures for high school teachers therefore varies across states (more on this in chapter 9).

FINDING COMPARISONS THAT FACILITATE COLLABORATION AMONG TEACHERS

Debates about education tend to assume—falsely—that teachers work in isolation with their students. This is one reason that teacher accountability seems so attractive. Every classroom has a teacher who is officially in charge, implying that student outcomes should be attributable to that teacher.

But, as Aristotle suggests, the whole of a school is a greater than sum of its teacher parts. Teachers are dependent on each other and their administrators in ways that may really matter. To function effectively, teachers must coordinate the curriculum across grades, share resources and knowledge, help maintain order and consistently enforce rules and norms of behavior, serve on committees with other teachers and administrators, help younger and less effective teachers to improve practice, and provide a shoulder to lean on after those really bad days. It could be that Ms. Bloom got her innovative and effective class project idea from another teacher or that she had been encouraged or mentored to use project-based learning by a colleague or school principal.

Teachers also depend on noninstructional staff and administrators (and vice versa). Administrators are responsible for creating and supporting a common mission, developing a sense of trust, providing instructional leadership, mentoring teachers, resolving disputes among teachers and staff, creating committees to carry out the core work of schools, keeping schools in compliance with rules and regulations, keeping students and staff safe, and garnering resources to help teachers do their jobs—just to name a few. If administrators do these jobs poorly, it can be reflected in student outcomes.

For all of these reasons, education scholars view schooling as an "intrinsically social enterprise."[3] And, in the larger field of education research, ideas such as *trust* and *community* play a central role in school effectiveness. This is partly why principals, when my colleagues and I asked them what they look for when hiring teachers, responded by saying they look for someone who will get along with others and fit in well with the school culture.[4] Teachers do spend a lot of time on their own with their classes, but that makes their interactions with colleagues that much more important.

This social aspect of education affects the types of teacher performance comparisons that are appropriate. One of the most common complaints about teacher merit pay is that the policy fails to recognize the teamwork that goes into the job and therefore tends to undermine collaboration and pit teachers against one another. This is especially true when only teachers within a single school—where interaction and collaboration are most common and important—are compared. Accountability systems that undermine collaboration are especially problematic because many education leaders and scholars believe the current level of collaboration is already insufficient. This is partly why mentoring, induction, and group planning periods during the school day are increasingly popular. Within-school comparisons could push collaboration in the other—and wrong—direction.

Value-added measures should be designed to encourage collaboration. If the state governments furnish teacher value-added performance measures to schools and districts so each teacher is compared with many other teachers across the state (as I did in chapter 4), then there is no incentive for destructive competition. If one teacher mentors another and there are thousands of other teachers around the state in the "similar" comparison group then the odds of this lowering the mentor's rating or compensation is nearly zero.

With this additional information about teacher value-added, it is now possible to compare and contrast the teacher and school value-added approaches more directly.

TEACHER VERSUS SCHOOL VALUE-ADDED

It is widely believed, and with some justification, that school value-added measures are easier to use than teacher value-added measures. Teacher value-added measures contain more error—both random and systematic—than school value-added. But the difference with regard to random error is not as great as often thought.

Random Error and Statistical Confidence

Schools are responsible for much larger numbers of students than individual teachers, which reduces random error. However, while having more students is helpful, the fact that there is a mix of effective and ineffective teachers in every school means that school performance varies little across schools. And it is a basic maxim of statistics that it is harder to have confidence when differences in measures are small.

Figure 6-3 shows how this maxim plays out with two teachers and two schools. First, consider only the school value-added measures, represented by the dots on the right-hand side of the figure. As I showed in chapter 5, school value-added measures are often close together, and the confidence intervals frequently overlap or, as in this case, are just far enough apart to create statistical confidence that the schools are different. The situation is different with the two teachers in figure 6-3. The value-added measures (the dots) are much farther apart, but the confidence intervals are also much larger. It can therefore not be conclusively stated in this case that Ms. Stuart really has higher value-added than Ms. Brown.

FIGURE 6-3 Sample size in teacher versus school value-added

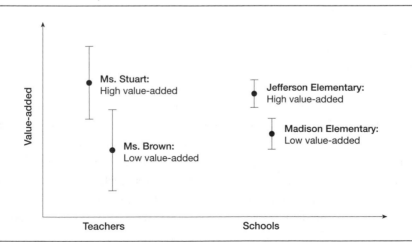

Again, there are two differences between school and teacher value-added that affect the statistical confidence behind our conclusions. One is the difference in the value-added estimates themselves—the larger the difference, the easier it is to be statistically confident. However, because each teacher has a small number of students, the confidence intervals are wider for teachers. Back to the college basketball RPI example: if team A's RPI index is dramatically higher than team B's RPI index, then it will be much easier to be statistically confident that the two are really different. In contrast, it is usually hard to confidently distinguish the top-two teams from one another. When the tournament teams are finally announced, there are often recriminations from fans of the teams that just barely failed to make the tournament. In terms of statistical confidence, they have a point—the teams just barely making the tournament are very similar to those that just barely miss the cut. This is true in the same way that we have less confidence in school value-added because actual school performance seems to fall within a narrow range. But the problem would be much worse if, as with teachers, the tournament selection was made after each team played only five games, instead of the usual thirty. More games (or students) and large differences in performance translate into greater statistical confidence. So, while there are more students per school, this does not necessarily translate into much greater statistical confidence.

Tracking and Systematic Error

I showed above that student tracking may cause systematic error in teacher value-added measures. The same is true of school value-added, though tracking into particular schools (sometimes called sorting) also takes place in more subtle ways. While students are not assigned to schools based on their test scores, there are clear patterns in which types of students end up in which schools. This is partly a function of family income, which can be measured and accounted for when creating value-added measures, but it is also related to things like how important education is to parents. Prior achievement also helps to account for these differences across students (test score snapshots are related to family income), but value-added measures are imperfect when accounting for tracking and sorting—better than with snapshot measures, but still imperfect.

At the school level, only tracking across schools is an issue, so measurement is less of a problem. With individual teachers, both forms of tracking—school-level and teacher-level—introduce error into teacher value-added measures.

Accounting for (Uncontrollable) School Resources

Chapter 4 includes a lengthy discussion of uncontrollable factors that might be accounted for in school value-added measures. Table 6-1 provides an analogous—and longer—list for teacher value-added. The teacher list is longer because everything that affects schools also affects teachers within schools, and then some. The question is, what school-specific factors are uncontrollable and measured for individual teachers?

Table 6-1 includes most of the original list from chapter 4, along with additional factors in **bold**. Teacher aides might improve student learning. But perhaps the most notable additions are teachers' overall and grade/subject-specific experience. As I showed in chapter 1, experience over at least the first five years of teaching provides a meaningful boost to student achievement. Therefore, for at least the early years of a teacher's career it might make some sense to account for this factor, essentially giving less-experienced teachers a bit of a break as they learn the job. On the other hand, an argument could be made that novice teachers should not expect to be among the high performers unless they are unusually talented. This is a case where the decision to account for a school resource depends partly on how the value-added measure will be used. If teacher value-added measures were going to be used for tenure and dismissal, then accounting for experience would seem essential. It would make little sense to deny tenure to inexperienced teachers because they are not as good as teachers with ten years of experience when the decision is whether to allow these young teachers to stay on the job and garner more experience.

Grade-level experience is also important. New research shows that it is not only teachers' overall experience that determines their effectiveness, but their experience in the specific grades and subjects.[5] Teachers have some control over these decisions, though opportunities for such varied experiences often arise from teacher turnover, retirements, and leaves of absence that require a pinch hitter—someone to step into a new area and take over for a short time.

TABLE 6-1

Factors to consider accounting for in creating teacher value-added measures

	Uncontrollable	Partly controllable
Measured *(Maybe account for)*	*Unmeasured* *(Can't account for)*	*Measured* *(Shouldn't account for)*
School Resources		
Class size	District leadership	Teacher credentials
Funding	District funding	
Staff positions	District policies	
Teacher experience	Collaboration among schools	
Grade/subject experience	**School leadership**	
Teacher's aide	**School policies**	
	Collaboration within schools	
Student characteristics		
Prior test scores		Program participation (e.g., special ed, gifted)
Race/income (?)		
Mobility		
Variation in snapshot achievement		
Student absences		
Courses		

Note: Bold text indicates additional factors to those used in creating school value-added measures (table 4-1).

In middle and high school, the specific course being taught is also important because the content of different courses aligns differently with state standardized tests. Tim Sass and I have found that teacher value-added measures can be quite sensitive to the inclusion of course indicators. Most states at this point do not have good information about the courses taught by individual teachers or schools. Finally, student absences, only marginally controlled by the school, are controlled even less by individual teachers; therefore in considering teacher value-added, I have moved them from the partly controlled to the uncontrollable category.

As the cardinal rule suggests, there is reason to account for the factors in the uncontrollable category. The partly controllable factors should generally not be accounted for, since teachers influence those factors, and their effect on student achievement is part of what we are trying to measure. I have therefore excluded most of the controllable factors from this list—notably, instruction.

For both teachers and schools, most of the important uncontrollable factors are also unmeasured—and inherently difficult to measure and account for. As Albert Einstein put it, "Everything that can be counted does not necessarily count; everything that counts cannot necessarily be counted."

There is a way to take these unmeasured resources into account, but the prescription may be worse than the disease. Accounting for unmeasured school resources requires comparing teachers *within* schools. Since factors such as school leadership and collaboration are in principle applied schoolwide, it is reasonable to make such comparisons. But this approach has a number of disadvantages. First, comparing teachers with their colleagues within schools pits them against one another and undermines the collaboration that can improve teaching and learning. Second, it greatly reduces the number of comparisons that are possible; as I will show later, it is preferable to compare only within grades, which would only allow comparisons with one or two other teachers.[6]

What this means is that teachers in schools with greater unmeasured and uncontrollable resources will have an advantage over other teachers. Even if true individual performance levels are the same, the school-level resources will be wrongly attributed to the teachers' performance and unfairly increase their value-added measures—a systematic error. If the most effective teachers really do seem to migrate to more advantaged schools, then the additional bonus they receive from the additional school resources will only add to their measured advantage and make it less likely that teachers in low-scoring schools will be judged as high-performing. This in turn could continue to dissuade effective teachers from moving to those schools, though it is difficult to imagine the problem of attracting teachers to low-scoring schools could be much worse than it is today.[7]

Limited Applicability

A final and quite significant issue is that, while all schools can be evaluated for achievement, all teachers cannot—in fact, depending on the state testing regime, only about one-third of teachers are in tested grades and subjects. This raises some issues of equal treatment, though there are two sides to this. On the one hand, we do want to evaluate teachers in broadly similar ways, and value-added measures cannot be used for all teachers. On the other hand, even if we were to instead evaluate teachers based, for example, on classroom observations or portfolios (something I recommend later as a complement to value-added), those evaluation tools do not, and should not, apply the same criteria across all teachers either. We wouldn't use identical criteria for evaluating twelfth-grade math teachers and kindergarten teachers.

Although the lack of teacher data has led some schools to consider greatly expanding the number of tested grades and subjects, I consider this impulse to be misguided. I'll discuss this topic in detail in chapter 9.

VALUE-ADDED FOR SCHOOL PRINCIPALS AND TEACHER TEAMS

Many school districts already try to evaluate school principals by student test scores, and this is likely to continue as federal policy makers require increasingly aggressive efforts to turn around failing schools. Presidents George W. Bush and Barack Obama both made school turnaround key pillars of their education agendas. They also share the idea that excellent school leadership may be one promising avenue to make those turnarounds successful. At the local level, school superintendents also embrace this logic, though the ways in which superintendents might be using student achievement scores to make their own pseudo-value-added assessments is not well known. Most likely, they are using federal accountability measures, which I have already shown to be inadequate for schools. This makes them even more problematic at the principal level, since principals do not control everything in schools.

The simplest approach would be to attribute school value-added measures to the principal. The principal is ultimately responsible for everything that happens in the school and can potentially influence everything through effective leadership and management. Further, if the conventional wisdom is right that teachers are the most important school resource, then principals can be evaluated based on how well they hire and retain high-value-added teachers, how the value-added of teachers improves over time, and how well principals dismiss or "counsel out" persistently low-value-added teachers. In most districts, principals do have at least some control over staffing decisions.

On the other hand, when a principal first takes over a school, most of the teachers are usually tenured. And, even when principals have positions to fill, they can only select from among those who apply, so administrators in high-poverty schools often have fewer experienced teachers to choose from. This is partly because poorly designed accountability systems almost always judge these schools as failing (see chapter 1), but there is more to it than that. The average teacher may be uncomfortable working with (or ill-trained for) low-income students. In any case, there is ample evidence that certain kinds of teachers (e.g., the more experienced ones) end up in schools with more advantaged students.[8] There are ways to address this, such as placing principals in buckets and comparing principals who are responsible for similar student populations, but it will be difficult to account for all of the factors that make a school attractive to potential teachers. For example, schools located near universities with teacher training programs have an easier time attracting teachers than others.

Given the importance of quality teachers for student learning, accounting for differences in the supply of teachers across schools will be an important challenge for evaluating principals. Nevertheless, if we are going to measure the performance of teachers and schools with value-added, then it stands to reason that we would do something similar for the people leading those schools. It is important that accountability provisions be aligned so that everyone in the system is moving toward the same goals.

Another potential approach to value-added focuses neither on the school nor individual teachers and principals. A key problem with value-added analysis is that the organization of schools does not match the assumptions that must be made when the value-added measures are created. Teachers do not work in isolation; noninstructional staff influence instruction indirectly; and so on. In addition, teachers work through grade- and subject-matter departments, team teaching, and partnerships between classroom and special education teachers. If teaching is really a team sport, then why not treat it like one and evaluate the team as a whole?

This is certainly feasible. It really amounts to just defining many different "mini-schools" within each school. Scores could be the basis for team-based accountability or, since each teacher will likely belong to multiple teams, each teacher's team measures could be used to create a value-added index used for individual accountability. In addition to better reflecting the actual organization of schools, this approach could address the issue of fairness since many individuals in schools are part of teams but not directly responsible for students in ways that allow for individual value-added measures. Random error could also be reduced if the teams cover a large number of students, as would be the case with grade-level teams. One potential problem, however, is that such a system could undermine the collaboration it is intended to facilitate. Teachers might battle one another to work in particular grades and subjects where other teachers are thought to be effective and have high value-added. Nevertheless, since the idea has received so little attention, it is something worth exploring.

Oakville Data Example: Value-Added as a Diagnostic Tool for Teacher and School Performance

I showed earlier how the confidence intervals for teacher value-added measures are larger than they are for school value-added measures. Here, I go further by highlighting this point for a group of specific teachers and schools from Oakville.

Figure 6-4 focuses on three Oakville elementary schools. The left bar in each group reflects the school's value-added, taken directly from chapter 5. As before, we can say with statistical confidence that Quincy as a whole has higher school value-added than the other two. Teacher value-added measures are shown for three fifth-grade teachers in each of the schools (to the right of school value-added).[9] As I illustrated in figure 6-3, there is much more variation in teacher performance compared with school value-added. Some teachers are far above average and others far below, even within the same schools. Also, the confidence intervals are wide. Of these nine teachers represented in figure 6-4, none can be clearly distinguished from the others.

FIGURE 6-4 Comparing school and teacher value-added

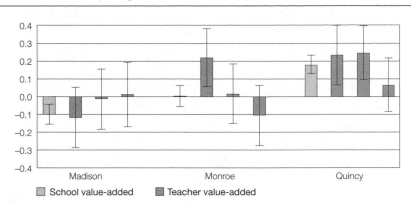

Note: First bar indicates school value-added and others at right indicate teacher value-added within the school.

The first teacher listed for Quincy can be nearly distinguished from the first teacher in Madison and the third teacher in Monroe, but that is as close as we come. None of the other teachers can be distinguished with statistical confidence. As I show in chapter 7, the difficulty of distinguishing teachers is a general problem and, as with the other patterns shown throughout the book, not unique to Oakville.

SUMMARY

Teacher value-added is an attractive extension of school value-added because teachers seem to vary considerably in their performance and because each teacher is, at least in many respects, responsible for specific students. Having some type of meaningful performance measure for individual teachers could be useful for both personal and external accountability.

Unfortunately, with those opportunities come some major challenges. Compared with school value-added, teacher value-added probably suffers from greater statistical errors. The random error problem is not as different between teacher and school value-added as it might seem because the differences in actual school performance appear much smaller for schools than teachers.

Moreover, the unintended consequences of value-added are amplified at the teacher level. With school value-added and accountability, there is a buffer between the accountability system and teachers.[10] To the degree that performance measures are sometimes wrong, this buffering is a good thing because it reduces the negative consequences. Perhaps Ms. Bloom would have fared poorly under teacher value-added measures because they didn't capture her considerable contributions to my motivation and long-term growth (alternatively, perhaps my increased motivation carried over to the standardized tests). On the other hand, when the performance measures are right, this same buffer creates the free rider problem that allows individual teachers to put forth less effort.

This chapter has discussed teacher, school, principal, and team value-added in the abstract. It may be that random error, while probably greater for teachers, is a manageable problem. Likewise, the systematic error caused by tracking might just be an illusion. To really understand the strengths and weaknesses of the measures, we have to go beyond theory and look at the evidence.

7

Marshaling the Evidence
About Value-Added

Senator Moynihan was right. In the aftermath of the U.S. financial crisis, books were written and congressional hearings held to investigate its cause. While there is still disagreement about how to prevent such another such crisis, the investigations uncovered important facts about what went wrong: Investment bankers had incentives to take on too much risk. Banks had too little cash on hand to cover the losses their risky investments might incur. Rating agencies were pressured to inflate their assessments of mortgage investments. We may disagree about what to do about these problems, but facts are facts.

With value-added, we also need to separate fact from opinion. In the previous two chapters I explored value-added's potential for systematic and random error (chapter 5), and showed why value-added measures for individual teachers and principals are more prone to error than for whole school measures (chapter 6). In this chapter, I examine the evidence about the true size of those errors. Research on value-added is moving ahead quickly—and dozens of new studies will no doubt be published even before this book goes to press—but there is now general agreement on some key issues, and it is important to understand these fundamental issues so that future research can be correctly interpreted. The vast majority of evidence pertains to teacher value-added, and therefore this is where I focus my review. Further, based on the evidence, I show that some studies have over-stated the variation in teacher performance and therefore the potential of accountability based on teacher value-added.

This chapter, like chapters 5 and 6, is organized by systematic and random error, although in some cases the issues pertain to both types of errors. Where possible, I report only value-added evidence based on what I consider to be the most appropriate statistical methods, in particular that: (a) the value-added method adjusts or *shrinks* estimates for sampling error; and (b) it combines value-added measures over two to three years. I, along with most researchers working on value-added, recommend these approaches: they allow us to judge value-added measures at their best—with the best methodology.

EVIDENCE ON SYSTEMATIC ERROR

One of the main arguments I make in this book is that snapshot measures of school and teacher performance introduce systematic error into performance measures, violating the cardinal rule of accountability and introducing unintended consequences into accountability systems. Value-added measures account for factors outside teacher control and therefore reduce systematic error. In the language of chapter 4, the key strength of value-added is the prospect of obtaining a more accurate prediction line for every teacher.

But value-added measures do not completely eliminate systematic error. In particular, student tracking, unequal (and uncontrollable) school resources, and misalignment of the timing of test-taking and school actions (specifically, student summer learning loss and mobility) are three major factors that could prevent value-added measures from getting rid of all systematic errors. Alignment of the curriculum with the test, the possibility that some teachers are more effective with certain types of students, and test ceiling effects pose other possible problems, although their effects are less influential. Table 7-1 summarizes these factors, along with the evidence.

Student Tracking

Every educator knows that students are tracked into lower and higher levels and that certain teachers (usually the more experienced ones) are

TABLE 7-1

Evidence regarding factors potentially introducing systematic error into value-added measures

Main Factors	Evidence
Student tracking	Students are tracked; worse in middle and high schools; mostly, but not completely, addressed by value-added, especially if specific courses are not accounted for
Unequal uncontrollable resources	Resources are unequal, but some can be accounted for; significance of unmeasured resources for value-added may be modest
Timing of tests versus timing of school actions • Summer learning loss • Students switching schools	Clear misalignment of timing; worse in high-poverty, high-mobility schools; summer learning loss is a particular issue for value-added with only annual testing
Other Factors	
Alignment of test content with curriculum	Affected by the choice of textbooks in schools, but teachers and schools also make relevant choices; variation in the "enacted curriculum" is large, but arguably the responsibility of the teacher
Certain teachers more effective with certain students	Does not appear to influence value-added much
Test ceiling effects	Does not appear to influence value-added much on average, but could in states with low test ceilings and schools where almost all students are advantaged

more likely to end up in the higher-track classrooms. Obviously, the students taking algebra in eighth grade, for example, are going to have higher snapshot scores than those taking basic math. While a great advantage of value-added measures is that they account for starting-gate inequalities, the inequalities are so large and complex that it is unlikely teacher value-added measures eliminate systematic errors of this type.

David Monk is one of few researchers to study the ways in which principals track students to particular classrooms and teachers in elementary school.[1] In a small sample of sixteen elementary schools, he found that almost all the principals either randomly distributed students or distributed more challenging students evenly, apparently because they want to even out the workload among teachers. Only one principal tried to match students to teachers whose skills were particularly well suited to students' needs. Systematic error in teacher value-added is most likely in these cases where principals deliberately match students.

Jesse Rothstein has published a series of widely cited reports showing that value-added measures do not completely account for tracking.[2] As the Monk study suggests, principals know things about students that are not captured in the data systems used to create value-added measures. I noted in chapter 5 that these unmeasured differences might not be a problem if they are constant across time for individual students or if they are spread out among teachers, but there are almost certainly teachers for whom this is not the case.

Rothstein also identifies a related tracking problem. Random error creates regression to the mean (see chapter 5), suggesting that students who score very high in one year are likely to fall back the next year because some portion of their high scores was probably due to random chance. At the extreme end, a student at the ninety-ninth percentile has nowhere to go but down, and those in the lowest percentiles have nowhere to go but up. Suppose that principals assign students to tracks in the beginning of the year based partly on their previous test scores. Teachers of higher-track classes might actually appear to have lower performance because their students are likely to regress to the mean. Further, if only certain teachers have higher-track classrooms, this tendency will affect all of their classrooms and show up as lower performance year after year.

Rothstein finds that tracking does seem to distort value-added measures somewhat, at least when he measures value-added for only a single year. However, Cory Koedel and Julian Betts show that this problem largely disappears when using at least three years of data for each teacher.[3] Tim Sass and I have confirmed the Koedel and Betts's finding for the majority of schools districts in Florida.[4]

As further evidence, Thomas Kane and Douglas Staiger conducted a clever experiment involving seventy-eight classrooms in the Los Angeles School District.[5] The researchers asked school principals to randomly assign teachers to classes. They then compared the value-added measures before the experiment to those calculated on the basis of random assignment. Random assignment eliminates any potential role of tracking within schools, so this is a good test. And value-added seems to pass the test: schools received similar ratings on average with and without random assignment.[6] This suggests that while tracking might introduce some systematic error, it does not prevent value-added measures from providing useful performance information.

The tracking problem could also arise across schools because some schools serve a much higher percentage of low-performing students—a sort of informal tracking. But this circumstance is unlikely to create the tracking problem suggested by Rothstein because those low-performing students are truly low-performing, making regression to the mean irrelevant. Accounting for where students start, as value-added measures do, should therefore do a reasonably good job of accounting for this cross-school informal tracking when creating school value-added measures.

Even though we know that tracking occurs, it is important to emphasize that not all forms of tracking introduce systematic error into value-added measures. Rothstein's key point is that the student assignment might introduce error when it is based on student achievement or factors that are not directly accounted for and not constant across time.

Unequal District, School, and Classroom Resources

Solving the student tracking problem is arguably the first order of business with education performance measures, but it does not by itself create an even playing field. As I showed in chapter 4 (for schools) and chapter 6 (for teachers), many school factors are uncontrollable and unmeasured, yet have important influences on student achievement. District-level actions affect schools, and school-level actions affect teachers.

Unfortunately, the fact that most of these factors are unmeasured means there is very little evidence about just how important they are. More is known about the effects of some measured factors. Some of my own work with Tim Sass reveals that many factors outside of teachers' control do seem to affect student achievement, and therefore affect value-added measures.[7] For example, larger classes, student mobility, and new school principals seem to reduce student achievement.

Misaligned Timing of Test Administration

I previously noted evidence that students from more disadvantaged backgrounds are more likely to experience summer learning loss, meaning that their knowledge and skills deteriorate when they are not in school. Because achievement tests are administered only once per year, summer learning loss gets attributed to the student's teacher the following year even though the teacher has no control over summer activities. Teachers do not even know who their students will be until just before the school year begins. Teachers can recommend a current student for summer school, but that student's learning would show up in the value-added of next year's teacher (who is likely not the same as the summer school teacher).

The summer learning loss appears to be quite large—on the order of 30 percent of the entire achievement gap between advantaged and disadvantaged students. (Given its size, summer loss is the most likely reason why student demographics still appear somewhat related to student growth.) It is not that most schools are letting these students down or giving up on them, but that students end up losing what the schools give them. This creates a misalignment because year-to-year changes in student test scores include both school year activities, which educators control, and summer activities, which they do not. If all students grew at the same rate during the summer, of course, this would not be an issue.

A second timing issue is student mobility—movement in and out of schools during a given school year. In some schools, the rate of mobility is greater than 100 percent, making it very difficult to say that any given teacher or school is really responsible for a student. Social scientists agree that high mobility is rarely due to school performance, but more likely the result of issues like the loss of a parent's job, change in parent custody, eviction from a home or apartment, or other change in family circumstances. Schools control neither student mobility nor most of its effect on student learning. In most schools, mobility is low and thus not much of an issue. But for those schools where mobility is greatest (usually high-poverty schools), value-added measures are less viable. Student mobility creates a misalignment because, once again, the timing of student growth does not neatly correspond to student attendance in a single school.

Alignment of Test Content with the Curriculum

I have assumed up to this point that the academic standards, as well as the textbooks and other materials teachers have to work with, are aligned with the student standardized tests that are the basis for value-added. In reality standards and textbooks may not be well aligned. Research shows tremendous variation in what is taught across classes within any given state.[8] This is likely driven by a variety of factors, including limitations of the standards and textbooks.

I consider this variation to be a less significant concern compared with student tracking and others above, since an effective accountability system should address this problem. That is, if teachers have incentives to teach the tested material, as they now do under test-based accountability, then the variation in the "enacted curriculum" should be reduced. Deviations from the enacted curriculum are partly the teachers' responsibility and something they should be held accountable for. Although standards and textbooks are outside their control, teachers decide what do with those materials.

The degree of teacher control over what is taught depends on district and school leadership. Many districts have become more prescriptive about what teachers teach, even going so far as to use *scripted curricula*—teachers are expected to follow a rigid schedule and to be literally on the same page throughout the school year. I am not advocating scripted curricula, but only pointing that this probably increases alignment of teaching to standards.

With or without scripted curricula, the fact that tested material is becoming the de facto standard is a valid concern. The extent of the problem depends on how the tests are designed. If the test questions are known with a high degree of certainty in advance, then the standards are not really defined by content at all, but rather by test items. This is problematic and it's one of the big advantages of maintaining high and broad standards and designing tests that draw from a large pool of potential items across a range of key domains.

Certain Teachers Are More Effective with Certain Types of Students.

In Monk's study, one principal assigned students based on the perceived fit between students and teachers, suggesting that some teachers may be more effective with certain types of students. Is that principal right? Does teacher performance vary by student type? J. R. Lockwood and Dan Mc-Caffrey examined this issue and found that teacher value-added did not vary much at all by student type.[9] This analysis is limited because their study can consider only the differences in students that are measured (in this case, mainly achievement). It's possible that principals, as well as the teachers who are often involved in the assignment process, know much more about students—learning styles, classroom behavior, and other needs—than these measures tell us, and they may know that some teachers are better able to address those issues.

Test Ceiling Effects

High-stakes testing in American education initially emerged in the form of minimum competency testing in the 1970s. If any adult were to go to the local elementary school, squeeze into one of those tiny chairs and take a third-grade math test, he or she would almost certainly get 100 percent of the questions right. The third-grade test would therefore be of little use in determining the math achievement of adults. Unfortunately, the same problem arises in more realistic situations where the skills of top-performing third-graders are not reflected in their scores. They are capable of much more than they are being asked to do. Likewise, to use to the basketball example, the very good teams in weak basketball conferences have the same problem, and it places a ceiling on their RPI ratings. They can do no better than win every game and even this is not enough to get them invited to the national tournament. The test is too easy to determine how good they really are.

Since the core idea is that value-added is based on student growth, the implications of test ceilings are evident. If students cannot show their true level of knowledge and skill because the test cannot measure more advanced skills, then growth in test scores will clearly be smaller than real learning growth. This is a particular problem in states using minimum competency testing. If state tests measure only low-level skills, then a high proportion of the students will hit the test ceiling and their growth measures will not accurately capture their learning. Federal policy under No Child Left Behind reinforced this problem by focusing on basic proficiency, which encouraged states to continue focusing on minimum competency.

Cory Koedel and Julian Betts examined this issue using data from San Diego schools.[10] The district uses one test that is not affected by ceilings; it is norm-referenced and thus designed to cover a broad spectrum of learning. Koedel and Betts imposed an artificial test ceiling, assigning a certain percentage of the highest-scoring students a score at the specified ceiling. Their analysis suggests that ceiling effects have little effect when the ceiling is set so that only 10 to 25 percent of student scores hit the ceiling. But the problem becomes more serious with lower ceilings that reduce scores for more students. The reason should be intuitive: If only 10 percent of students are affected by the ceiling, then the vast majority of student scores are unaffected. The larger the proportion of students whose scores are affected, the greater the impact on teacher value-added. This could be a real concern in states where a high percentage of students reach the highest performance standard defined by the state, especially in schools within those states that have high percentages of advantaged students (who are also most likely to be at the test ceiling).

Overall Assessments of Systematic Error

So far, I have tried to break down the potential sources of systematic error and analyze them separately. But there are two other forms of evidence that can contribute to an overall assessment of systematic error in value-added: the relationship, or correlation, between value-added measures and other measures of performance, and fade out in value-added measures.

Correlation Between Value-Added and Other Performance Measures. One indicator of the degree of systematic and random error in teacher value-added measures is the relationship between value-added and other performance measures—in this case, confidential assessments by school principals. I will discuss the strength of these relationships, as well as others later in the chapter, using statistical correlations, so the first step is to consider what correlations mean.

Suppose a group of twenty teachers was evaluated on two different performance measures, These two measures each put teachers into one of four performance categories: 1, 2, 3, or 4, with 1 being the highest and 4 the lowest. If there was a 0 correlation between the two performance measures, then half of the 4s with the first measure would be 3s in the other measure and the other half of the 4s would become 2s, and so on for 1s, 2s, and 3s. This is no better than flipping a coin to determine performance and, in that case, there would be no reason to believe that the measures were really reporting anything meaningful about teacher performance. On the other hand, if none of the teachers switched performance categories, then the correlation would be +1.0. (Correlations can also be negative, but such cases will not be considered in this book.)

Figure 7-1 illustrates this scenario. The left-hand column in each of the six panels reflects the performance category of teachers under the first performance measures and the right-hand column reflects the performance category under the second measure. The panel for the correlation of +0.8 shows that 1s and 2s remain in the same performance category, but the 3s and 4s all swap categories. This means half the teachers switch, but they only switch one category over. Under the correlation of +0.4, one teacher drops two performance levels, from 1 to 3—that is, the teacher goes from being a top-performer to below-average. The fact that this is the instance of a two-level drop is reflected by the faint line. The thicker dashed line

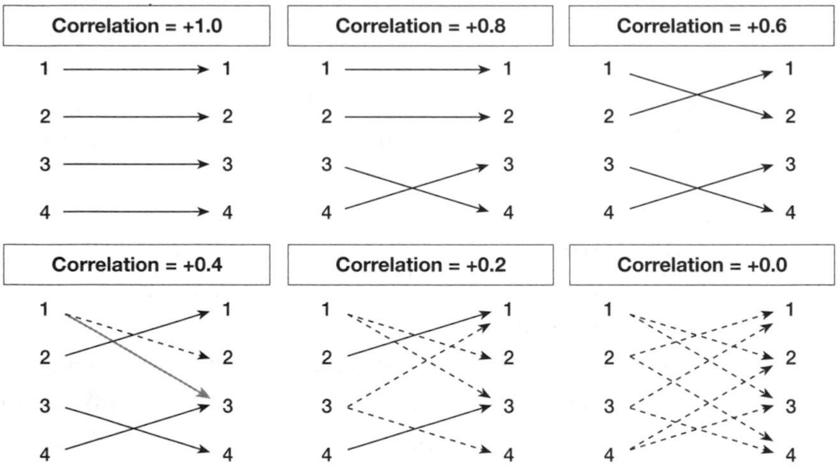

FIGURE 7-1   Illustration of correlations: Comparing two different performance measures

from 1 to 2 indicates that most of the 1s are still switching to 2s. The frequency of switching and the number of levels teachers move both increase as we continue down to correlations of +0.2 and 0. (There are many different combinations of moves that generate a given correlation. I have chosen ones that are visually clear.)

Researchers use correlations to define the strength of the relationship between two numbers, including performance measures. We would not expect teacher value-added measures to be identical to principal evaluations (+1.0) because, in addition to systematic and random error, principals are likely to judge teachers on factors other than how they affect student test scores. This means the correlation should be less than +1.0. But, since principals almost certainly value the skills measured by student test scores to some degree, correlations can be expected to be greater than 0.

Several studies have considered the relationship between teacher value-added and principal evaluations. In my own work with Tim Sass, I estimate the correlation between the two measures (without sampling error corrections) to be in the 0.2–0.3 range.[11] A second study, by Brian Jacob and Lars Lefgren, finds correlations in the 0.3–0.4 range. The numbers are larger partly because Jacob and Lefgren make the shrinkage adjustments discussed in chapter 5.[12] This is like the bottom-left and bottom-middle panel of figure 7-1 where all the teachers switch categories and some move two performance levels up or down. More recent evidence by Jonah Rockoff and colleagues yields similar results.[13]

We would not expect a perfect correlation between these two performance measures, though the correlations here are low enough to generate some concern. Principal assessments contain systematic and random error as well, and we don't really know how large these errors are. Even if we were confident that confidential principal assessments were accurate, there is a big difference between asking principals to give their assessments confidentially to a researcher, as in the above studies, and making a public assessment that could influence a teacher's career or compensation. Public assessments of teachers would likely be inflated because the principals (or any other assessors with a personal relationship to the teacher) would want to avoid discord and hurt feelings. Thus certain teachers would receive preferential treatment that is unrelated to any objective notion of performance. Value-added measures, though not perfect, are not subject to this type of inflation and error because they are based on standardized student achievement scores.

Fade-Out. In their study of the Los Angeles Unified School District, Thomas Kane and Douglas Staiger show that teacher value-added fades out over time—meaning that the effect of a teacher on one year's scores does not show up in the subsequent year's scores.[14] For example, suppose that a high-value-added teacher increases a student's fourth-grade achievement by 10 points per year relative to the average teacher. With fade-out, the effect of this fourth-grade teacher on fifth-grade scores is only half that amount, or 5 points above the average. This example suggests a 50 percent rate of fade-out, which is what Kane and Staiger report.

Some have interpreted this evidence as suggesting that teacher value-added measures are not meaningful. If we think effective teachers have a lasting impact on students (as Ms. Bloom did for me), then we would not expect increased learning to fade out in this way. There must be something wrong with the performance measure, right?

Not necessarily. One likely explanation for fade-out is that knowledge and skills tested in one year are not completely dependent on knowledge of skills acquired in prior years. This is easiest to see at the high school level. When a student walks into a high school physics classroom for the first time in, say, eleventh-grade, it is not clear whether much of the content the student has learned before (with the exception of math) will really have much impact on the student's score. Physics is very different from any other subject the student may have studied. The value-added of the biology teacher on students' tenth-grade science scores is likely to appear to fade out in eleventh-grade because knowing biology does not help students studying physics. While this is an extreme example, the same general principle holds in other subjects and grades.

So, fade-out might not reflect a diminution in what students learned. To figure that out, we would have to retest students in biology again one or two years later and compare results with previous learning levels. This is in some sense the same problem as the misalignment of the curriculum and tested content discussed earlier. Fade-out studies are likely measuring the effect of teachers on subjects that are largely unrelated to the content that is part of their responsibilities.

Again, the banking example provides a useful analogy. The activities of investment bankers in one year are likely to have more of an effect on this year's profits than next year's profits (except of course for activities that take place toward the end of the year). This does not negate the value of this year's contribution to profits. The bottom line is that the general presence of fade-out is not necessarily something to worry about—and in fact, calling it *fade-out* is somewhat misleading because it implies that something is wrong. It's simply not clear at this point whether this is a problem.

Overall, the above evidence suggests that systematic errors are reduced but not completely eliminated with value-added measures. The Kane and Staiger's Los Angeles experiment, as well as the studies of value-added and principal evaluations, suggest that teacher value-added measures provide at least some useful information about teacher performance. Given that estimating teacher value-added is arguably more difficult than school value-added, we can reasonably extend this conclusion to school value-added, though I am not aware of any comparable evidence (it is difficult to imagine an experiment in which all students and teachers are randomly assigned to schools!).

EVIDENCE ABOUT RANDOM ERROR

If only systematic error was all we had to worry about. In previous chapters, I identified three main sources of random error in value-added measures. First, we are dealing with small groups or samples of students—and sampling error is particularly problematic with value-added measures because they are created from student growth measures. Second, test measurement errors arise because test designers cannot include every potential question on a test and because scaling techniques are imperfect. Third, sampling and test measurement errors are compounded in measures like value-added that depend on growth. The larger the random errors, the more we have to worry that value-added measures do not reflect actual differences in performance. Table 7-2 summarizes these sources of random error and the relevant evidence.

TABLE 7-2

Description and evidence of factors potentially introducing random error into value-added measures

Factors	Evidence
Small samples	• Wide confidence intervals for teacher value-added measures put teachers in wrong performance categories
	• Smaller confidence intervals for school value-added, but smaller differences in actual performance among schools make comparisons difficult
	• Some instability in teacher value-added, but improves when using rolling averages and adjustments for sampling error
	• Small samples are a bigger issue in elementary schools
Test instrument (including scaling)	• Results sensitive to test scale and correct scaling method is unknown
	• Difficult to separate sensitivity to test instrument from sensitivity to alignment

Evidence on Sampling Errors and Confidence Intervals

I provided some evidence about confidence intervals in chapter 6 for Oakville, but others have examined this issue as well. Jacob and Lefgren looked at random error in teacher value-added measures and showed that our statistical confidence in teacher value-added measures is low enough that, by the usual standards of statistical confidence, it is only possible to clearly distinguish very low-value-added teachers from very high-value-added teachers.[15] The example I used in chapter 6 is a case in point: I showed two teachers who have very different performance levels, yet wide confidence intervals imply that their true performance levels are not clearly different. We are statistically confident that very low-value-added teachers are not terrific, but we are not so sure that they are worse than average teachers.

What kinds of comparisons can we make with statistical confidence? First, suppose that the goal was to identify very high-performing teachers for some type of reward system and this was done by identifying teachers whose value-added measures were above some cutoff. Because we are using a specific cutoff, there will certainly be some teachers just above the cut-off whose actual performance is almost identical to teachers just below the cut-off. That is a concern because the large random errors mean that some average teachers might end up in the very low- or very high-value-added categories (and vice versa). The only consolation is that very high value-added teachers are unlikely to end up in the very low performance category when multiple years of data are used. So sampling error is a particular problem with policies that place teachers into broad performance categories in this way.

Instability from Year to Year

A related side effect of random error is that value-added measures for individual teachers, especially when based on a single year of data, can bounce around from year to year in ways that are unrelated to changes in true performance. Because this error is random, an error in each individual teacher's value-added will differ from year to year and the value-added measure will change along with it—even when true performance is unchanged. This is sometimes called the instability of teacher value-added.

In their study of San Diego schools, Koedel and Betts examine the stability of value-added measures for individual teachers.[16] They divide teachers into five equal-sized categories—much like the categorization I used in figure 7-1. (Recall that individual teacher value-added measures have more random error than those for whole schools and this means we can expect more switching in this case compared with school value-added.[17]) They find that only 50 percent of teachers ranked in the top-fifth on teacher value-added one year were still ranked in the top-fifth in the subsequent year (the equivalent of a solid straight arrow in figure 7-1). This suggests that half of high-performing teachers got worse relative to their peers over a short period of time—some, dramatically worse. A similar pattern emerges, but in reverse, for the teachers in the lowest category. Roughly 43 percent remained in the lowest category and the remainder moved into higher categories. Koedel and Betts do not report correlations, but their findings imply a correlation of about +0.37.[18] These results are not driven by regression of the mean—that is, of random error affecting teachers at the extremes more than those in the middle.[19]

Daniel McCaffrey and colleagues find similar results and also show that stability is much higher in middle school, as is to be expected because there are more students per teacher.[20] For elementary teachers, they report correlations of 0.2–0.5 and, for middle school teachers, 0.4–0.7. These analyses, as well as those of Koedel and Betts, calculate each teacher value-added measure using data from one cohort of students for each teacher and then estimate correlations across these single-year estimates.[21] The situation improves considerably when more cohorts are added. McCaffrey and colleagues also find that adding one more cohort of students increases stability by 40 to 60 percent, and adding a third increases it further (but not as much).[22] Again, this is predictable because data on more students mean larger samples and larger samples mean lower random error—and less switching of categories.[23]

Everything I have said so far is based on the assumption that instability is due entirely to random error and that actual teacher performance does not change much from year to year. This is a fairly reasonable assumption. Naturally, some teachers will have bad years when an external problem (e.g., divorce, health issues) distracts them from school work. Teachers also improve as they gain experience (at least in the early parts of their careers), and perhaps there are large jumps in performance as a result of particularly effective professional development or the intervention of another instructional leader in a school in a given year. Some researchers have tried to isolate what they call the *nonpersistent* aspects of teacher performance, which roughly translates to factors other than sampling error that make value-added measures differ for individual teachers over time.[24] Many of these nonpersistent factors are outside of teachers' control. For example, as I noted earlier, value-added measures do not account for certain forms of tracking, and if the nature of tracking varies over time, then this would reduce stability in value-added measures. A school principal might assign a teacher to students who are having some short-term behavioral issues that affect the learning environment (not picked up with prior achievement in the value-added measures), but the next year it might be a different teacher's turn to work with these students.

But by and large, we do not expect teacher performance to bounce around in the ways recorded in the above studies. This is why it is reasonable to assume that the instability we observe above in value-added measures is due mainly to random error.

Test Measurement Errors and Scaling

Students' knowledge and skill, as I showed in chapter 2, do not have a clear scale of measurement—an inch is an inch but 10 points is not 10 points (in growth) on a standardized test. The real issue is whether value-added measures are sensitive to the scaling method. If we identify the same teachers as effective and ineffective no matter what scale is used, then the scaling issue is not a problem of practical concern.

In a study of the sensitivity of teacher value-added measures to extreme changes in the test scale, Dale Ballou compared typical scale scores to an alternative in which student growth is simply the change in the student's (relative) ranking.[25] This alternative is intuitive: if a teacher takes students who start at the fiftieth percentile and moves them to the fifty-fifth percentile, then the teacher would appear to have high value-added, whereas a teacher whose students remain at the fiftieth percentile would be average.[26]

Ballou finds that teacher value-added measures are sensitive to whether the scale score or ranking approach is used. On the one hand, only 1 percent of teachers switch from the top fourth to the bottom fourth of teachers when the measure is switched from scale scores to rankings. On the other hand, only 40 percent of teachers ranked in either the top or bottom fourth remained in the same category. These differences in rankings are similar in size to those noted above for instability in teacher value-added across time. However, Ballou only estimated teacher value-added using a single year of data. The number of changes would be reduced, perhaps considerably, with more years of data.

Derek Briggs and Jonathon Weeks also consider sensitivity to test scale, although they consider less extreme options.[27] All of their scaling procedures use the item response theory (IRT) method, but they change specific assumptions within that framework. The comparisons in Ballou's study are like comparing baseball to football, while the comparisons by Briggs and Weeks are like comparing baseball with wooden bats to baseball with aluminum bats. Briggs and Weeks also focus on school rather than teacher value-added. For both reasons, the Briggs and Weeks results suggest that the test scale has only limited influence on school value-added measure.

One way to reduce scaling sensitivity is to compare only schools with similar initial average test scores (an example of bucketing). If two teachers have groups of students who start at 70 points when they walk in the door and each group gains 10 points, then those 10 points are more likely to be comparable because they come from the same part of the scale. In contrast, if the comparison was between two teachers whose students started averaging 30 and 70 points, respectively, then a 10-point gain might mean something different.

Even in comparisons of teachers and schools whose students start at similar parts of the scale, scaling problems will add some random error to value-added measures. This is because the exact distribution of scores with each school is distinct; the average might be the same in the comparison schools, but some schools will have few students at the extremes and others will have a wider range. Such error might even be called systematic because it is systemically related to the distribution of test scores within a school. There is so little known about this issue that it is hard to say which schools and teachers are at a systematic disadvantage.

Overall Sensitivity to Test Instrument

Sensitivity to the test scale is only one element of a larger issue—sensitivity to different testing instruments. In addition to scaling procedures, tests differ in their content, item formats, number of questions, and method of item selection from the item pool. Some comparisons have only limited use—to return to my earlier example, a biology teacher should not expect to have much effect on the physics exam. A more realistic question is, to what degree do different math tests given at the same grade differ in content?

Several studies have examined this question. For example, Tim Sass and I found that whether National Board Certified teachers had higher value-added than others depended on whether we used Florida's low-stakes or high-stakes test to calculate value-added.[28] Two studies have focused on the correlations between teacher value-added measures with different tests. These studies, by Lockwood and McCaffrey and another by John

Papay, find correlations of 0.52–0.65 between teacher value-added measures based on different subscales from the same test (for example, comparing numeracy and fractions from a single math test).[29] These studies find similar correlations of 0.48–0.58 when comparing entirely different tests. It remains somewhat unclear what accounts for these differences. Papay concludes that measurement error and the different timing of the two assessments are the main reasons why the correlations are not higher. Another possible explanation—and one that seems likely, given what we know about how much the enacted curriculum varies—is that tests vary in what specific strands are emphasized and that different teachers simply place different amounts of time and energy on each strand. If this is the correct explanation, then it also means that variation in teacher value-added resulting from different tests is affected by how well teaching generally aligns with the tested content. As I said earlier, it is reasonable to expect alignment when accountability and quality standards are in place. Two different tests cannot be perfectly aligned and still be considered meaningfully different.

The evidence summarized in table 7-2 shows that random error is a limitation of value-added and therefore a problem when using the measures to draw conclusions about performance to make high-stakes decisions. Some teachers will be placed in the wrong performance categories for reasons outside their control—by random chance alone. Random error will always be an issue in value-added measures for three main reasons: (1) small samples of students per teacher and school; (2) test measurement error; and (3) the increased error that comes with any type of growth measure. This is, again, why value-added measures should be "shrunk" to reduce the chance that random error will lead to unjustified punishments or rewards. However, it should be recognized that teachers and schools with few students will rarely have a chance to be considered different from average (i.e., there will be many type II errors). This may be a price we have to pay to avoid the reverse problem of placing teachers and schools with small numbers of students in the extreme performance categories (perhaps subject to accountability sanctions or rewards) for reasons unrelated to their actual performance.

EVIDENCE ON TEACHERS AS THE MOST IMPORTANT SCHOOL RESOURCE

One of the primary reasons there is so much interest in teacher value-added is that there seem to be such large differences in effectiveness between the most and least effective teachers. Below, I discuss three specific studies on this topic by authors who have generally supported the use of teacher value-added: one by Gordon, Kane, and Staiger; a second by Hanushek and Rivkin; and a third by Sanders and Rivers.[30] These studies suggest that simply reassigning teachers could eliminate achievement gaps between students of different races and income groups within three to five years.

Good teachers are very important, and low-scoring students tend to have less-effective teachers, so it stands to reason that reassignment would indeed reduce the achievement gap. But the above evidence suggests a reason why these conclusions are almost certainly overstated. In particular, the fade-out phenomenon implies that the effect on students while they are still with that teacher is much larger than the effect of that teacher on longer-range scores. The likely explanation is that content changes over time—learning biology this year doesn't necessarily help much in learning physics next year.

The fact that fade-out influences the apparent benefit of teacher accountability has apparently gone unnoticed, however, in the three key studies that support the benefits of teacher accountability. Consider the following back-of-the envelope calculations that are similar to those used by value-added advocates: Suppose that low-scoring students typically have teachers with below-average value-added—specifically, students with these teachers can be expected to grow by 5 scale score points *less* than they would have if they were in the average classroom. Conversely, high-scoring students earn 5 scale score points *more* than they would have with typical teachers because they have high value-added teachers (a difference in teacher value-added of 10 scale score points). In other words, the advantaged students receive still greater advantages in the form of better teachers. Let's also assume that there is no systematic error in these estimates so that these numbers can be taken at face value.

Value-added supporters have calculated the benefits by, first, assuming that low-scoring students with less effective teachers switch to high-value-added teachers, and then simply adding up the estimated achievement gains across grades. If swapping teachers this way increases achievement by ten scale score points on each of the respective grade-level tests, then this implies: 10 + 10 + 10 = 30-point reduction in the achievement gap between low-and high-scoring students. Each reports different specific numbers and goes about the thought experiment a little differently, but the basic logic is similar to this. The research on fade-out suggests, however, that the effect of the current teacher on next year's achievement is about half what it was on current year achievement. Two years later, the effect appears to be cut in half again. This implies that the correct calculation is more like: $(10 \times 0.25) + (10 \times 0.5) + 10 = 17.5$-point reduction in the gap. This is a little more than half the effect on the achievement gap that has been reported.

Random error also makes each of the above ten-point differences look larger than they really are. That is, teachers with very low or very high value-added receive that designation partly by chance and their true value-added is probably closer to the average. So, if the real difference between low- and high-value-added is only 7 scale scores points instead of ten, then the calculation might be more like $(7 \times 0.25) + (7 \times 0.5) + 7 = 12.3$-point reduction in the gap, less than half of original 30.

Potential reductions in achievement gaps may also be over-stated because of systematic error. As I have shown, all the important school and district factors cannot be accounted for in estimating teacher value-added because many are unmeasured. If those omitted factors are also positively correlated with teacher value-added, teacher performance will look more varied than it really is. In other words, some of what these three studies by supporters are calling teacher value-added are really partly capturing school and district value-added. For example, schools with strong leadership might hire more-effective teachers. The effective leadership, because it is unmeasured, would be attributed to the teachers and make effective teachers look even more effective than they really are—and exaggerate the benefits of teacher accountability.[31]

One of the three studies suggesting large reductions in the achievement gap also suggests that firing the bottom 25 percent of teachers and replacing them with inexperienced teachers would eventually generate $500 billion in economic benefits per year in the United States.[32] But this economic analysis assumes that increasing test scores increases students' later productivity in ways similar to increases in other types of tests. This is a fairly standard type of analysis (and I myself have done similar analyses), but the assumption is especially problematic in this case.[33] The studies linking test scores and worker productivity are tests of general *cognitive skills*, not achievement on state tests. There is considerable evidence that cognitive skills are important, allowing workers to learn their jobs more quickly and carry out their roles more effectively.[34] But there is little evidence to suggest that faster growth on *state standardized tests* are associated with either growth in cognitive skills or worker productivity. Growth in state standardized tests may just reflect new academic knowledge (e.g., how to do algebra) and not new cognitive skills, in which case these estimated economic gains may be illusory.

Again, since students spend almost all of their school time in classrooms with teachers, it stands to reason that teachers would be very important. To say that the most important school inputs are teachers is like saying the most important parts of basketball teams are the players. But just how important are they? How much could teacher accountability reduce achievement gaps and improve education overall? Probably a fair amount, but still only a fraction of what these three studies have suggested.

SUMMARY

The evidence in this section provides a mixed picture about the usefulness and meaning of value-added measures. Value-added measures will probably never stack up very well in terms of random error, especially for individual teachers who are responsible for only a small number of students. However, value-added measures almost certainly reduce systematic error relative to snapshot measures.

While the individual limitations of value-added seem to add up to significant limitations, some of the evidence suggests that the problem might not be as bad as it seems. The study conducted by Kane and Staiger in Los Angeles suggests that value-added measures might provide estimates with little systematic error.[35] Likewise, the three studies by value-added advocates I noted above now show that teacher value-added measures are at least modestly correlated with other measures of teacher performance. Value-added measures also look better—in terms of both systematic and random error—when more years of data for each teacher and school are added. For this reason, I advocate using at least two years of data for each teacher and shrinking estimates to reduce the effects of measurement error.

But the questions addressed in all of these studies of value-added concern what happens on average: Are some teachers more effective with certain students *on average*? Do teacher value-added measures without random assignment of students provide accurate predictions of teacher value-added with random assignment *on average*? While these are relevant questions for researchers, they are not necessarily the right ones for policy makers. If these measures are to be used for accountability, they really need to work for *all* teachers and schools, not only the average ones. For this reason, value-added measures might never be very useful, for example, when teachers and schools whose students who are all near the test ceiling and when there is tracking based on student achievement.

In addition, most of these studies have been conducted in individual school districts. Schools in the United States are nothing if not diverse and it is possible that results might hold in some districts but not others. A good example is the test ceiling effect: it depends on the breadth of knowledge and skill the tests are designed to measure, which varies across states. Student tracking is another example; Monk's study suggests wide variation in the ways that students are assigned to teachers.

No matter how good or bad we decide the measures are, at the end of the day, the validity of a measure depends on what conclusions one wishes to draw with it. Many of the criticisms of value-added, described in chapter 8, are based on the assumption that value-added measures should be used alone to make high-stakes decisions. This is not the only option. Whether and how statistical errors translate into decision errors depends on education policies—the topic to which I now turn.

8

Evaluating Value-Added Measures and Avoiding Double Standards

"When I hear somebody sigh, 'Life is hard,' I am always tempted to ask, 'Compared to what?'"

—*Sydney J. Harris, journalist*

There is a great deal of debate about how to interpret the evidence on value-added discussed in chapter 7. On the one hand, no measure of teacher performance is perfect. On the other hand, there are clearly some significant limitations and many unknowns. So, even though the fog around value-added is being cleared away, the big picture remains a bit blurry. To bring things into greater focus, I next discuss how to interpret the value-added evidence, especially when designing and implementing policies that use value-added measures. The debate is important not only because it will determine what policies are adopted in the short term, but also because the long-term debate is likely to spill over into the court system.

The value-added debate comes down substantially to two perspectives: that of a researcher or that of a policymaker. As a researcher, I naturally believe that research should play an important role in determining how to proceed with value-added measures, but policy decisions must ultimately be made by policy makers. Statistics and analysis are useful starting points, but policy making also requires judgment and comparison of alternatives. Debates about value-added often ignore this simple fact and instead apply a double standard—taking it easy in judging credentials and setting a higher bar for value-added.

VALIDITY: A RESEARCHER PERSPECTIVE

Much of the debate about value-added is rooted in a single word that I have avoided using thus far: validity. As commonly used, valid means something like legitimate. But in statistics and research, the term has a more precise meaning. Statistical validity is a characteristic of a conclusion, not of the measure (e.g., value-added) used to draw that conclusion. What we really mean by a valid measure is one that allows us to draw valid conclusions—for example, that teacher A is better than teacher B. These conclusions then affect decisions about those same teachers. Consider again the example of measuring the length of a pencil with a ruler. Most people would probably agree that it's possible to draw valid conclusions about the true length of the pencil from that measure—because there is general agreement that rulers can be used to measure length. If only life were so simple.

Determining a valid measure of *performance* is unfortunately far from easy. Not only can systematic or random errors increase the likelihood of false conclusions errors in decisions, but some people—especially researchers—are also much more worried about concluding that two teachers are different when they are the same, than they are about concluding that two teachers are the same when they are different.

The validity of value-added measures has been assessed by well-respected researchers, including a recent assessment of value-added measures by the National Academy of Education (NAE) and National Academy of Sciences (NAS). There are also more general standards for measurement created by the American Education Research Association (AERA), American Psychological Association (APA), and the National Council on Measurement in Education (NCME).[1] The discussion below is drawn from a debate I had with Heather Hill.[2] She and I were asked to consider whether teacher value-added measures should be used to make high-stakes decisions about teachers (and schools). I was asked to take the "pro" side and she was asked to argue the "con" side. We each presented what we saw as the strongest arguments in favor of our assigned positions. In figure 8-1, I quote directly from Hill's arguments. She focuses her remarks on the AERA-APA-NCME standards, and clearly and explicitly outlines what assumptions must be held in order for value-added measures (VAM) to

FIGURE 8-1 Researchers' validity standard applied to value-added

Assumption I: Scores represent quality. In a properly specified value-added model, teacher/school scores are valid indicators of the "effectiveness" or "quality" of those teachers and schools.

    A: VAM rankings converge with results from other ratings of quality, such as classroom observations, parent surveys, and so forth.
    B: Different student-level assessments within the same domain yield [the] same results.
    C: VAM scores are not affected by inputs (curriculum materials, class size) that vary across districts, schools and classrooms.

Assumption II: Scores are accurate (reliable) enough. In a properly specified value-added model, teachers/school scores are accurate enough indicators of [performance] to sustain their use in accountability systems.

    A: Schools and teachers can be accurately distinguished from one another, particularly around the cut-points used in specific accountability systems.
    B: School and teacher rankings should be relatively stable over time, as the quality of teachers' instructional practice and school conditions are thought to rarely change quickly.
    C: Scores are unbiased, in the sense that the "items" used to compose VAM scores—individual student performances—are exchangeable among schools and classrooms.

Assumption III: Scores are free from manipulation. In systems with accountability attached to VAM scores, these interpretations do not change. As rewards/sanctions appear or increase, VAM scores remain an indicator of effectiveness rather than the extent to which teachers "game the test."

Source: Quoted from Heather Hill.

reach the researcher standard of validity. I discuss each of these assumptions in turn.

Assumption 1: Scores Represent Quality

Hill and I addressed three explicit arguments about the way scores might represent quality, which are discussed below.

Assumption 1a: VAM rankings should converge with results from other ratings of quality. Hill argues that "VAM rankings [should] converge with results from other ratings of quality, such as classroom observations, parent surveys, and so forth." In other words, to be valid, value-added measures should produce very similar results to other teacher performance measures. To the degree that all of these alternative measures capture the same educational goals, this argument makes sense. But one of the complications in measuring teacher performance is that the goals of education are multifaceted, encompassing not only academic skills, but also social skills, citizenship, and the like. For this reason, each measure of teacher performance captures contributions to different educational goals. This is why, as I described in chapter 7, differences between value-added measures and principal evaluations are difficult to interpret.

Assumption 1b: Different student-level assessments within the same domain yield the same results. Similarly, Hill argues that "different student-level assessments within the same domain yield [the] same results [and] . . . one would hope that teachers identified as exemplary in reading by one assessment are similarly identified by another [reading assessment]." In other words, the results from different math tests taken by the same students (in the same grade) should yield the same educator value-added measures. Again, this makes sense as long as the specific content of the tests is the same. But two third-grade math tests can actually measure fairly different math content, and thus produce less-than-perfect correlation across tests. Also, teachers vary dramatically in the amount of time they spend teaching specific subjects and even specific strands of subjects (e.g., one-digit addition).[3] The effect is almost like comparing different academic subjects. Research comparing value-added measures across tests is important, but interpreting the results requires more in-depth comparisons of the test content and test scaling procedures than are available at present.

Assumption 1c: VAM scores are not affected by unmeasured inputs. Hill writes that "VAM scores are not affected by inputs (curriculum materials, class size) that vary across districts, schools and classrooms." This assumption is closely related to the cardinal rule. What Hill is really saying here is that we need to take into account inputs that are outside the control of educators. Some factors can be accounted for and others cannot. The more important question is, just how important are those unmeasured (and uncontrollable) factors? While there is no clear evidence on this point, the fact that teachers have considerable autonomy and are the ones directly interacting with students suggests the roles of these other factors are probably smaller than the factors that teachers control.

Assumption 2: Scores Are Accurate (Reliable) Enough

As with assumption 1, assumption 2 is comprised of three sub-parts that Hill and I considered in our debate.

Assumption 2a; Schools and teachers can be accurately distinguished from one another. Hill argues it is important that "schools and teachers can be accurately distinguished from one another, particularly around the cut-points used in specific accountability systems." The vast majority of evaluation and accountability policies place teachers into broad performance categories based on cut points. (In some cases, like compensation, this is unnecessary because compensation can be paid incrementally for small improvements in performance rather than a few broad categories.) With up-or-down decisions like tenure, placing teachers into broad categories is a necessity, which also means that being in one category versus another must be truly meaningful in terms of actual performance. Given what we know about random error, performance above the bar is unlikely to differ much from performance below the bar. However, as I showed in chapter 6 for Oakville and in chapter 7 for other districts, we can be confident by the usual standards that teachers with very low performance measures are not actually very high performers (and vice versa). Fine-grained distinctions are harder to make with any performance measure.

Assumption 2b: School and teacher rankings should be relatively stable over time. Hill posits that "school and teacher rankings should be relatively stable over time, as the quality of teachers' instructional practice and school conditions are thought to rarely change quickly." On this point as in assumption 2a, she and I are largely in agreement. Actual teacher performance is more stable than teacher value-added measures. The reason, again, is random error.

Assumption 2c: Scores are unbiased. Hill's full expression of this point is, "Scores are unbiased, in the sense that the 'items' used to compose VAM scores—individual student performances—are exchangeable among schools and classrooms." This is another way of talking about the tracking problem I discussed in chapter 7. Again, the issue is that teachers and schools may be evaluated differently based on the types of students assigned to them (which they do not control).

This is arguably the main concern with performance measures in education because we know that many nonschool factors influence student outcomes. In fact, the main reason value-added is considered better than the snapshot approach is that it at least tries to address the tracking problem by taking into account prior achievement.

Hill concludes, and I again concur, that value-added does not completely solve the tracking problem. Although the evidence discussed in the previous chapter shows that the problem is significantly reduced when value-added measures are created in the way recommended by researchers—using at least 2–3 years of data—random error does not completely disappear.

Assumption 3: Scores Are Free from Manipulation

We have certainly seen a lot of gaming in traditional accountability systems, such as teaching students the tricks of test-taking, focusing on the bubble kids near the performance standard cutoffs, and making sure low-scoring students do not take the test, either by suspending them on test day or putting them into a category like special education that is untested or tested differently. So, there are reasons to be leery of setting performance standards for value-added measures as well. I showed in chapter 3 that some of this gaming of measures can be reduced using value-added. But, like the other problems, these cannot be eliminated either. Teaching students how to answer particular types of test items, for example, is not addressed by value-added and not a particularly constructive use of student and teacher time.

Hill makes many good points. But rather than calling these assumptions and concluding that their violations negate the worth of value-added, I suggest thinking about them as criteria that we should try to meet as best we can. This is more than just an academic debate about competing definitions. We need to expand our discussion to the various

alternatives facing policy makers—in the real world, waiting for the perfect accountability measure is not a viable option.

VALIDITY: A POLICY MAKER AND PRACTITIONER PERSPECTIVE

None of the assumptions in figure 8-1 includes anything about alternative performance measures. Are value-added being compared with the current credentialing/checklist approach? To some new and more advanced credentials? To a more sophisticated measure of instructional practice? Whether teacher value-added is valid from a practical standpoint has to depend on the available alternatives.

Policy makers and practitioners have to compare policies and make decisions in this way every day. Making decisions is what legislators and school board members are elected to do and what superintendents and school principals are hired to do. Sometimes they do not even realize they are doing it. School principals and district administrators have to decide how to evaluate teachers and which checklist to use. State officials have to decide what requirements to impose on teacher training institutions and on certification standards. Now, you might be thinking, "How is this really relevant? Educators and policymakers almost never have conversations about these issues, let alone make explicit decisions about them." That is certainly true. These decisions almost never show up on any meeting agenda. But that is precisely the problem. Given what we know about these credentials and checklist evaluations (see chapter 1), educators and policymakers should be having these conversations. The decision to leave things as they are gets made every day, whether or not it is discussed or even recognized as a decision.

The job of researchers is quite different. Researchers are scientists, and science is about drawing conclusions about how the world works. A reasonable case can be made that researchers shouldn't say that the world works a particular way unless they are very sure—that is, to avoid type I errors. But policy makers and practitioners are also obligated to consider type II errors. As a school leader, is it OK to falsely conclude that two teachers are performing equally well when they are really different? Is it OK to allow a teacher who is almost certainly ineffective to stay in the classroom because that ineffectiveness cannot be proved absolutely? Of

course not. Thus, both types of errors are relevant for policy makers, who need to avoid making them as much as possible. Practitioners cannot defer actions until there are solutions that have the levels of confidence that researchers demand because those solutions may never appear. Problems don't wait for clear solutions.

This does not mean that we should let value-added off the hook and ignore the criteria from the NAE-NRC report, AERA-APA-NCME standards, and Hill's arguments above. On the contrary, the problem is that policy makers have to apply researcher standards to *all the various policy alternatives* and then decide what is the best path forward. I show in the next section that this has not happened in the debate over value-added— *we have been evaluating value-added incorrectly.*

THE DOUBLE STANDARD FOR VALUE-ADDED

Opponents of value-added measures, sometimes explicitly, but usually implicitly, apply the researcher standard to value-added, without applying the same criteria to current credentialing and accountability policies. Below, I apply the assumptions and criteria mentioned in figure 8-1 to the current teacher master's degree and formal teacher evaluations. While these might seem like different policy topics, teacher value-added is being proposed as an alternative to credentials and checklist indicators of teacher performance. Value-added measures address performance more directly, by focusing on student outcomes; master's degrees and evaluations do this indirectly. But the goal is the same—providing measures and indicators of teacher performance that help ensure that students receive effective instruction and learn the curriculum. Whether to continue the credentials/checklist approach or switch to value-added (or some combination) is a very real policy question that is now being faced around the country.

The validity assumptions described above cannot be applied in exactly the same way to these alternatives. For example, it makes little sense to consider the assumption about "different student assessments" because master's degrees and typical teacher evaluations are not based on student assessments. Therefore I focus instead on the three broad assumptions (1, 2, and 3) in figure 8-1.

Assumption 1

Few would argue that either the master's degree or the current teacher evaluations represent quality as expressed in assumption 1. I presented evidence in chapter 1 that that there is little reason to believe that degrees add very much to teacher performance, or even that teachers who have those credentials tend to be higher-performing. Likewise, teacher evaluations omit the intellectual core of instruction. If we consider student learning to be the ultimate gauge, value-added seems to come closer to meeting this assumption than do credentials and checklists.

Assumption 2

Given that the current master's degree and evaluations are largely unrelated to quality, it is irrelevant whether they are reliable, or precisely measured. I'll use another baseball example. Suppose a coach's performance was judged on the basis of the team batting average—a highly invalid measure. It would be silly to then argue that the team batting average should continue to be the criterion for evaluating the coach because it's reliable and stable over time. The current master's degree and teacher evaluations are reliable in the same sense. The teacher who holds a master's degree today will have it tomorrow. The teacher who scores well on the evaluation checklist may score well tomorrow as well. So the criteria are reliable, but they are reliably bad measures of performance. They give the same wrong answer about performance almost every time.

The master's degree is also an unreliable measure around the cut-off. A sophisticated evaluation of classroom practice would consider a range of instructional dimensions, but the overall evaluation would still boil down to a single number. Just as with value-added, the difference in effectiveness between teachers just above or below the line is going to be slim. In the case of the master's degree, the cut point is the difference between those who have taken few or no graduate courses (but not enough to graduate and get a bump up on the salary schedule) and those who have finished their degrees. Again, the evidence suggests little reason to be optimistic that the master's degree meets this standard of validity.

A related problem is that the reliability of teacher evaluations is essentially never reported. Value-added estimates the confidence interval based on the variation in student growth and sample sizes. In theory, it would be possible to do something similar with evaluations of instructional practice, if multiple evaluations were administered in a given year. Obtaining a large number of these observations would be quite expensive, and the practice is rare even in the most sophisticated of current alternatives. If confidence interval estimates *were* based on a few observations per year, the reliability of such estimates might turn out to be just as bad as with value-added. But confidence intervals are almost never estimated or reported with other teacher performance measures, so they are never subjected to the same scrutiny as value-added.

Assumption 3

Are master's degrees and teacher evaluations free of manipulation and gaming? No. Typical teacher evaluations are in fact easy to manipulate because teachers often know well in advance when they are going to be observed in the classroom and can be sure that they are well prepared on that day, even if they are not on other days. They can also cater to the evaluator's preferences in an attempt to gain an advantage (especially if the teacher knows the evaluator). Also, in the case of master's degrees, it would be easy for teachers put minimal work into those graduate courses—enough to get by. Given that most are working forty to fifty hours a week already, it is little wonder.

The bottom line is that when the research standard of validity is applied to current credentials and evaluations of teacher performance, they fail the test—and make teacher value-added look good by comparison. Of course credentials and evaluations should not be the only measures against which value-added is compared. Other viable alternatives such as better classroom observations for teachers and team- and school-level accountability should also be part of the discussion. I will discuss these alternatives in chapter 9.

VALIDITY OF VALUE-ADDED IN USE

I frequently hear people say that value-added measures are "not ready for prime time." The previous discussion of the researcher standards of validity illustrates one reason for that. But ready for what? The conversation so far has focused only on whether value-added measures (and some alternatives) are good measures of performance. But what policy makers really want to know is whether performance measures can be used to improve performance. For this reason, I suggest a different way of thinking about validity—what I call *policy validity*.[4] (Others refer to it as consequential validity.[5]) This term is intended to account specifically for the types of decisions that get made through education policy.

There are dozens of ways that value-added measures can be used. One of the most important distinctions is between low-stakes uses like creating professional development plans for teachers and high-stakes uses like tenure and compensation decisions. Although their impact may be greater or smaller, none of these uses are "no stakes." In my conversations with them, teachers express the most concern about making performance results public and/or using performance measures for tenure and compensation systems.

This leads to another rule, almost as important as the cardinal rule: The stakes attached to performance measures should be proportional to the quality of the performance measures. One goal I have for this book is helping to provide some sense of what accountability systems might be consistent with this rule.

RULE 3

Attach stakes to performance measures that are proportional to the quality of those measures; that is, inversely related to the degree of statistical error.

Rule 3 is also affected by Campbell's Law: "The more any quantitative social indicator is used for social decision-making, the more subject it will be to corruption pressures and the more apt it will be to distort and corrupt the social processes it is intended to monitor."[6] In this case, the social indicators are educator performance measures of all sorts, including value-added. Corruption of the measures includes, for example, teaching students how to answer particular test items. So the fact that the stakes might initially seem proportional to the quality of the measure does not necessarily mean that it will continue to be proportional over time as people adjust their behavior.

There is unfortunately very little evidence to work with at this point about the best way to use value-added measures. One study by researchers at the Rand Corporation focused on a Pennsylvania program that provided teacher value-added measures to school principals and district officials.[7] Principals received training about the meaning and interpretation of teacher value-added, though the performance measures were not officially part of any high-stakes decision. This is a fairly low-stakes use of the measures.

Even though the information was not officially part of any high-stakes decision, it is possible that it did influence principals' decisions. For example, the Rand study was conducted just after No Child Left Behind was adopted, so principals and district leaders might have felt compelled to respond to these results. However, the researchers found that the information derived from the value-added measures was generally not used much in decision making and that other sources of information continued to be used much more extensively. To the extent that the value-added information was used, curricular and professional development decisions were the most common applications.

District administrators seemed to use the value-added information more often than school principals. One reason is that more than one-third of the principals in the study reported that they were unaware of the program or, if they were, had never seen their teachers' value-added scores. It may be that principals already had considerable information about teacher performance from their own observations and word of mouth. But district officials have less information than principals about teachers, so for them teacher value-added measures were filling more of an information vacuum.

Given that the program did not influence decisions much overall, it is unsurprising that the study also found no effects on student achievement. But there are several reasons why these results are difficult to interpret. First, since there were no stakes attached, this use of value-added measures was unlikely to impact the larger decisions principals make that might have influenced student learning, such as evaluations related to tenure. The measures could, in theory, have influenced how principals mentored teachers or created professional development plans, but since the measures were not officially part of those decisions, the principals may have been reluctant to report their use. Since many principals' actions are directed by rules and compliance, the lack of rules (or incentives) to use value-added makes it unsurprising that principals paid little attention to the new information.

The importance of context, and especially the degree of test-based accountability that goes along with the value-added measures, is highlighted in a second study. As in the study just described, researchers, led by Jonah Rockoff, randomly assigned principals to receive value-added measures for their teachers.[8] But this time the study was done in New York City which, unlike Pennsylvania, has been long known for its aggressive test-based accountability. The researchers conducting this study found compelling evidence not only that principals changed their views of teachers as a result of the value-added information, but that teachers with low value-added scores were less likely to stay in their jobs. The exact mechanisms for the job losses are unclear, but it is unsurprising that teacher value-added measures would have a greater impact on both decisions and achievement in settings where school-level test-based accountability is already strong.

Finally, a third study of Milwaukee looks not so much at the effects of value-added measures, but at educators' perspectives on them.[9] Conducted by district leaders as well as researchers at the University of Wisconsin at Madison, the study finds that schools with high value-added measures see the results as a validation of their performance. However, schools with high scores that were judged to be low value-added viewed their value-added scores "with some disbelief." This is not surprising, since the standard snapshot scoring measures to which U.S. schools have grown accustomed give an unfair advantage to high-scoring schools. I explore how Milwaukee is using value-added measures in chapter 9.

Evidence regarding teachers' and administrators responses to value-added is arguably the most important evidence in the entire book. Even if a measure had zero systematic and random error, it would not matter if it could not be used to improve teaching and learning. In the end, the policy validity of value-added will depend on what happens in schools when value-added is used in different ways. Do lower stakes uses have any impact—on teaching? On learning? Do high-stakes uses work, while avoiding unintended consequences?

These are all important questions, and they cannot yet be answered. One reason is that accountability systems are examples of *systemic reforms* that are intended to change the basic decision-making process and the pressures influencing decisions.[10] In the wake of the financial crisis, for example, the federal government instituted systemic financial reforms, including new regulations governing investment banks (such as how much capital and cash they needed to keep on hand in case some investments lost money) in order to avert another collapse. With accountability in education, the goal is to inform and improve decisions at all levels—from the district down to the classroom—in the hopes of improving teaching and learning.

Three special challenges make it difficult to establish whether a systemic reform "worked."[11] First, systemic reforms, by design, change schools gradually over time, making it hard to see immediate and noticeable improvement in student outcomes when reforms are introduced. This means that even if we ran an experiment involving a large number of states, we might have to wait a while—possibly years—to see any improvement. Recall the various potential benefits of performance measures discussed in chapter 1: accountability (personal and external), mission, and messages. These things do not change overnight. Policy makers must stay the course to see whether systemic reforms are effective, though as Hess's work in *Spinning Wheels* shows, patience is not a virtue of a general public clamoring for change.[12]

Second, systemic reforms are adopted in ways that make it difficult to know how students would have fared in the absence of the policies. Researchers like nice clean experiments, like the Rockoff study of New York City school principals, where one group of principals was randomly assigned to see value-added information about their teachers while others were randomly assign to continue their usual practices. Such experiments work relatively well with policies involving curriculum, professional development programs, and so on because these can be applied in specific, randomly selected classrooms. Not so with systemic reforms. Because the goal is to change the system and decision making at all levels—from the teacher all the way up to the school board and state officials—comparing individual classrooms or even schools would miss much of the story. The problem with accountability is even thornier, as it would seem unfair to hold educators in a given district to different standards in an experiment.

Third, systemic policies are adopted at the state and federal levels, so in a research sense there are few examples to analyze. Researchers do try to tease out the effects of policies by comparing states that adopt them to those that do not, but this is challenging when there are so few states, and only one federal government. No Child Left Behind is a case in point. How do we know whether NCLB is working when every state had to adopt it? There are fifty NCLB states and zero non-NCLB states. Researchers have devised some clever ways to discern effects, but these studies face major obstacles because they are studying a systemic reform and it is therefore no surprise that they have come to contradictory conclusions.[13] The same problem arises in a recent experiment with merit pay where just a portion of the potential ways in which the policy might influence teaching and learning outcomes was captured, and only the short-term effects of that narrow set of outcomes. The study is very important and the authors did an excellent job addressing the concerns, but there are inherent limits to our ability to learn about the effects of systemic reforms in this way.[14]

For these and other reasons, there remains much we do not know about school-level accountability. Similar problems arise in evaluating extensions of value-added accountability to teachers.

LEGAL ISSUES

This chapter is about the policy debate and, in the case of teacher evaluation, this also means a legal debate. If value-added measures are used in employment decisions about individual educators, then questions about the legality of particular policies will certainly end up in court. The controversy surrounding the measures will guarantee that suits are brought and those suits will involve both the specific technical issues I have discussed thus far as well as the ways in which evidence is interpreted.

At least three main areas of federal law could come into play. First, Title VII of the 1964 Civil Rights Act establishes that employment decisions cannot have a disparate impact on protected groups. For example, teachers of different racial backgrounds might end up with consistently different average value-added measures. Minority teachers might end up with lower value-added scores because, for example, they are more likely to be teaching minority students, and this group is more likely to suffer summer learning losses—which value-added measures generally do not account for. (Whether this would occur would depend somewhat on what factors are accounted for in the prediction stage of value-added calculations.) But differences in value-added measures across racial groups are not enough to make the use of value-added measures illegal. According to education lawyer Scott Bauries, if an employer can show that the value-added measure is "job-related," meaning that it fairly and accurately measures a teacher's ability to perform the essential functions of his or her job, and "consistent with business necessity" then unequal outcomes would pass muster under Title VII. Whether value added measures can satisfy that standard remains to be seen.[15]

Second, federal due process provisions require that the same *procedure* for employment decisions be used for all potential applicants. Specifically, districts need to show that they have provided: "(1) sufficient notice of impending termination or demotion; and (2) an opportunity to be heard (usually in a hearing before the [School] Board or its designate)."[16] There is nothing distinctive about value-added that would prevent either sufficient notice or an opportunity to be heard.

In addition to procedural due process, *substantive* due process prevents decisions from being "arbitrary or capricious deprivation of property," which is often defined to include employment. According to Bauries, some state laws similarly prohibit "arbitrary government action."[17] Here, the case for arbitrariness could be built on the degree of random error. Even using multiple years of data and making shrinkage corrections leaves room for enough random error that value-added measures could be considered arbitrary.

The legal reasoning in some cases helps illuminate how the issues might be argued in court. One legal scholar argues that, for the purposes of making high-stakes decisions about students on the basis of their test scores, courts will require that "the [tested] skills be included in the official curriculum and that the majority of the teachers recognize them as being something they should teach."[18] While this is a case about high-stakes decisions about students, this logic suggests that courts, in evaluating the use of standardized tests to evaluate individual educators, will also require that the content of the tests be aligned with state standards. Although states are beginning to improve their standards, many have standards that are ambiguous enough to have questionable alignment.

One court case is interesting not because of the legal basis and reasoning, but because of the remedy. In *Golden Rule Life Insurance Co. et al. v. Mathias et al.*, the Educational Testing Service (ETS), as part of an out-of-court settlement, agreed to select test questions that minimized the difference in scores between minority and nonminority candidates.[19] This suggests a potential way to minimize Title VII suits with value-added: districts and states, to show that they tried to address potential racial differences, could create their value-added measures in a way (e.g., accounting for student racial status) that minimizes differences in value-added by teachers' racial groups.

Existing legal reasoning has many things in common with the analysis I have presented. First, the "courts seem to take a somewhat less rigorous and more practical view on validation [than the psychometric community]."[20] That is, as I have argued above, the AERA-APA-NCME standards provide useful criteria, but not all the criteria have to be met completely. Second, in another case about the use of standardized tests to make decisions about K–12 students, the court ruled that "while the [graduation test] does adversely affect minority students in significant numbers, the TEA has demonstrated an educational necessity for the test, *and the Plaintiffs [opponents] have failed to identify equally effective alternatives*" (italics added).[21] This is similar to my point that the use of value-added should be compared with the alternatives.

Of course, the above only sketches out some potential roadblocks for value-added measures under federal law. State laws and agreements may provide others, particularly where value-added measures are being used for disciplinary or termination proceedings for which just cause must be shown. A showing of just cause is more rigorous than showing simply that the measure is not arbitrary.

So, do value-added measures provide a legal basis for making employment decisions? The answer is not entirely clear. Prior legal precedent under federal law seems to favor the proponents of value-added, but state laws are generally more restrictive. More importantly, the legal prospects for any policy obviously depend on the particulars of policy design—specifically on: (a) how much weight is given to value-added measures (the above analysis assumed essentially 100 percent, and few if any districts or states are considering this); (b) the nature of the decisions being made (employment versus lower-stakes decisions); (c) what other information is brought to bear in making those decisions; and (d) what efforts are taken to minimize differences between minorities and other educators. Even if the courts don't strike down the use of value-added for individual employment decisions, a policy that is legal is not necessary wise. We still need to learn more about whether and how value-added measures can be used to improve teaching and learning. Conversely, if the courts do reject value-added measures for individual employment decisions, this would not preclude using the measures for lower-stakes decisions like educator professional development and compensation.

CONCLUSIONS

It may sound strange—even self-defeating—for a college professor to tell policy makers not to look at research the way researchers do. But that is my key message here. I look at value-added not only from my current, official perspective as a university researcher, but as an educator, parent, and adviser to local, state, and national policy makers, as well as former school board member and legislative aide. Policymaking requires a perspective and judgment that research does not and the point of this book is to inform that perspective and improve the judgments that are ultimately rendered.

We do not know whether adopting value-added accountability would improve true student learning. More than a decade after NCLB became the law of the land, there is still debate about whether school-level test-based accountability improves learning. And even if we believe that high-stakes school-level accountability is completely ineffective, it would still be unclear what this would mean for teacher value-added accountability. If school accountability fails, is it because the free-rider problem made the school approach ineffective or is it because of the inherent limits of our ability to measure student outcomes and design appropriate accountability? The correct answer—still unknown—leads us in opposite directions when it comes to teacher accountability. What we do know is that many elements of existing accountability policies are broken. If value-added measures do not meet the criteria laid out by Hill and others, then certainly credentials and checklists do not either.

To paraphrase Sydney Harris, measuring performance and designing accountability systems is hard, but compared to what? Should we use teacher accountability based on value-added? What about alternative teacher evaluations and school-level accountability? The answers to these questions may not turn on legal constraints, but the availability of policy options certainly doesn't ensure good policy choices.

How do we approach these comparisons? Do we have to prove beyond a reasonable doubt that value-added is better than the status quo and viable alternatives? Or, do we think there are enough problems with the current system that the burden of proof is really on the credentialing/checklist status quo? The answers to these questions depend partly on how you interpret the evidence I presented in chapter 7. In my view, the evidence suggests that we can do better than credentials and checklists. I cannot absolutely prove that view, partly because there is insufficient evidence about the use of value-added. But there is a strong rationale behind using value-added as at least one part of the overall system of ensuring effective instruction. The main goal of education is to help students learn, so measuring and rewarding teacher and school performance based on measured learning seems logical and important.

If we accept that test-based accountability has potential, or at least believe that it is here to stay, how should we use the information we gain from value-added measures to improve teaching and learning? This is the question I address in chapter 9.

9

Using Value-Added to Improve Teaching and Learning

"In theory, there is no difference between theory and practice. But in practice, there is."

—Yogi Berra

Measuring the performance of teachers and schools is hard. Holding people accountable for that performance—in a way that improves teaching and learning—is even harder. That much should be clear from the previous chapters. Yet we also know that performance measures are important for personal and external accountability, for establishing and implementing missions, and for sending the right messages to the outside world. So, how should we design and use performance measures and accountability in education? How can we take advantage of the strengths of value-added without falling prey to unintended consequences?

To answer these questions, theory and evidence are useful but, as Berra's quote suggests, a healthy dose of reality about practice also needs to be mixed in. In this chapter, I identify key policy issues surrounding value-added and make recommendations about how value-added should be used. Given that there is very little evidence about the use of value-added, my suggestions are necessarily somewhat speculative. But the first eight chapters show that we do know some important things about value-added measures, allowing us to make some informed judgments about how to proceed. In most cases, using value-added measures involves important trade-offs—this is where judgment becomes important. I do my best to explain these trade-offs and to prioritize and interpret them in drawing my recommendations. My judgments are based on a combination of factors—awareness of the various alternatives to value-added and their strengths and weaknesses, remaining unknowns about value-added measures, and my own goal of developing an accountability system that would reward teachers like Ms. Bloom. Of course, my personal biases also come into play—this is unavoidable in any policy argument—but I've been transparent about my thought process so that you can use these recommendations in ways that make sense for your own situations.

RECOMMENDATIONS FOR USING VALUE-ADDED

A basic principle of measurement, as I have said, is that the validity of a measure depends on what conclusion one is trying to draw from it. A well-functioning thermometer, for example, is likely to provide a good measure of temperature, but not of rainfall. And we might be comfortable trusting cheap household thermometers when deciding whether it's warm enough to wear shorts outside but we probably want something more precise and reliable for measuring the temperature of a room storing combustible materials that could explode at high temperatures. Likewise, value-added measures are valid for some purposes and not for others.

Educators want to improve and value-added measures provide an additional tool in the arsenal to make this happen, both by holding individual educators and leaders accountable and by holding practices and programs accountable. The sections below set forth my recommendations for doing just that (see "Summary of Recommendations for Using Value-Added Measures").

Recommendation 1: Use value-added to measure school performance and hold schools accountable.

The new accountability that started in the 1990s got one thing right—it focused attention on schools. Most teacher-coworker interactions occur within their schools. Principals lead teachers within their schools. More experienced teachers help younger ones within their schools. Decisions about student discipline, the curriculum, and teacher hiring are primarily made at the school level. So, if you are going to hold educators accountable, the school is a good place to start.

Summary of Recommendations for Using Value-Added Measures

1. Use value added to measure school performance and hold schools accountable.

2. Carefully implement and evaluate pilot programs using value added performance measures as one part of individual teacher accountability.

3. In creating performance measures, combine value-added with other measures more closely related to classroom practice.

4. a. Consider extending value added to other grades, subjects, and student outcomes . . .

   b. . . . but don't let the tail wag the dog. Design performance measures to improve practice, don't design practice to improve performance measures.

5. Avoid the "air bag" problem. Don't drive value-added measures too fast.

6. Don't create perverse incentives in elementary schools.

7. Use value added to identify effective practices and to evaluate school, district, and state programs.

8. Use value-added to determine how well schools serve different groups and drive improvement with underserved groups.

9. Develop programs collaboratively, learn from mistakes, and adapt over time in a process of continuous improvement.

A second reason for using school value-added is that there are fewer opportunities for systematic error (as discussed in chapter 6). Using teacher value-added involves tracking of students both within and across schools. With school value-added, only the latter is an issue.

Third, school performance measures are probably here to stay. Even if one disagrees ultimately with the idea of high-stakes testing and school performance measures, we can at least agree that, if we're going to do it, we should do it as well as we can and value-added measures are simply more consistent with the Cardinal Rule compared with snapshots.

Recommendation 2: Carefully implement and evaluate pilot programs using value-added performance measures as one part of individual teacher accountability.

This is arguably the most controversial issue surrounding value-added, and it is easy to see why. The vast majority of teachers, effective and ineffective alike, care about their students (and not just about their test scores), and to tell these teachers they are failing in their jobs is to tell them they are failing the children they care about. So we really need to get this right. Unfortunately, teacher value-added measures have high random error and some systematic error, and they cannot be applied to most teachers at present.

I don't know how Ms. Bloom would have fared if teacher value-added had been used in those days, but I do know that what I remember most from my time with her was not the type of knowledge and skill that would show up on today's standardized tests. This doesn't necessarily mean, however, that value-added measures cannot be used productively. As I showed in chapters 1 and 8, credentials and checklist evaluations have arguably even greater flaws. (Ms. Bloom probably looked good on those measures too, but this wouldn't mean much because almost all teachers look good and Ms. Bloom would be lumped together with mediocre teachers.)

Some experimentation with teacher value-added therefore seems warranted. There is some debate about what constitutes a reasonable pilot program, given the uncertainties and the fundamental shift that teacher accountability entails. It is difficult to learn much from systemic reform programs such as accountability without implementing them at least on a district level—otherwise, some of the main effects are likely to be missed. So, *pilot* in this sense cannot mean a program limited to a few schools. Rather, it might mean a system to be implemented districtwide on a trial basis, scheduled to be reconsidered at a defined future date. Whether intended as pilot or permanent programs, the case studies I describe later will highlight how important it is to carefully phase in the various program elements.

There are also some types of programs that would be difficult to justify under any conditions. Given what we know today, high-stakes decisions like tenure, compensation, and dismissal should not be based on teacher value-added *alone*—which leads directly to the next recommendation.

Recommendation 3: In creating performance measures, combine value-added with other measures more closely related to classroom practice.

In any discussion of accountability, the phrase "multiple measures" comes up a great deal, though it can mean many things; for example, giving students more than one standardized test, or providing a wide range of measures to capture the full breadth of education goals. There are four main advantages to combining value-added with other measures. First, some provide formative information about how teachers can improve. Strictly speaking, these are not formative assessments if they also have a high-stakes use, but nevertheless these additional measures can provide information that helps teachers move forward—a key goal of accountability.

Second, additional measures help reduce random errors by contributing important information to the overall performance assessment. Recall from chapter 2 that adding more items to a test reduces measurement error in student scores. The same principle applies here—the more information contained in the evaluation, the lower the random error.

Third, additional measures can help capture information about teachers' contribution to student outcomes that are hard to measure—Ms. Bloom's class project, for example. To capture teachers' ability to develop students' creativity, the overall performance measure could include an evaluation of practices that might facilitate creativity. This allows student outcomes to be captured in more indirect ways. We can view this as a reduction in systematic error because ignoring teachers' contributions to student creativity (and other skills not captured on standardized tests) systematically disadvantages teachers who are stronger in developing typically unmeasured student skills.

Fourth, and finally, it might be possible to develop other measures that have an absolute scale. This would offset the concern that value-added measures are inherently relative, though, again, the relative measures are a basic part of the principle of continuous improvement and are not a primary limitation of value-added.

All four of these rationales point to observations of classroom practice as the best general alternative measure of teacher performance. They provide formative information, reduce random error, reduce systematic error (by indirectly capturing contributions to other student outcomes), and increase the possibility that all teachers can achieve excellent scores. On one

175

level, this is just common sense. If we want to evaluate how well a teacher is doing we have to observe what the teacher is doing. Credentials don't help in this case; this is one of the problems with credentials that is driving current interest in value-added.

There are growing numbers of frameworks for evaluating teachers' classroom performance, including the Danielson framework, Teacher Advancement Program (TAP), Connecticut's Beginning Educator Support and Training (BEST) program, and CLASS™.[1] I have been particularly impressed by the framework used by the National Board for Professional Teaching Standards (NBPTS) because of my research on NBPTS-certified teachers and because I served on the NBPTS Task Force on Student Learning Student Achievement (SLSA). It is also a useful example because it includes many components that could be used individually or adapted for teacher evaluations.

Developed as an attempt to further "professionalize" teaching, the three main components of NBPTS certification are: (a) portfolios that include videotaped instruction in actual classroom settings, samples of student work, and written commentary by the teacher regarding his or her own teaching practices; (b) documentation of interactions with students' families, colleagues, and other educational actors; and (c) computer-administered tests of content knowledge.

One strength of the original NBPTS standards is their focus on the link between teaching and student achievement. This link might seem obvious, but recall that most certifications and evaluation frameworks have been only loosely related to instruction, let alone student learning. The NBPTS-SLSA Task Force has recommended going even further, partly by experimenting with direct assessments of student learning like value-added, but more importantly by ensuring that teachers understand how to develop and use student assessments for diagnostic and formative purpose, including giving feedback to students.

A second strength of the NBPTS-SLSA report is that it is endorsed by the entire task force, which comprises a wide range of educational thinkers and scholars.[2] This suggests that it is possible to develop sophisticated evaluation systems that stakeholder groups with different perspectives can agree on.

Finally, the close alignment between practices and student learning is supported by evidence that NBPTS scores are related to teacher value-added measures.[3] This might seem to contradict my argument in chapter 1 that teachers with NBPTS certification are not much more effective than others. However, this is more of a problem with how the NBPTS measure is used than it is with the measure itself. As I explained in chapter 2, any time a performance standard like proficiency—or in this case, *certified*—is set, a lot of useful information is wasted. The more fine-grained scores, rather than the certified/uncertified designation, show significant differences in performance between teachers who are at the top versus the bottom of the NBPTS scoring scale. The fact that NBPTS scores are used for certification therefore masks the fact that the exact scores are really useful indicators.

My point here is not to endorse a particular model. While NBPTS links teaching to student learning, has broad support, and is backed up by research, the NBPTS process takes 200–400 hours per teacher to complete. This makes it impractical for annual evaluation purposes. Nevertheless, NBPTS might provide the framework for a more streamlined evaluation that could be used on a more regular and widespread basis. The most important thing is that teacher evaluations become more accurate indicators of classroom instruction.

Using Multiple Measures for Teacher Evaluations. One of the most important unintended benefits of the move toward value-added is that educators around the country seem to be taking this recommendation to heart and paying much closer attention to classroom observations. Most states and school districts that are experimenting with value-added measures are using them as only one component of the overall teacher evaluation. Given their concerns about value-added, they are taking a closer look at alternative approaches.

The recommendation of multiple measures begs the question, how do we combine them? One answer is they can be combined into a single composite or index score. Scale scores on student standardized tests are like indices because they combine information from all the different individual answers into a single score. Combining value-added with a measure of quality of instructional practice could be done in similar fashion, except that the measures would not necessarily be weighted using a fancy statistical technique like IRT, but with more subjective value judgments about which outcomes are most important and which evaluation scores are most valid.

Here is a simple numerical example: Suppose a teacher receives a score of 80 on the classroom evaluation and 90 on value-added (for now, assume that both are on a scale of 0–100). The simplest index would just be the average of the two, or $(0.5 \times 80) + (0.5 \times 90) = 85$. But we might decide that the observation measure is more important than the value-added measure. In that case we might instead take a weighted average as follows: $(0.7 \times 80) + (0.3 \times 90) = 83$. The index is now lower for this teacher than the simple average (85) because the teacher's lower evaluation score (80) is now given more weight.

The assumption that both measures were already on a scale of 0–100 is unrealistic, however. The problem with indices is that each measure is usually on a different scale. Obviously, if we combined a number that ranged from 0–10 with one that ranged from 0–100, the first one wouldn't have much influence on the overall evaluation even if the two parts appeared equally weighted. A 0–10 scale can be converted to 0–100 simply by multiplying by 10, but this wouldn't completely solve the problem if the two measures had different distributions. For example, while the classroom observation measure might be on a 0–100 scale, it could be that almost all the teacher scores are above 80. (I found exactly this pattern in my own study of principal evaluations with Tim Sass.[4]) If the scores are more evenly distributed from 0–100 in the value-added measure, then the value-added score will tend to dominate the overall score even if they are appear equally weighted. There are ways to address this concern through weighting schemes, but it is important to be aware of the potential problems so that they will be taken care of when the index is created.[5]

Rather than being combined, the separate measures could be part of a multistep evaluation. For example, because value-added measures are inexpensive, they could be used as an early warning system, indicating teachers who might warrant additional classroom observations and assistance, and these additional observations which might then serve as the primary basis for decisions about professional development, tenure, and so on. The value-added measures in this case would influence only the frequency of evaluation. Alternatively, classroom observation could be a standard aspect of evaluation for all teachers and then value-added could function as an additional marker when the classroom observations scores are especially low (or high).

Extending Multiple Measures to Schools or Teams. Some of the same basic principles apply to school-level measures, but in this case the measure is of the "practice" of the school rather than individual classrooms. Surveys represent one way to collect this type of information. Schools already use climate surveys of school staff to provide a sense of how the school is functioning. These might be considered as part of the evaluation for school leaders. Some policymakers have also considered surveying students and parents, as is almost universal in higher education. One concern is that some people will not fill out surveys and their views may differ from those who do fill them out. A second concern is that the evaluations may reflect factors either outside the control of educators or unrelated to sound instruction. (While I mentioned earlier how much I valued student evaluations of my college-level teaching performance, research also shows that teacher ratings by students are associated with a wide variety of factors unrelated to what we would typically think of as instructional quality: instructors' physical attractiveness, student demographics, student interest in the course, lower- versus upper- division course level, and perceived course difficulty.[6]) Also, student evaluations could take on an even different character if they were used for high-stakes purposes, and might be less useful as a result—Campbell's law again. Nevertheless, how students perceive what is happening in schools has an important influence on their motivation and actions, so surveys may be useful as one of multiple measures.

There are also some non-survey measures that could be useful for evaluating schools that are less subject to manipulation that can undermine the use of surveys. For example, the availability of courses in nontested subjects might be one useful indicator of the breadth of the curriculum. At the high school level, college-going rates could be used. Later in this chapter, I will discuss the issue of nontested grades and subjects and the ways in which value-added measures can indeed be applied to other student outcomes.

Another possibility, as I suggested in chapter 6, is that instead of teacher value-added, some type of team value-added measures be used.

While these have the advantage of reduced random error and reduced systematic error (because the role of tracking is diminished), they might still have more problems than either teacher or school value-added. Although one intended use of team value-added would be to increase collaboration, given the practical realities of schools, the main effect of team accountability might be to create competition between teachers to be on the best teams, doing little to help students. Also, team value-added measures could not easily be used for tenure, dismissal, and promotion decisions, which inherently pertain to individuals. Team measures, might seem good in theory, but they might not work at all in practice. But, like surveys, they might have some productive use.

Recommendation 4a: Consider extending value-added to other grades, subjects, and student outcomes . . .

One of the limitations of value-added measures is that they are typically applied only to teachers in grades 4–8 in math and reading, omitting the vast majority of teachers. It is worth considering possible extensions.

In my workshops and presentations, some district officials have indicated they are considering extending value-added to untested subjects and grades by creating their own district assessments. This is possible in some large districts that have greater resources. However, given that all school districts are subject to state standards, this approach is at best inefficient and at worst likely to result in some bad test instruments and test scales. Good standardized tests do not come easily or cheaply.

In high school, many states use end-of-course exams, and value-added can be applied to these tests. An advantage of end-of-course exams is that the curriculum is probably more tightly aligned with test content, so that changes in scores are more likely to represent differences in classroom teaching. The disadvantage, however, is that there is no interval scale linking, say, eighth-grade math tests with tenth-grade end-of course exams. This is especially true in cases where the end-of-course scores have no logically prior starting point. For example, what would be the right prior test score for ninth-grade biology? Perhaps a general science test in states that have one. The lack of an interval scale increases random error in this case, but prior scores in other subjects will still likely be good predictors of high school end-of-course exams, making value-added feasible.

Given that state standardized content testing is less common in high school, it should come as no surprise that we know less about the statistical properties of value-added at this level. Almost all of the research on value-added is based on elementary school and, to a lesser, extent middle school programs. There is no obvious reason to think the statistical properties will be dramatically different at the high school level, but new rigorous studies must still be conducted at this level.

Another potential extension of value-added is to outcomes other than academic achievement. Value-added can be applied to any student outcome measure. Graduation from high school and college attendance are commonly reported outcomes in state and federal accountability policy, but these are snapshot measures, with all the accompanying problems. Value-added-like measures from predicted outcomes are necessary for any meaningful judgment of school performance. While we cannot calculate growth for outcomes like high school graduation and college attendance, we can predict them with measures like prior achievement scores and demographics. This prediction approach is the essence of advanced value-added, but simply extended from student achievement to other outcomes.

On the other hand, as the next recommendation makes clear, it is possible to extend the idea too far.

Recommendation 4b: . . . but don't let the tail wag the dog. Design performance measures to improve practice, don't design practice to improve performance measures

While expanding the application of value-added to other grades and subjects is worth considering, there is a real danger that enthusiasm over value-added may lead policymakers to go too far. In my presentations and workshops about value-added, I hear more and more people talking about how they need to change the way their schools work so that they can expand the use of value-added.

I frequently hear states and school districts trying to rapidly expand student testing to essentially all grades and subjects. There might be good reasons to extend testing, but doing it solely for measuring educator performance could be a grave error. Decisions about standardized testing should be driven by the testability of particular subjects and with an eye toward ensuring that they don't distort teaching in unproductive ways.

Music education is a case in point. On the one hand, music is one of the easiest subjects to test because there are clear standards for music performance—performance means playing music, and playing it well.[7] Also, there are some aspects of music education, such as the ability to read notes and scales, that make it feasible to apply paper-and-pencil standardized tests, as Kentucky has done. On the other hand, those tests do not capture the ability to play music, nor the student's creativity and love of the subject. Given how little we know about how value-added might improve teaching and learning, the idea of making fundamental changes in educational practice to support performance measurement in subjects like music is highly questionable.

One alternative option would be for teachers in hard-to-test grades and subjects to set their own (nonstandardized) goals, working in conjunction with school principals and senior teachers. While calculating value-added with such nonstandardized measures is not possible, this approach could still improve teaching and learning, inducing additional thought among teachers about what they are hoping to accomplish and providing some other metric to measure progress toward those goals.

Changes in school practice that are more tangential to teaching and learning might be more reasonable. For example, most elementary schools already seem to assign students to teachers at random or at least evenly distribute more difficult-to-teach students. Taking the practice from very common to universal might make sense to improve performance management.

Design performance measures to improve practice, don't design practice to improve performance measures.

Recommendation 5: Avoid the "air bag" problem. Don't drive value-added measures too fast.

It would be easy to get overconfident about value-added measures. In fact, if you had stopped reading this book after chapter 4, you too might have been tempted to become a strong value-added supporter. But the takeaway message from chapters 5 to 7 is "not so fast." That is why I introduced rule 3: Attach stakes to performance measures that are proportional to the quality of those measures; that is, inversely related to the degree of statistical error. I also emphasized in chapter 8 that there are few, if any, success stories in which value-added has clearly improved teaching and learning.

This problem is similar to the one faced by auto engineers who keep trying to make cars safer, only to see people drive faster as a result. Air bags and antilock brakes are cases in point. For any given speed and driving conditions, these features undoubtedly reduce the risk of serious injury. But the security of having an air bag or antilock braking system may unintentionally encourage riskier driving behavior.

I know some of the engineers who were involved in the early development of air bags. They, more than anyone else, were cautious at first about using them because air bags are small bombs that go off in the driver's (or passenger's) face. Likewise, some of the most cautious people about value-added are the people who have spent the most time studying them—people who see the statistical problems and the potential for explosive and harmful consequences for educators as well as students. Given how little is known about the effective use of value-added measures, implementors should move forward carefully, avoiding the temptation to see them as a panacea for our concerns about accountability and the education system as a whole.

I have already noted one example where this recommendation has already been clearly violated. The *Los Angeles Times* commissioned calculations of value-added measures for more than six thousand district teachers and published teacher value-added measures on its web site, along with teacher names. This is clearly a case of the driving the measures too fast. The newspaper's measures are based strictly on value-added for student achievement. Even if those reports contained no error—that is, even if they captured teachers' contributions to all student outcomes, which they demonstrably cannot—this is hardly a policy that would lead to school improvement.

Recommendation 6: Don't create perverse incentives in elementary schools.
In chapter 3, I explained how focusing on growth is important because it helps account for where students start and, therefore, for factors outside schools' control. But students in grades K–3 are not tested. This not only prevents the use of value-added in those grades but creates the potential for perverse incentives. Suppose that elementary schools were evaluated

based only on value-added in grades 4 and 5. This would actually create a strong incentive for schools to ignore students in grades K–3 and place their weakest teachers in those grades. Lowering the third-grade score makes fourth- and fifth-grade growth look higher. Given how important grades are to child development, undermining grades K–3 is the last thing we want to do.

One option for addressing this problem, as suggested with high school grades, is to expand K–3 assessments. This is a possibility, since most schools already administer assessments to students in grades as low as kindergarten. However, these assessments were designed for diagnostic purposes, not summative ones. Because K–3 students cannot as easily manage paper-and-pencil tests, the tests are usually administered directly by school personnel, opening up concerns about manipulability. A second, and more viable, option is to combine third-grade snapshot measures with fourth- and fifth-grade value-added. This way, schools would still have incentives to focus attention on those important early grades, while taking advantage of value-added in higher grades.

Recommendation 7: Use value-added to identify effective practices and to evaluate school, district, and state programs.

From the opening page of this book, I have focused on using value-added for accountability—for measuring the performance of individuals. Here, I shift gears and consider another possibility: using value-added to identify effective practices and programs.

The Logic of Value-Added for Program Evaluation. Suppose we used value-added to identify the highest value-added schools. The obvious next step would be to gather more information about these schools and their practices. We might discover that most of the high value-added schools were using a particular curriculum, had specific after-school programs, or used instructional technology in distinctive ways. This would obviously be useful information and it would be worth experimenting with expanding those practices to other schools.

The same logic applies to formal school programs. With the rapid expansion of test data, there has been a veritable explosion in studies using value-added techniques to study programs ranging from certification and university degrees to in-service professional development.

The logic of these studies is exactly the same as with value-added for accountability. In determining the performance of a practice or program, we need to take into account the factors that are outside the program that might influence student achievement—students' prior student achievement still being the most important. It is then possible to predict what student achievement would have been in the absence of the program and compare this with actual outcomes.

Consider again the class size example I used in chapter 4. I showed that we can create two different prediction lines for teachers, and the appropriate one would depend on whether the teacher had a small or large class. The difference between those prediction lines represents the impacts of a program—class-size reduction—on student achievement. So the statistical analysis is almost identical (some differences are noted in chapter 10), but the focus has shifted from the teacher value-added measures (accounting for class size in order to measure the impact of the teacher) to the class size value-added measure (accounting for the teacher in order to measure the impact of class size). There is no limit to the number and types of practices and programs that could be studied in this way.

As a second example, consider a study I conducted with Tim Sass on teacher professional development (PD).[8] Could we just compare the snapshot achievement of students whose teachers had a particular PD program with those whose teachers did not? No, because certain teachers are more likely to engage in PD. It is easy to see how this might happen. Suppose that teachers who were performing poorly were encouraged to seek out PD to improve. In this case, if we compared the student outcomes of teachers with and without the PD, it might appear that the PD actually made things worse, when in reality these teachers were lower performing to start with. Value-added helps to solve this problem by first focusing on student growth and taking into account student differences, and second by comparing teachers to themselves, before and after the PD took place. That is, value-added allows the evaluator to see whether teachers typically improve as a result of PD. More teacher growth means more student growth.

The same idea holds with school-level programs. We can estimate the effect of a program, like a new curriculum, by comparing the value-added of schools before it was adopted to the value-added of the schools after adoption. In some cases, it might take more than one year to see effects, but value-added measures can be designed to be "patient" and wait for longer-term effects to emerge. There are also districtwide and statewide program examples (I'll discuss one—Milwaukee—later in this chapter).

Evaluating Colleges of Education, Teach for America, and More. One question I get asked in a lot of workshops is whether value-added can and should be used to evaluate university-based colleges of education. These programs have been under the gun for many years because evidence shows that teachers who graduate from these programs seem no more effective than other teachers.

In principle, value-added measures could be used to evaluate individual colleges of education simply by comparing average teacher value-added across programs. This information could be used to hold university programs accountable and, at the very least, might provide useful information for aspiring teachers as they choose colleges and majors.

Many of the challenges to using value-added to evaluate colleges of education in this way are the same as those discussed earlier—the limited scope of student standardized tests and other forms of systematic error and the limited number of teachers to whom this can be applied, to name just two. But there is one additional issue as well: colleges of education and certification programs actually serve two different functions at the same time. Most obviously, they train people to become teachers. But they also serve as gatekeepers into the profession. While there are increasing numbers of alternative routes to teaching, most teachers still pass through a college. No doubt some of these programs do a better job than others in preparing teachers. But just as there are starting gate inequalities among K–12 students, so too are there important differences in prospective teachers entering various preparation programs.

A case in point is the research about Teach for America. This program puts applicants—high-achieving college students, mostly from elite and competitive colleges—through an extensive screening process, which includes teaching a practice lesson (something most colleges of education and public schools do not do). Those selected for TFA then undergo an intensive summer training course before being placed in some of the nation's most difficult schools. What makes TFA teachers distinctive is not only their strong academic and leadership backgrounds, but the fact that *they have not had any formal training in education before being selected for TFA*. They walk into the classroom with just the single training course under their belts.

Research using the value-added technique suggests that TFA teachers are about as effective, or perhaps even more effective, in raising student test scores than the average non-TFA teacher.[9] This could mean that the TFA summer training course is stupendously effective, allowing trainees to instantly develop the many complex skills they need to be effective in the classroom. A more probable explanation is that TFA selects very smart, ambitious, hardworking people who would excel in almost any job. The training program provides some basic useful building blocks, but that is all. In this sense, TFA appears to be a more effective gatekeeper than colleges of education.

This does not mean that TFA is a better learning model than the traditional certification route. Realistically, TFA can only attract so many bright and talented applicants, and most of them leave the classroom within two to four years. When using value-added to draw conclusions about the performance of colleges of education, we need to distinguish the gatekeeping function from the training function and, for example, avoid punishing or shutting down colleges of education that do a good job of turning less academically prepared college students into solid teachers.

District Research and Evaluation. While states are increasingly making data more available to researchers wishing to evaluate different types of teacher preparation programs, some districts have gone further and integrated value-added research into their program evaluation and overall management systems. The most well-known example is the Consortium on Chicago School Research. The Consortium is a partnership between the Chicago Public Schools, the University of Chicago, and a group of philanthropic organizations committed to improving the city's schools. While it is a separate entity, the Consortium works in close collaboration with the district and has broad access to the district's student achievement data. Leaders from the Consortium meet with district officials regularly to discuss research and evaluation studies, many of which use the value-added methodology, to assist the district in its school improvement efforts.

President Obama gave a boost to the idea of district-research consortia by appointing former Chicago schools superintendent Arne Duncan to the post of Secretary of Education. Duncan in turn selected Consortium cofounder and director John Q. Easton to direct the federal Institute for Education Sciences (IES). The Obama administration's stimulus programs gave further impetus to the Consortium approach by placing a premium on careful evaluation in district proposals for funding under its set of education stimulus programs, such as the Race to the Top. As a result, new consortia and new opportunities for value-added-based program evaluation are developing around the country.

The promise of the Chicago Consortium model is its integration of careful evaluation and program planning—what is sometimes called *performance management*. As almost any district official can attest, these two activities are usually far from integrated. While evaluations are sometimes carried out, the continuation or discontinuation of programs is more likely to be determined by program popularity than objective evidence about how programs affect teaching and learning. The quality of district evaluations are also hampered by limited resources devoted to it.

Just as we need to hold people accountable, so too do we need to hold programs accountable.

Recommendation 8: Use value-added to determine how well schools serve different groups and drive improvement with underserved groups.

I discussed in chapter 4 the fact that accounting for student background factors like race and income could be interpreted as lowering expectations for disadvantaged students. I also presented the alternative perspective that accounting for student background could provide useful barometers for how well a school or district is doing with different groups, including minority students and those below proficiency. Finally, I also discussed the possibility of continuing current accountability practice of giving greater weight to achievement of disadvantaged students when measuring educator performance as a way of driving improvement specifically for these students.

The same general approach could be used in identifying effective practices and programs. We can measure not only the impact of class size and PD on the average student's achievement, but also for particular groups. For example, in my study with Tim Sass on NBPTS certification, we found that NBPTS-certified teachers were in some cases more effective with disadvantaged students.[10] This implies that policies to encourage these teachers to work in high-poverty schools could improve learning for those students.

It is important to recognize, however, that when any group's achievement is given more weight than that of others, there can be a tendency to reclassify students into that group. For example, if the scores of racial minority students count more, then schools might reclassify students who are mixed race to a racial minority category. This type of reclassification could be even more pernicious if the category is one that affects the type of education students receive, e.g., reclassifying students as special education if special education scores counted more.

Recommendation 9: Develop programs collaboratively, learn from mistakes, and adapt over time in a process of continuous improvement.

It is a basic maxim of educational policy that how programs and policies are adopted is often as important as what the policies look like on paper. Even a "good" policy can go wrong if the implementation process is fraught with mistrust, miscommunication, and stakeholder resistance.

Value-added-based policies are most likely to be effective when they are based on collaboration among teachers, school leaders, and policymakers. As I show in the next section, school districts are some of the main trailblazers in value-added. Most uses of value-added for accountability that involve even moderate stakes require negotiations between districts and teacher unions because they pertain to teacher evaluation and in some cases compensation and dismissal that are part of almost any labor contract. Many unions, including those in Chicago, Pittsburgh, Tampa (Hillsborough County), and the state of Colorado, have signed agreements to use teacher value-added measures for accountability purposes.[11] Moreover, hundreds of others made commitments to growth models (in many ways similar to value-added) as part of applications for President Obama's Race to the Top initiative. This type of collaboration between teachers, school leaders, and district leadership is most likely to minimize mistakes and show long-term success.

No matter how carefully initial policies are crafted, mistakes will be made, and problems will develop over time, requiring adaption. In the case studies below, I show that value-added policies have not been static and all have changed at least a little over the years.

CASE STUDIES

It is easy to discuss recommendations in the abstract, based on theory, but now I will consider some specific practices using value-added in states and school districts—and, in one case, another country. In some cases, value-added is being used in ways consistent with my recommendations, in other cases not. I begin with some trailblazers—Tennessee and Dallas, both of which began using value-added almost two decades ago. I then consider more recent adopters—Milwaukee, Houston, and England.

State of Tennessee

Tennessee's value-added accountability system was first implemented in 1992 as part of a comprehensive school reform plan. The measures were developed by Bill Sanders, who has since gone on to be arguably the most ardent support and marketer of value-added (his Educational Value-Added Assessment System [EVAAS] is sold through the company SAS). The Tennessee version, which goes by the analogous acronym TVAAS, makes school value-added publicly available. Internally, school and district personnel use value-added reports to pinpoint problems by subject and grade in order to make decisions about resources and efforts.[12]

TVAAS uses the Tennessee Comprehensive Assessment Program (TCAP) tests. Students in grades 3–8 are tested in five academic content areas (math, science, reading, language, and social studies) using norm-referenced tests. However, they are responsible only for those students who spend a minimum of 150 days in their classrooms.[13] TVAAS data are also used in academic planning, curriculum evaluation, and program evaluation.

TVAAS value-added measures have been used to varying degrees in teacher evaluations since 1996; however, in January 2010 the Tennessee legislature decided that up to 50 percent of teacher performance could be determined by value-added measures. Also, teacher development plans are drawn up from the TVAAS teacher value-added measures that school administrators receive, and teacher evaluations include an assessment of how well each teacher completes his or her plan.

While TVAAS is one of the oldest value-added accountability systems in US education, we know little about the program's success with teaching and learning. In 1996, in response to questions raised by administrators and teachers, the state commissioned an independent audit of the system. The evaluation generally supported the validity of the basic statistical approach, but concluded that there were too few questions in the science and social studies tests to achieve sufficient reliability. In addition, the auditors recommended that the way the statistical model stabilized teacher effects should be changed.[14] The Tennessee legislature agreed to add more test questions to the science and social studies, but the rest of the system has remained largely unchanged.

Overall, the Tennessee approach is strong because it focuses on school value-added and program evaluation and uses teacher value-added in a low-stakes way. However, the state has not carefully evaluated the system, focusing on the statistical properties of the measures rather than on the impact the system is having on teaching and learning. After two decades, it remains hard to say whether TVAAS has improved Tennessee's schools.

Dallas Independent School District

The Dallas Independent School District's value-added system was the apparently the first adopted by a school district. Initially adopted in 1992 as part of a comprehensive reform initiative led in part by future NCLB architect Sandy Kress, the Dallas system provides public reports on school- and district-level data. The district and schools use the reports to develop continuous improvement plans, and schools are required to address any reported areas of weakness in their plans. Stakes are attached. Schools are ranked based on value-added, and financial rewards are paid to staff in the most effective schools. (Initial rewards totaled $25 million; every staff member in the most effective schools received financial rewards in varying amounts, including teachers, administrators, aides, maintenance staff, and others.) In addition to incentives for effective performance, the Dallas accountability system provides consequences for ineffective schools that can include replacement of administrators and restructuring.

Initially, reports provided teacher value-added measures, but these proved difficult for principals to understand, in spite of the two-day training they received. After 1995 the reports were simplified, graphs were added, and training for principals was expanded. Principals now develop assistance plans for teachers who show weaknesses on value-added measures. Teachers also develop personal improvement plans, including changes in their teaching behavior that will directly improve student outcomes.[15] The program has recently been expanded to include incentives for individual teachers whose students perform significantly above expectations.[16]

Teacher effectiveness reports subdivide teachers into three categories: high, middle, and low. Teachers ranked high receive formal evaluations only every three years, and the value-added measures are essentially all that are used in between. Middle-ranked teachers receive yearly evaluations. Teachers ranked low, however, receive an abundance of extra attention, including classroom observations, extra assistance from school and district staff (e.g., curriculum and instruction specialists), and supplemental evaluation instruments, including teacher portfolio, peer review, structured classroom observations, surveys, content knowledge assessments, and the like. This extra assistance continues until the teacher ranking improves.

Critics of the Dallas system argue that its complexity makes it too difficult for principals and teachers to fully understand how it works and that the value-added-based incentives should be part of more fundamental reforms.[17] In addition, the Dallas system excludes students with missing data and does not consider the point at which students start on the developmental scale.[18]

While I take no position on Dallas' use of financial incentives, one positive element is that its value-added accountability system is aligned across levels, so that district and school leaders and teachers are all paying attention to the same performance measures.

Milwaukee Public Schools

The Milwaukee Public Schools (MPS) has been using school value-added measures since 2002. As in Tennessee and Dallas, results are available on the district website, with interactive menus allowing for comparisons throughout the district. However, MPS is distinctive in reporting results in four quadrants that reflect value-added measures on one dimension and snapshot measures on the other, so that schools are high-value-added/high-snapshot, or high-value-added/low-snapshot, and so on. Value-added measures can also be linked with survey information about practice and perceptions of practice, although this approach has seen limited use so far. This approach provides a holistic picture of school strengths and weaknesses.

Since 2005, the district has also created by grade-within-school measures (examples of team value-added) for internal use and is also exploring uses for classroom/teacher value-added measures. To produce all of these various value-added measures, MPS has worked with the Value-Added Research Center (VARC) at the University of Wisconsin at Madison, led by Robert Meyer.

Much like the Consortium in Chicago, the MPS-VARC partnership also includes an extensive set of program evaluations that begin with value-added measures, but often go beyond them. The partners not only produce value-added measures, but plan professional development so that all staff in the district understand what value-added measures mean and how they are being used. A team of leaders, including district staff and some school principals, has been trained extensively about the meaning and calculation of value-added, and these leaders are assigned to schools. In this way, the district helps educators use the data productively.

As in Tennessee and Dallas, value-added measures are integral to the MPS management system and have been used in school-closing decisions and differentiated management of schools. Value-added results were also used in the early years of implementing sanctions for schools identified for improvement under NCLB; that is, low-scoring schools with high value-added received greater autonomy from district-prescribed interventions.

So, like Tennessee and Dallas, Milwaukee started by using school value-added and is carefully considering extensions to teacher value-added. Despite being a more recent entrant to the value-added arena, MPS appears to have learned from the experiences of others and created a system that is better in several ways: engaging stakeholders in the process, training educators about what the measures do and do not mean, and making value-added part of a comprehensive system of continuous improvement. As my discussion of research in chapter 8 suggests, the district is also engaging researchers in using the data to evaluate programs in ways that can guide district decisions.

Houston Independent School District

In 2007, the Houston Independent School District (HISD) also began using school- and teacher-level data as the basis for a merit pay program that is now called ASPIRE (Accelerating Student Progress, Increasing Results and Expectations). Teachers can receive a bonus up to $1,500 if their school is in the top half of the district in value-added, and up to an additional $7,000 if their teacher value-added measures are in the top half of the district in the respective grade and subject. Since teacher value-added cannot be calculated for many teachers, team value-added measures are used instead for a large number of teachers in tested grades and subjects. Because some teachers with low teacher value-added scores are in high-value-added schools, well over half of teachers receive some type of award. One positive element of the program is that all school staff, including noninstructional employees, are eligible to receive funds under the school-level award component, emphasizing the collaborative element of schooling.[19]

The district is also paying close attention to teacher viewpoints about the merit pay system; it conducts annual surveys, the results of which are made publicly available on the district website. While the surveys pertains more to merit pay than to value-added per se, two results are worth noting. First, the majority of teachers support (favor or somewhat favor) the ASPIRE program, and this number has grown slightly since its initial inception, from 57 percent in 2008 to 64 percent in 2009.[20] The fact that the surveys are coming from the district, which clearly supports the program, is a point of caution, but these results are still noteworthy.

One limitation of the Houston system is that there are essentially two parallel evaluation systems—one that uses only value-added (for compensation bonus decisions) and one that mainly uses measures other than value-added (the standard evaluation system for decisions like tenure and dismissal). This dual system is partly driven by state laws, but creates a dilemma because the two sets of evaluations surely differ and both cannot be right. It is even conceivable with this approach that a single teacher could receive a merit bonus *and* be denied tenure in the same year. In any event, compensation based solely on value-added is hard to justify.

The Houston case also highlights the importance of implementing programs carefully from the outset. When the district first started in 2007, district staff created the teacher value-added measures in-house. However, some errors were made in these calculations and neither teachers nor school administrators checked their own measures at first. Compounding the problem, the local newspaper, the *Houston Chronicle*, submitted a freedom of information request, which the district fulfilled before telling teachers what their bonuses would be. The teacher bonuses ended up on the newspaper's website even before the teachers themselves knew what their bonuses would be.[21] Then, because of the errors, some of these bonuses were misreported: ninety-nine teachers were actually paid bonuses that were too large, and had to return the extra amount. Houston has made great strides since the program's initial rollout, but the district also should have moved more carefully to start with.

Houston's public reporting of results bears comparison with the Los Angeles example. While I found some fault with the Los Angeles school district's release of value-added measures (by name) to the newspaper, the situation in Houston is different because compensation of public employees is typically considered public information. By releasing the salary information, Houston therefore released the teacher value-added scores indirectly but had no choice given state laws and its decision to use merit pay. (The case of the Los Angeles Unified School District was only slightly different in that most of the relevant law seemed to require the district to provide the data to the *Los Angeles Times*, though there were more legal ambiguities in the case.) Nevertheless, the fact that the measures are likely to become public, and without obvious educational benefits, only reinforces distrust and undermines the potential for long-term success.

England

Value-added is also used in other countries. Most European and Asian countries have longer histories with high-stakes testing. However, in contrast to the United States, these countries have typically held students accountable for their own scores, but not schools. Starting early in students' school careers, standardized tests have a major impact on what track students end up on and what college they get into. (In the United States, ACT and SAT scores also affect college entrance, but not to the same degree; and these college entrance exams are not usually directly linked to the state curriculum or state high-stakes tests.)

England is an exception. The national government introduced value-added measures in 1998 and, since then, has made them a key component of the nation's school accountability system. School value-added measures are published in national *league tables*, the equivalent of US school report cards. The league tables are based on evaluations by school inspectors, who have the power to intervene in very low-performing schools.[22] The national inspectors will not intervene, however, in schools with high value-added scores.

Value-added measures are also used to evaluate teachers. While teacher results are not publicized or used for decisions like compensation and employment, teachers seeking career advancement must use value-added measures to document that their students are making progress.

One recent study finds that parents do not use the value-added data in league tables when making decisions about their children's schooling. One reason for this, echoing the Pennsylvania study of school principals (see chapter 8), is that the value-added measures do not directly affect school rankings, but are only shown alongside the rankings for further information. Another reason may be that parents are interested in outcomes other than those measured by narrowly defined tests.

One noteworthy difference is that England's Department for Education provides detailed reports that permit school staff to analyze question-level data to investigate pupil performance as well as to develop targets for future goals. Beyond that, however, the England case is in many ways similar to the US cases described above. The accountability system focuses on schools and the stakes are growing. For teachers, the stakes remain modest, but those too are expanding.

CONCLUSION

Ultimately, the usefulness of value-added depends on what it does to improve teaching and learning. The recommendations in this chapter are aimed at that exact goal. Because of the almost complete lack of research on the use of value-added measures, these recommendations are based mainly on reasoned judgment and common sense—though in my experience one person's common sense is another's blasphemy. But, at the very least, these recommendations provide a starting point for debate.

The case studies provide a sense of perspective, describing how some districts, states, and countries are using value-added and what directions they might be headed in. They are not necessarily exemplars, though most of the cases include some positive elements. Even with its initial missteps, Houston has moved in a better direction. In the coming years, the number of cases will surely multiply, affording greater opportunities to carefully study and report on how the systems affect teaching and learning. Tennessee and Dallas, despite having blazed the trail, have not left a very clear track for others to follow. Districts like Milwaukee are poised to fill that gap—indeed, they already have with one study that evaluates value-added-based policies through research collaborations that will tell us much more about the promises and pitfalls these measures pose.[23]

In the next chapter, I expand my set of recommendations to encompass a closely related issue—creating and reporting value-added measures.

10

Creating Value-Added Measures
That Match Their Uses

"The devil's in the details."

—Anonymous

In chapter 4, I briefly explained how value-added measures are created—that is, how to predict achievement for each student and then compare that prediction to actual achievement. One reason I didn't go into more detail is that the process of creating value-added measures depends very much on their uses—the topic of chapter 9. Now I can return to this topic and discuss the creation of value-added measures in more detail.

There are three reasons why value-added measures should not be created until decisions have been made about how they will be used. First, using them to inform high-stakes decisions—tenure, dismissal, and promotion—means that they must be very reliable, and requiring more years of data might be justified. There is a trade-off in this case: the more years of data used, the less the measures will reflect teachers' and schools' current performance. But decision makers would want to lean more toward reducing random error by using more years when the decisions are high-stakes.

Second, every effort should be made to account for factors outside the control of the educators being evaluated, but the ways to do this depend on the local context. For example, in a district where schools largely control teacher hiring and assignment, it might make sense to account for initial teacher effectiveness in schools when evaluating the school principal.

Third, value-added for program evaluation requires accounting for different factors than value-added for accountability. In particular, I argue that teacher value-added measures should be based on comparisons across schools to facilitate collaboration and cooperation. But in the case of value-added for program evaluation, the general absence of consequences for individuals means that there need be no concern about undermining collaboration. The goal is simply to learn whether the program works. This is why, for example, in my study of NBPTS teachers with Tim Sass, we compared NBPTS teachers with other teachers in the same school who were not NBPTS certified.[1] I recommend against such an approach when using value-added to evaluate individual performance, but it is arguably the best approach for program evaluation. To keep things focused, I limit my recommendations below to the use of value-added for accountability over program evaluation.

Conversely, appropriate uses also depend on how measures are created: if the tests are not well designed, then the value-added measures we create with those test scores will not be very good—garbage in, garbage out. Missing or inaccurate data would be another reason not to trust value-added measures for high-stakes uses.

The rest of the chapter comprises my recommendations for creating value-added measures for accountability. I then discuss how well the five case studies—Tennessee, Dallas, Houston, Milwaukee, and England—apply the recommendations.

RECOMMENDATIONS FOR CREATING AND REPORTING VALUE-ADDED MEASURES FOR ACCOUNTABILITY PURPOSES

Over the course of my research, I have developed ten basic recommendations for creating value-added measures that apply across almost all uses (see "Summary of Recommendations for Creating and Reporting Value-Added Measures"). These are discussed below.

Recommendation 1: Use student tests that reflect rich content and are standardized, scaled, and criterion-referenced.

I have deliberately made this my first recommendation because high-quality tests are so crucial to the success of any system of test-based

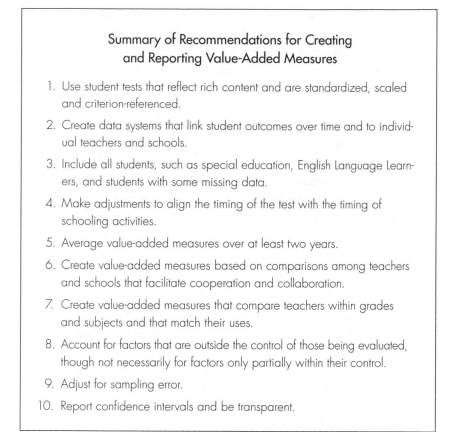

Summary of Recommendations for Creating and Reporting Value-Added Measures

1. Use student tests that reflect rich content and are standardized, scaled and criterion-referenced.

2. Create data systems that link student outcomes over time and to individual teachers and schools.

3. Include all students, such as special education, English Language Learners, and students with some missing data.

4. Make adjustments to align the timing of the test with the timing of schooling activities.

5. Average value-added measures over at least two years.

6. Create value-added measures based on comparisons among teachers and schools that facilitate cooperation and collaboration.

7. Create value-added measures that compare teachers within grades and subjects and that match their uses.

8. Account for factors that are outside the control of those being evaluated, though not necessarily for factors only partially within their control.

9. Adjust for sampling error.

10. Report confidence intervals and be transparent.

accountability. What gets measured gets done. While this is true regardless of whether value-added techniques are applied, the fact that value-added might produce more aggressive accountability systems makes the issue even more important.

In addition to requiring tests that are standardized and properly scaled (see chapter 2), value-added measures will work best if student tests capture a broad range of content and skill. This is a real limit of today's tests, though it is not a problem inherent to all standardized testing. To see why, consider a less-typical form of assessment—International Baccalaureate (IB) exams. I use this example because one of my own children went through an IB program and took these tests. If only every child were so lucky. The IB test is an authentic assessment, meaning that it captures skills like inquiry and problem solving that are important not just in the classroom but in the real world.

While they capture richer content and skills, authentic assessments also involve greater random error. First, they generally require open-ended (constructed response) questions. Even well-trained scorers often do not agree when rating answers to particular questions. Because the content is rich, it is also more subjective; and because it is subjective, it is more difficult to place on an interval scale even within grades. Linking items are impractical, partly because authentic assessments have fewer items in total, so scaling across grades is also difficult. However, given how much the test drives the curriculum in any high-stakes accountability setting, the additional random error is almost certainly a price worth paying.

Whether they use multiple-choice or authentic assessment, tests must be criterion-referenced. A shortcoming of some criterion-referenced tests is that they are designed to capture knowledge and skills right around the cut points of the standards—near the achievement level of the average student. But part of the point of this book is to reduce the focus on such arbitrary performance standards. Tests should be designed to capture a range of content and difficulty levels, which requires selecting items from large item banks, making it harder for teachers to guess what specific content will be covered.

More generally, there are three important trade-offs in designing tests with value-added in mind:

- *Broad content versus measurement error.* The more content we hope to measure, the more test items we need to capture it well. But the number of test items is essentially fixed (children can be expected only to spend so much time on the test), which will limit the amount of information on how students are doing on any given content domain. The increase in measurement error also means that tests of broad content are not *instructionally sensitive*, in the sense that covering a broader range of content means that some of the things teachers teach will not be captured on the test. This means there is a trade-off between instructional sensitivity (some information is not captured) and narrow content (teaching to the test is more prevalent).

- *Vertical scale versus measurement error.* Creating a vertical scale requires linking items across grades and years. But, again, if the number of items is fixed, and the linking items really only serve to create the scale, then the creation of the vertical scale adds measurement error to the test.

- *Measurement error versus cost.* The above problems can be reduced, but not without costs. Longer tests cost more to produce and score. Currently, less than 2 percent of current K–12 expenditures go to fund the entire state and federal systems of standards, assessments, and accountability, and switching from tests now in use to IB tests, for example, would increase costs from $15 to $34 per student to $113 to $161 per student.[2] However, given the importance of the test in high-stakes contexts, putting more money into the tests seems like a worthwhile investment. Helping to reduce measurement error and facilitate broad content and a vertical scale would be an added bonus. Another important potential cost is time. Some states have multiple standardized tests and some districts add their own tests, not to mention the classroom assessments and diagnostic tests. The time involved in testing begins to add up, taking time away from the very thing that can make scores rise—quality instruction.

While I have focused on testing issues that relate to value-added, it is really only the second trade-off—involving the vertical scale—that is truly unique to value-added. The other trade-offs and choices arise with snapshot measures as well, but they are more important with value-added where random error is an important problem to contend with.

Recommendation 2: Create data systems that link student outcomes over time and to individual teachers and schools.

I explained in chapter 3 how the word growth is used in many different ways, but that the only relevant form of growth for performance measurement is individual student growth over time. This obviously requires having a data system that links students and their outcomes (such as achievement) over time so that growth can be calculated.

Student data should also be linked to individual teachers and schools. Even if value-added is never used to measure individual teacher performance for accountability, the student-teacher linkage is necessary if value-added is to be used for program evaluation. Many states still have laws that explicitly prohibit linking student data to teachers. Those laws should be repealed.[3]

There is much more that can be said about developing data systems, such as the importance of linking K–12 and higher education data systems to examine students' long-term outcomes. While the scope of this book does not allow for a detailed discussion, there are many other excellent sources of information on this topic.[4]

Recommendation 3: Include all students, such as special education, English Language Learners, and students with some missing data.

The idea that all students be included in value-added measures is really a rule that applies to any measure of educator performance, even snapshots. If students are excluded, then schools have incentives to pay less attention to these students. Partly for this reason, federal law now requires some form of assessment for all students.[5] The main two groups whose assessments differ from the typical state tests are English Language Learners (ELLs) and special education students whose individualized education programs (IEPs) stipulate test changes.

As one way of addressing their needs, ELL and special education students often are given regular tests, but with accommodations. In special education, accommodations can include, for example, the use of a calculator or dictionary, a reader, a scribe, extended time, or a small group setting. ELL students might be tested in their native language. In addition, for the purpose of calculating AYP, districts can permit up to "1 percent of students . . . who score 'proficient' or 'advanced' on an alternate assessment based on alternate achievement standards to be counted as proficient."[6] This rule is intended for students with the "most severe cognitive disabilities."[7]

While the basic principle of including all students is not very controversial, implementing it can be a challenge when ELL students take reading assessments or any assessment that requires substantial English literacy skills (e.g., a social studies assessment). A test in English is not going to be an accurate gauge of language skill for a student whose primary language is Spanish. But even in math, ELL students are at a disadvantage because math problems also involve some language skills.

The challenges also extend to special education. One concern is that accommodations might give schools an incentive to classify more students as special education, in the hopes that the accommodations will boost their scores. Excluding special education students from testing could have the same effect, as it did during 1990s when test-based accountability began to expand. For the excluded students, this decision is obviously unfair, but it affects others as well, since it also creates incentives to reclassify students into the excluded categories.

When alternate assessments are used, the question of test scaling returns. The most advanced scaling methods are not being used in alternate assessments.[8] While this is a limitation, using a nonscaled test seems a reasonable price to pay relative to the unintended consequences of completely omitting whole groups of students.

As an aside, it is noteworthy that NCLB assessment rules for ELLs include a mandate for assessing the "English Language proficiency *gains*" (italics added) of all ELL students in addition to assessing their proficiency in other academic subjects (reading, math, science).[9] So federal law currently recognizes the importance of growth for ELL students but not for the majority of students. My recommendation to use value-added for school accountability would bring the law on regular students into alignment with current ELL policy.

Even in cases where efforts are made to include all students, data for some students may simply be missing. This is a common problem with mobile students (those who switch schools often). The move from district to state data systems helps solve this problem because students can move to any public school within a state and still show up in the data. But there are various ways students can still get lost from a data standpoint. For example, students might go by different names or spell their names differently. So, a single student might show up twice in the data system without anyone knowing it. From the standpoint of value-added, half the data for each of these "different" students appears to be missing. Whatever the reason for missing data, the students in question should not be excluded because this would create an incentive to pay less attention to them, or to deliberately lose data. Instead, there are more sophisticated methods that can be used to include students with incomplete data.[10]

This is the only place in the book where I recommend holding schools accountable for something that is largely outside their control. The reason is simple: While the cardinal rule is key, it does not trump the fact that *all* students deserve a quality education. Excluding students provides incentives to ignore them. The fact that the students under discussion are ELL and special education only reinforces my belief that we cannot exclude them—they are the ones who need the most help. So, even though mobility problems cannot be laid at the feet of the schools, an exception must be made to the cardinal rule, and schools held accountable for student outcomes.

As I have noted, as long as all students are included in the calculations, value-added should reduce incentives to exclude students because the approach takes into account prior achievement, making it more difficult to predict which students will make the schools and teachers look good.

Recommendation 4: Make adjustments to align the timing of the test with the timing of schooling activities.

When it comes to bonuses for investment bankers, we automatically tend to think that the bonus should be related to a specific time period—say, one year—and that the information used to assess performance comes from that time period. This is just common sense. This is why I implicitly assume in earlier chapters that the timing of achievement tests coincides with the timing of the school activities of educators whose performance is being measured. I assumed that students take tests at the end of each school year, that learning during the summer is irrelevant, and that students remain in only one school during the school year. Unfortunately, none of these assumptions is entirely correct—and they can be wildly wrong in some schools.

One timing issue, discussed earlier, is summer learning loss. A partial solution to this problem is accounting for student demographics, which have been shown to be related to summer learning loss—but doing leads back to the larger controversy about accounting for demographics. Also, schools can assign students to summer school, placing this issue partly within their control.

Some students switch schools in the middle of the school year. As long as the data are not missing, the achievement of these students can still be accounted for by (a) allocating the student to more than one school and weighting by the amount of time in each school, and (b) accounting for the number of students who enter the school during the school year, since complete accounting requires adjustments not just for the students who move but, because of how mobility harms the learning environment, those students who stay in the receiving school as well. As suggested by the prior recommendation, mobile students should be included in value-added calculations.

A final timing issue is that states do not administer tests at the end of the school year. January through May is a typical—and wide—range of months for test administration. But some states, such as Wisconsin, give their tests in November or December. This is problematic because each year of student growth has to be somehow split up between two (or more) different teachers. This can be done by weighting each student's growth by the amount of time spent with each teacher. Suppose that each student's test score gain from November to November involves spending three months in one school and six months in another. Then, one-third of each student's growth is assigned to the first school and the remaining two-thirds is assigned to the other. This process adds random error to the estimates, but it still makes value-added estimates feasible.

In fact, splitting up the gains in this way also solves another problem— the big "letdown" that occurs in schools after the tests have been administered. The flurry of activity leading up to the exams can be followed by field trips, watching movies, and generally relaxing. Why? Partly because students and teachers alike are worn out after testing time, from all the testing pressures. But it is also because any learning that might take place after testing will not show up in teacher performance measures. It might not show up in school performance measures either, even for students who remain in the school the following year. If the fourth-grade test is in January, then about the only way for the fourth-grade teacher to influence future test scores is by switching over to the fifth-grade curriculum in February. This makes little sense and at the very least raises questions about the alignment of grade-level standards to teacher activities. So, by giving the test late in the school year, schools have greater incentive to continue working hard through the entire year. But positive incentives can also be maintained in midyear testing by identifying how much time each student spends with each teacher and schools and weighting each student's contribution to value-added based on time spent.

Recommendation 5: Average value-added measures over at least two years.

A basic principle of statistics is that the more information there is available, the lower the random error. And since random error is not a strong suit of value-added, taking steps to address this is a must. The number of students that a given teacher or school has cannot be controlled, so the main way to reduce random error is by averaging value-added scores across multiple years. As I showed in chapter 7, averaging across years also reduces systematic error.

This standard could be set even higher to an average of three or four years of value-added measures. But this time frame creates two key problems. First, decisions about teacher performance (e.g., professional development and tenure) might have to be made early in their careers—before information about those additional years is available. A second disadvantage is that, in most cases, it is less important how teachers performed in the distant past than more recent years. Many teachers improve quickly in their early years of teaching. If the goal is to decide whether a teacher should continue teaching in a school, how much does it matter that the teacher *used to be* effective or ineffective? In addition, if measures are meant to give teachers a sense of how they are doing now, then a value-added measure averaged over, say five years will not be very helpful—especially if the teachers have recently tried to make changes in their practice and want to know whether the changes helped.

The data issue is less about the number of years than it is about the number of students for whom there are test scores for a given teacher. Recall that in middle and high school, each teacher is responsible for many more students than in elementary school. Even so, evaluators might still want to require two years of data in middle and high school, because it would give teachers time to improve if they are doing poorly in a particular year.

While the optimal number of years depends on the use of measures, as well as the level of accountability—teacher or school—the fact that averaging significantly reduces both systematic and random error means that averaging over two years is probably a wise minimum for any conceivable use.

Recommendation 6: Create value-added measures based on comparisons among teachers and schools that facilitate cooperation and collaboration.

One of the biggest concerns I hear when giving presentations and workshops on value-added is that teachers do not want to undermine collaboration. As I discussed in chapter 6, there is an easy way to avoid this: compare teachers across large numbers of schools—preferably an entire state or very large district—so that no teacher's score has a meaningful impact on anyone else's. The same is true for evaluating schools. Comparing schools only within districts might account for unmeasureable contributions by district leaders, but might undermine collaboration across schools. Statewide comparisons address this problem and have the added benefit of improving measurement accuracy. The more comparison schools there are, the better the measures will be and the fewer incentives there will be to undermine collaboration. One goal of performance measurement should be to induce educators to work together towards better performance, not to drive them apart.

It is worth noting that this approach does come at a cost because, at the teacher level, school-level factors that contribute to student achievement and are unmeasured and outside teachers' control cannot be accounted for.

Recommendation 7: Create value-added measures that compare teachers within grades and subjects and that match their uses.

I often get asked, "How can we know whether a third-grade teacher is better than a fifth-grade teacher?" The fact is that we probably cannot. The main issue is that comparing test gains across grades is problematic due to differences in content and scaling. This is why most value-added measures are based on comparisons within grades. Likewise, comparisons should only be made within subjects.

The basis of comparison in accountability policies also depends somewhat on their specific use. For example, for compensation purposes, it might make sense to compare each teacher, team, or school to all others of the same subject and grade. However, if the decision is about teacher tenure, then it makes more sense to further restrict comparisons to other young teachers. From a policy standpoint, this helps account for the fact that, if a teacher is denied tenure and terminated, the replacement teacher is likely to be inexperienced.

Recommendation 8: Account for factors that are outside the control of those being evaluated, though not necessarily for factors only partially within their control.

In chapters 4 and 6, I outlined factors that are uncontrollable, some of which are measured and others not, and factors that are partly controllable. The factors that are uncontrollable and measured (like class size) should be accounted for, and it should be recognized that unmeasured ones, such as school and district leadership, may be creating some systematic error in the performance measures of teachers and schools, respectively.

Notice that my statements here are not unequivocal. In rule 2 (my amendment to the cardinal rule), I argued that it might be better not to account for factors that are partly within the control of those whose performance is being measured because this would create an incentive for educators to ignore those factors. Summer learning loss is a case in point. Teachers have only a little control over what happens to students during the summer, but, given the importance of the summer learning loss, we should be hesitant to induce teachers to ignore this critical time in children's lives.

Recommendation 9: Adjust for sampling error.

One way to reduce address random error is to shrink estimates based on the amount of information available. If there is less information about a teacher or school, then the shrinkage process essentially pulls the estimate back toward the overall teacher average to reduce the chance that we will conclude falsely that a teacher is extremely effective or ineffective.

One disadvantage of shrinking the estimates is that it makes it much less likely that a teacher with few students who is also truly low- or high-performing will be recognized as such. But this really just reflects the limited information available about the teacher or school. It is not really the sampling error correction per se that is reducing the probability of being in a low or high performance category, but the fact some teachers and schools have less performance-related information to work with.[11]

The shrinkage adjustments also represent a clear trade-off, reducing type I errors, but increasing type II errors. The only way to reduce both errors is, again, to increase the quality and quantity of data used to create the value-added measures.

Recommendation 10: Report confidence intervals and be transparent.

Using two or more years of data and making sampling error corrections helps to address the problem of random error, but it does not completely eliminate it.[12] There will always be uncertainty about teachers' true performance and, to the degree possible, that uncertainty should be quantified and reported. I have already defined the range of likely values as the confidence interval; these should be reported along with value-added scores themselves.

I have heard some argue that confidence intervals should not be reported because they add confusion, but their exclusion not only hides important information but creates a new problem. Recall that random error causes teacher value-added estimates to bounce around from year to year. It is critical that teachers understand that these year-to-year changes may reflect random error rather than changes in their actual performance. Therefore, the solution is not to hide random error, but to report it with confidence intervals and explain how random error may cause year-to-year bounces.

Another issue of transparency involves the inner workings of the value-added approach. For example, the approach developed by Bill Sanders, and now sold by SAS, is not fully disclosed because it is considered proprietary—the same rationale that food companies use for not revealing their "secret formulas." But this is not a situation where secrecy is acceptable. People have to understand how they are being evaluated.

Again, decisions about creating and reporting value-added measures are closely connected to how the measures will be used. Therefore what I have done is establish a minimum bar—one that applies to almost any conceivable use of value-added. In some cases, it might make sense to apply more stringent rules, but it is hard to think of circumstances where the rules should be less stringent than my recommendations.

The Omitted Recommendation

Some of you may be disappointed that do I not recommend using a particular value-added model. Sanders' EVAAS approach—used by Tennessee, Houston, and others—is the oldest and most widely known, but there are other approaches such as those being used in Dallas, Milwaukee, and England. There are three reasons why it is difficult to recommend one over another:

- It is inherently difficult to know which specific approach is "correct." To really know whether one approach did a better job than others, we would actually have to know true teacher or school performance, as a basis of comparison. But no such true measure exists.

- Value-added measures will always contain some element of random and systematic error and in some cases there are trade-offs between them. Judgments about how to prioritize systematic and random error, as well as type I versus type II error, are really for policymakers and practitioners to make. My only argument here is that all forms of error are important.

- The right value-added approach depends on how the measures will be used, and there are many potential uses. The clearest distinction is between value-added for accountability versus program evaluation, but this is not the only one. There are different forms of accountability—for example, compensation versus tenure—and these too affect the specific approach taken.

While it is difficult to make general recommendations about the correct approach, it is useful to recall some important distinctions. As I pointed out in chapter 4, basic value-added is really just simple growth, and "growth models" are usually not considered to be value-added measures because they do not take into account as much information as they could. In this sense, the term value-added generally means what I have described as advanced value-added. The distinction is important because taking into account factors outside the control of those being evaluated is necessary to be consistent with the cardinal rule.

The Colorado Growth Model has received particular attention and has been adopted by many states. As the name implies, the CGM is not a value-added model and is therefore probably not appropriate for making high-stakes decisions about teachers and schools. As of the model's developers, Damien Betebenner, puts it, "the emphasis of value-added toward school and teacher effects has skewed discussions about growth models toward causal claims at the expense of description."[13] Betebenner is absolutely correct: *describing* individual student growth is quite different (and easier) from the challenging task of measuring, with value-added approaches, how much individual teachers and schools contributed to that growth. The CGM is deliberately descriptive, projecting how much growth individual students will have to make over time to reach performance standards. It is not a value-added measure.

I wish I could say that the choice of particular model is unimportant, but value-added measures do vary depending on the specific approach used for the calculations.

RETURNING TO THE FIVE CASE STUDIES

Though I cannot say which specific value-added approach is best, it is worth comparing the above recommendations to the approaches used in the case study sites discussed earlier—Tennessee, Dallas, Milwaukee, Houston, and England.

Unfortunately, none of these cases really follow the first recommendation that tests cover broad and rich content. Nor do any of them account for many, if any, uncontrollable school factors. This probably does not have a significant impact on how schools and teachers are ranked, and there is a case to be made for not accounting for factors that are even partly within the control of teachers, but it is worth noting. More importantly, while the EVAAS model does a good job of reporting confidence intervals in intuitive ways and adjusting for sampling error, the statistical methods used to make the calculations are considered proprietary and are therefore not transparent.

Sites are split on including student demographics. Dallas, Milwaukee, and England account for student background, but the two EVAAS sites (Tennessee and Houston) do not. All five cases include student-teacher data linkages and all have moved toward varying degrees of high-stakes uses for teacher value-added measures. Likewise, the five sites use at least two years of data per school/teacher, make comparisons across large numbers of teachers and schools to avoid undermining collaboration, and limit comparisons to within-grade and within-subject.

The Dallas system excludes students who enter a school after the first six weeks. In Houston, students who do not have a test score for the year in which the analysis is conducted are not counted. These exclusions are problematic because schools have less incentive to focus attention on those students.

CONCLUSION

While there is much that is not known about value-added, this and chapter 9 show that there are still some commonsense steps that can be taken to improve the odds that value-added measures improve teaching and learning. It is useful to consider the broader goals underlying these recommendations:

- Reduce systematic and random error as much as possible. This is why I recommend accounting for factors that cannot be controlled, using at least two years of data for almost any purpose, and adjusting for sampling error.

- Create sensible comparisons among teachers and schools, comparisons that are consistent with the intended uses of the measures.

- Develop a system that works for all students and educators, not just average ones. This is why I recommend including data for all students, even mobile ones, despite the fact that this breaks the cardinal rule.

- Recognize that student test scores, and therefore value-added measures based on them, do not account for everything we think is important. This is why I emphasize the need to improve the tests and to combine value-added with other types of performance measures.

Then, there is the ultimate, overarching goal—improving teaching and learning. Different people define quality teaching and learning in different ways—I keep Ms. Bloom in mind—but keeping our focus on teaching and learning will no doubt help us to make better decisions about using and creating value-added.

11

—

Addressing Key Trade-Offs, Misconceptions, and Questions

"All [statistical] models are false but some models are useful."

—George E. P. Box, statistician

I started this book with a noneducation example. How did problems with performance measurement contribute to the 2008 financial crisis? How did this happen even in companies with one relatively simple goal—profit? By now, it should be much easier to see how such problems might arise. Performance measurement is a challenge, and using those measures effectively through accountability systems is an even greater challenge. This is especially true in education: where the goals are complex, where there are many ways to reach those goals, and where each student's results depend not only on the classroom teacher, but on home and community factors as well as previous teachers and other school staff.

This does not mean all forms of accountability are equally good—or equally bad. With its focus on credentials and checklist evaluations, the current accountability system—if indeed we can call it that—is hard to defend. Teacher autonomy has its place, but autonomy does not equal professionalism, and professionalism demands some accountability. We can do better.

MISCONCEPTIONS ABOUT VALUE-ADDED

Because doing better requires first addressing the misconceptions, I begin by revisiting the list from the introduction. I mentioned several persistent misconceptions, some that tend to be raised by opponents of value-added and others more often raised by supporters. Almost all of them have an element of truth, but also some significant misunderstanding.

Misconception 1: We cannot evaluate educators based on value-added because . . .

- *Different teachers have different students.* As I described in chapter 3, this is the problem that value-added is intended to solve, and it does so fairly well, though still imperfectly.

- *Value-added measures have flaws.* Value-added measures are flawed but, as I showed in chapter 8, many of the alternatives to value-added are even more flawed.

- *Student tests are inadequate.* Most standardized tests are indeed flawed, but this is not a problem created or worsened by value-added. As I argued in chapter 10 (recommendation 1), what is needed are more sophisticated tests that capture richer content, such as those used in the International Baccalaureate program. With their open-ended, constructed response questions, these types of tests preclude vertical scales and create more random error, but since what gets tested gets taught, this is a sacrifice easily worth making. We can still do value-added with these richer assessments.

- *Teaching is complicated.* Teaching is certainly complicated, but this is as much an argument in favor of value-added as it is against. The logic of test-based accountability is that the government should establish the goals of education, measure and encourage progress toward those goals, and then get out of the way and let educators figure out how to reach them. While policymakers are yet to get out of the way in terms of rules, this basic logic of test-based accountability recognizes the complexity of teaching, so much so that the value-added measures are criticized for being too complicated (see misconception 6 below). There are many ways to be a good teacher, and measures like

216

value-added that focus on student outcomes—used in well-designed accountability systems—allow each teacher to be effective in reaching accountability goals in his or her own way.

- *Student needs are diverse.* There is little question that students vary in what they bring to the classroom as well as learning styles and, in this sense, students have different learning *needs*. This is not the same, however, as saying they have different learning *goals*. In a world where education is increasingly seen as a right, and where the academic skills imparted by schools are increasingly important to life success, educational goals are similar across all students. This is partly why there is such broad support for academic standards. It also means that diverse learning needs are not an argument against value-added, since value-added measures encourage educators to identify each student's distinctive needs in order to facilitate growth toward the goals.

Misconception 2: Value-added is fair for teachers but not for students.

This point comprises several related concerns. The first is that, despite the arbitrary nature of performance standards such as proficiency, some still see this as an important bar that all students should reach. They also see these standards as a necessary element of an accountability system aimed at the lowest performers. Viewed this way, value-added might seem unfair to low-performing students because it takes the focus away from proficiency.

While I am concerned about meeting the needs of the lowest performers, it is not clear that current law really helps these students. Proficiency-focused systems place their attention on students nearest the standard, the *bubble kids*. In states where the bar is set very low, the bubble kids are also arguably the lowest performers, but this is not the case in states with higher proficiency bars—in those states, students who are far behind may be the least likely to get attention. It is also important to note that giving schools incentives to increase scale scores, as value-added does, also provides incentives to help students become proficient.

There are three ways that value-added could maintain, or actually enhance, the attention given to achievement of low-performing students. First, value-added measures could be weighted so that achievement of the lowest performers counts more than that of other students (see example in chapter 2). This highlights the fact that the decision to use value-added is entirely separate from the decision to focus on a particular group of students.

Second, snapshots can be included in the performance measures, in the same way that an index could be created that combines performance on student outcomes with measures of practice, much like the example in chapter 9 of combining teacher value-added measures with classroom practice measures. Suppose both snapshot and growth were placed on a 0–100 scale. The two measures could be averaged together to obtain a hybrid snapshot-growth measure.[1] Such an approach might be necessary in elementary schools to avoid undermining performance in grades K–3.

Because the lowest performers also tend to be minority and come from low-income families, accounting for student demographics is also a matter of concern. Value-added measures do not have to account for demographics; however, they can, and using demographics changes the teacher and school value-added measures somewhat. A reasonable argument can be made against accounting for demographic factors because it means schools serving disadvantaged students do not have to produce as much learning to reach the same performance level. But at the same time, accounting for them does not create any incentive for schools to work any less hard to help these particular students.

Misconception 3: Value-added measures are not useful because they are summative rather than formative.

Value-added measures provide summative assessments of teacher performance—they indicate whether teachers are high-performers, in terms of one important student outcome. But value-added is often criticized for not providing information about how educators can improve. This is a legitimate point, but no single measure can fulfill both formative and summative functions very well. For this reason, any use of value-added, especially for individual teachers, should be coupled with observational information from school principals or peer assessors that includes specific information about areas of weakness.

Formative and summative evaluations are also complementary. Having a formative evaluation with no summative evaluation means that there is a path to improvement but no incentive to follow that path. A summative evaluation without a formative one provides an incentive but no path. We need both.

Misconception 4: Because they involve comparing teachers to one another, and there are no absolute value-added standards, value-added measures are not useful for accountability.

I have already described the various ways in which relative comparisons among teachers and schools are constantly being made. Parents don't call the principal to make sure their children get teachers who are good enough; they want the best teachers. Parents do not move to neighborhoods because the schools got a stamp of approval, but because it got a higher stamp than other schools. This is not only inevitable but in many ways healthy. Everyone should always be trying to get better—it is the essence of continuous improvement.

Misconception 5: Because we know so little about the effects of value-added, we cannot risk our kids' futures by experimenting with it.

No one wants to put children at risk. Some are more willing to take chances than others, depending on how many problems they see with the existing school system. In a crisis, the odds of making things better are high, lessening risk. I think the evidence is fairly persuasive that, while our performance and accountability system might not be in crisis, it is at least seriously flawed.

The larger problem with this risk argument is that, if taken to its logical conclusion, it would prevent all changes whatsoever. If we cannot experiment, then we cannot discover productive new approaches. The current system of credentials and checklist evaluations was itself an experiment when it first began.

Misconception 6: Value-added is too complicated for educators to understand.

Part of my goal in writing this book is to explode this misconception. If you have made it this far, and feel that you have understood most of what I'm saying, then I would argue that you understand value-added well enough to be evaluated by it. You don't need to understand all the underlying math and equations, but you do need to understand the basics of how measures are created and what they mean.

Consider again the college basketball RPI ratings. The RPI is a key factor determining whether teams get into the national tournament each year. The rankings are based on a precise and moderately complicated formula. My guess is that only a handful of the thousands of college basketball players, even the ones on the teams most likely to be in the national tournament, know the exact formula. What they do know is that if they win more games, especially against good opponents, then they will get a high RPI rating. There is little serious concern raised about the complexity of the RPI—and there should be as little about value-added. Value-added measures should be as simple as possible while still being correct.[2]

Misconception 7: Value-added simply represents another step in the process of "industrializing" education, making it more traditional and less progressive.

It is easy to see how someone might get this impression. As I explained in chapter 3, the term value-added not only comes from business, but from industrial manufacturing processes. I explained value-added initially as the difference between the value of inputs and the value of outputs. Moreover, the goal of value-added, as in business, is to get results and improve the bottom line.

But to conclude that value-added industrializes schooling is misleading. First, the hallmark of industrialization is not so much the focus on standardized *results* but the standardization of *processes*. If policymakers concentrate on accountability results, they can reduce the rules that still constrain educational practice. In this sense, expanded use of value-added could actually *reduce* the industrialization of education.

Similarly, value-added can be viewed as a further shift toward traditional and away from progressive education. Whether this is true, however, depends more on the design of the standards and assessments than on the potential use of value-added over snapshot measures. *Progressive* education is closely related to the idea of inquiry-based learning, and there is nothing to prevent tests of those types of learning from being used to create value-added measures. More creative testing would increase random error to some degree, but this is a fairly small price to pay. That said, this is one area in which there is a danger of the tail wagging the dog. We should set standards and design assessments based on what we want students to know, not on any small challenges this might entail for value-added and other educator performance measures.

Value-added measures might also be seen as paths to industrialized, *traditional* education because they focus on student achievement—skills considered important for the workplace. While I have focused on applications to student achievement, I also showed that value-added can be applied to other student outcomes such as high school graduation and college attendance and success. If a goal can be defined and measured—traditional, progressive, or otherwise—then the value-added approach can usually be applied.

Misconception 8: Value-added is a magic bullet that by itself will transform education.

While the enthusiasm for value-added is understandable and to some degree well founded, there is no direct evidence that these measures will improve teaching and learning. As the federal NCLB shows, school-level test-based accountability can certainly change teaching, but not always for the better and not necessarily in ways that positively influence learning. Also, past efforts to hold individual teachers accountable, especially through merit pay, have been short-lived.

There are also reasons to be skeptical of value-added measures: the lack of confidence created by random error, remaining problems with student tests, and the expense and other challenges associated with classroom practice measures, to name a few. A failure to recognize these limitations could easily lead to both the "tail wagging the dog" and "air bag" problems. Better performance measures do not necessarily produce better performance.

But the magic bullet argument is also a bit of a straw man. *Nothing* is a magic bullet. The real question is, can value-added approaches improve education? I think the answer is yes, as long as the policies are well designed and carefully implemented. Unfortunately, history shows, and the Los Angeles fiasco reminds us, that we cannot always depend on policymakers to make careful and wise decisions.

TRADE-OFFS

Addressing misconceptions is one step toward clearer understanding of value-added measures, but this only tells us how *not* to think about value-added. This book is meant to provide a useful path forward on how the measures should be used. The issues around value-added are clearly not cut-and-dried, and require the judgments of policymakers and educators alike. That is because trade-offs lie at the heart of any policy decisions including those about the use of value-added measures. The fact that there are trade-offs is nothing particularly distinctive to accountability or to education. They may reinforce George Box's quote that "all models are wrong" in some way, but it's also the case that "some are useful." Below, I identify five fundamental trade-offs in choices about value-added measures:

1. Holding People Accountable for What They Can Control Versus Creating Perverse Incentives in Areas They Partly Control

As was made clear in chapter 4, the cardinal rule comes with a significant caveat. In theory, schools have at least a little control over almost everything. The home environment is very important and hard to control, and has a particular influence over student learning during the summer months. If we wanted to eliminate that factor from value-added measures, we could do so by testing students both on the first and last days of every school year. But this would reduce the incentive for educators to encourage students to read over the summer or to assign students to summer schools. There is a trade-off here, but encouraging educators to set aside important activities is arguably worse that holding them accountable for factors they only partially control.

2. Free Riding Versus Collaboration and Statistical Error

The reason policymakers want to create value-added measures for individual teachers and other educators is that they believe the new accountability focus on whole schools does not do enough to place pressure on each individual within schools. Less-effective individuals can ride free on the performance of the rest of the group.

But eliminating the free-rider problem requires individual performance measures, and such measures are more prone to random error because there is less information available for each individual. A systematic error may also arise: it is impossible to exactly measure how much an individual teacher contributes to the value-added of other teachers through collaboration. So even if policymakers create performance measures through comparisons across whole states, they may still undermine collaboration somewhat by inducing teachers to focus on things that will help the scores of their own students rather than other teachers' students.

One way to address this trade-off would be to include collaboration among the measures of practice. Another would be to use team- or school-based value-added, although this opens up potential for a free-rider problem and highlights the trade-offs.

3. Errors Versus Cost

Statistical and decision errors can be reduced by collecting more good information, especially by combining value-added with classroom observations. But this is expensive in terms of both money and time. Classroom observations, done well, are not cheap. Even if existing school personnel conduct the observations, and even if they are not financially compensated for this additional work, observing teachers still takes evaluators' time away from other activities.

4. Systematic Versus Random Error

Value-added measures reduce systematic error relative to snapshots but, because the measures are based on growth, they increase random errors. While both systematic and random error have difficult consequences, there are at least two reasons to think this trade-off is worthwhile: (a) it is possible to quantify the degree of random error (with confidence intervals), but this cannot be done with systematic error; and (b) there are ways to reduce the level and influence of random error, but no obvious way other than value-added to reduce systematic error.

5. Type I Versus Type II Decision Errors

In chapter 5, I described type I and type II statistical errors, and how those errors, depending on policy design, could lead to decision errors. The issue arose again in chapter 8 when I discussed how critics of accountability, following the lead of researchers, have focused on type I errors, even though type II errors arguably do just as much to affect students. Dismissing a high-performing teacher is a type I decision error, while keeping a low-performing teacher is a type II decision error. Both harm the quality of teaching and learning.

For any given level of statistical confidence, this is a pure trade-off. Larger samples, more frequent testing of students, and other adjustments reduce the chances of both types of errors, but as the third trade-off suggests, this comes at some cost.

Above all, it is important to note that these five fundamental trade-offs also apply to other measures, and so using them simply as arguments against value-added is not valid. For example, the credentialing system has less random error, but very large systematic errors. Classroom observations probably have less (or at least different) systematic errors, but possibly high random errors, depending on the quality and quantity of observations.

TOWARD WELL-ROUNDED ACCOUNTABILITY

This book has focused on only one element of accountability—performance measurement—yet decisions about performance measurement depend on other policy decisions. Test design, and the academic standards on which they are based, are obvious examples, but there are many more that deserve a brief mention, among them capacity, differentiation, alignment, and balance.

Capacity plays a big role in accountability. Research shows that the schools most responsive to accountability are those that have the resources—money, time, knowledge, experience, and skill—to respond positively and productively.[3] Not coincidentally, schools serving high proportions of low-income students have less capacity to work with. They have greater difficulty attracting teachers and fewer community resources to rely on.

Differentiation is also important, although sometimes hard to implement in a world with so many up-or-down decisions. Teachers are hired or not, tenured or not, terminated or not, promoted or not—there are only two options in these cases. But this is not true of all aspects of accountability. Public reporting of performance is a form of accountability (as the Los Angeles case clearly shows) as is compensation. In these cases, making more nuanced distinctions in performance is possible and worthwhile.

Because of the importance of capacity and differentiation, I previously proposed a school performance table like that in figure 11-1.[4] I argued that accountability would be focused mainly on value-added. The schools at the extremes would be subject to rewards and sanctions, while the schools in upper rows (with students from wealthier families) would receive additional resources to help offset student disadvantages and give all students a better chance of reaching basic academic standards.

To further highlight the roles of both capacity and differentiation, I have included in figure 11-1 where all of the Oakville schools fall according to these categories. They are all over the map. Quincy seems to deserve some type of award, producing very high value-added. Fillmore, Harrison, Tyler, and Van Buren are also doing well and might deserve a smaller award, or least some public recognition. At the other end, Adams,

FIGURE 11-1 School performance table with value-added and snapshot

% High-income	Advanced value-added percentile				
	0–19	20–39	40–59	60–79	80+
0–19	Adams, Jackson, Washington				
20–39		Jefferson			
40–59	Polk			Van Buren	
60–79	Madison				
80+		Taylor	Monroe	Fillmore, Harrison, Tyler	Quincy

Jackson, Madison, Polk, and Washington have very low value-added and, if that trend continued, might be subject to major interventions. Among those schools, however, Adams, Jackson, and Washington are differentiated by their extremely low-income population. Even with the threat of reconstitution looming, these three schools might warrant some additional resources to build capacity and perhaps increased compensation (or "combat pay") to help attract effective teachers. The one in the middle column, Monroe, with value-added near the average, might be largely left alone, but would still have an incentive to work hard to receive the rewards that come with the higher categories and to avoid the additional scrutiny that would come from being at a lower level.

Alignment of standards and standardized tests is obviously important in test-based accountability, but so too is alignment of incentives. Teachers, schools, and districts cannot afford to be working at cross purposes. At present, the system of school-level test-based accountability is misaligned: credentials and evaluation checklists are used to hold teachers accountable, while principals and district leaders are accountable mainly for achievement scores and other goals largely unrelated to teacher credentials.

This does not mean that incentives have to look identical. In the above example, the problem is not just that teachers are not held accountable directly for student outcomes but that the principals have very little direct authority over the vast majority of teachers. The school principals are therefore held accountable for factors beyond their control.

This leads to a final aspect of well-rounded accountability—*balance*. Balance is important to accountability in two ways. First, it is imperative to balance the many goals of education and the many roles we have in mind for our children when they become adults. Likewise, in designing accountability, there must be a balance between punishments and rewards. The current system, with its sanctioning of low-performing schools, is not balanced (not to mention unfair, since the focus on snapshots results in systematic misidentification of schools as low-performing). We need more rewards to bring the accountability picture into balance. Figure 11-1 highlights the need for responses at both ends of the performance spectrum.

These four concepts—capacity, differentiation, alignment, and balance—apply to any accountability system, including one focused on value-added measures. There is still a lot of room for interpretation and adaptation, especially in deciding what punishments and rewards to use and how to ensure that interventions for low-performing schools are targeted to their real weaknesses. In this sense, what I have provided is a compass more than a detailed roadmap.

VALUE-ADDED AND ACCOUNTABILITY: PAST, PRESENT, AND FUTURE

It is very difficult to create performance measures and design accountability systems that follow the cardinal rule, align individual and organizational goals, and, in the end, help organizations succeed in reaching their core missions. The possibilities for perverse incentives, unintended consequences, and corrupted measures are endless. Unfortunately, failing to even try to measure performance also has consequences we see today—failed accountability, failed missions, failed messages.

The struggle to get accountability right is not new. The snapshot problem goes all the way back to the 1800s, if not earlier. But by focusing on achievement at a single point in time, this approach has frustrated teachers, driven them out of low-income schools, and allowed complacency in high-income ones. The teacher who was relieved at the death of one of her low-scoring students is an extreme case in point, but still one that highlights the sometimes bizarre nature of the system.

The twentieth century saw evolution, but not revolution. The advent of mass scale standardized testing in the 1920s was followed by minimum competency testing in the 1970s, and then, in the 1990s, by accountability for schools in the form of school report cards and occasionally high-stakes responses like school reconstitution. The system still focused on snapshots, but at least the content became more sophisticated and comparable across schools.

Added along the way to this ill-designed accountability system was the credentialing strategy—an elaborate system of college degrees, certification, salary schedules, and pro forma evaluations that measures everything about teachers except what they do in classrooms. This system achieved some positive outcomes as well, addressing important problems such as the gross inequities in pay between genders and races and it stemmed the cronyism that previously pervaded hiring and compensation decisions. It moved teaching away from politics and in the general direction of professionalism. Nevertheless, few would argue that it did anything more than move us from an unsatisfactory system to a satisfactory—but not excellent—one.

In addition to reducing the role of politics, another admirable goal of new performance measures was ensuring that all students had the basic academic skills they would need to have real social and economic opportunities. Performance standards, as arbitrary as they are, set the same bar for everyone and, in theory, help ensure that even the most disadvantaged students are not left behind. Point-in-time achievement measures made sense by this logic because they told parents, educators, and stakeholders alike whether their students were meeting those basic standards.

Unfortunately, designers failed to realize two important things: First, lofty aspirations like 100 percent proficiency do not make for smart incentives. Snapshot-oriented systems punish low-scoring schools and educators, so much so that they have little hope of measuring up. Modest changes in snapshot achievement are possible, but a low-poverty school is twenty-two times as likely to be high-performing on state assessments compared with high-poverty schools.[5] This does *not* mean that schools cannot help low-income and minority students, or that all schools are equally effective. On the contrary, I and many others have shown clear evidence that some schools serving almost entirely low-income students have higher value-added than schools serving mostly high-income students. What it does mean is simply that snapshot measures, while they reflect lofty ambitions, do a very poor job of reflecting what schools contribute to student learning. Violating the cardinal rule has significant unintended consequences for the very students the polices are intended to help.

Second, the credentialing and accountability systems never fully recognized and addressed the importance of teachers and instructional practice. Even teachers themselves seem to agree that the credentialing strategy does not work. It fails to distinguish effective from ineffective teachers, even when research increasingly shows their vast performance differences, and the system provides no useful feedback to help teachers improve. This is another reason why the value-added debate has come to the forefront. Value-added offers the potential to measure, for the first time on a broad scale, each teacher's contribution to student achievement. Given the obvious limitations of the credentialing strategy, it is easy to see the attraction of this new option.

In chapter 1, I posed the deliberately provocative question, in aligning organizational goals with individual ones, "Are schools as bad as investment banks?" Apparently so. This is not for lack of effort or from bad motives. But there is a persuasive case to be made that our traditional approaches are, at best, outdated and need of change. It is not only the clear problems with the policies themselves that drive concern, but the nation's poor academic performance relative to other countries and stagnant scores on national assessments. Test scores should never be the sole arbiter of educational success for student, teachers, or the nation as a whole, but they are important.

Some might see the shift to value-added-based accountability as another wave of educational reform that sacrifices equity for excellence and efficiency. But value-added measures can avoid a trade-off on these grounds. By moving away from snapshot proficiency, and perhaps giving great weight to achievement growth of the lowest performers, we can provide better incentives for schools to educate these students, thus improving equity. In addition, by moving away from uninspired goals of "proficient" knowledge and "satisfactory" teaching, we can improve excellence as well.

We do not just need better performance measures, but a new way of thinking. The essence of education is about taking students where they start, even far down the ladder of readiness, and helping them grow as much as they can. Yet, our present accountability system does everything it can to prevent this healthy perspective. The reams of snapshot test data, however well intentioned, do not create the right way of thinking. If we want educators to help each student grow, we should provide the information they need to see student growth.

We do not yet know exactly how to use value-added measures. I have proposed some general principles and recommendations as a starting point, but the real process will be one of trial and error, fits and starts. It will include careful districts like Milwaukee and careless ones like Los Angeles; high-stakes programs like reformed tenure and compensation rules and lower-stakes, but possibly equally effective, programs like evaluation-based professional development; simple programs, such as providing performance information confidentially to individual teachers and principals; and more complicated ones like collecting mounds of data and turning them into complex indices. Some educational leaders continue the focus on schools and teams, while others will continue the present shift to individual teachers.

There is no single path forward, but there are principles and evidence. There are also important stories about teachers like Ms. Bloom. If we can all agree that the teachers who inspired and helped us over the long haul are the ones who deserve awards and praise, then we will have much more success in designing and implementing accountability in the coming century than we had in the last one.

Notes

Introduction

1. After reading several court cases and consulting education lawyers (who chose to remain anonymous), it appears that the school district may have been bound by the California Public Records Act (CPRA) to provide the data. However, there are privacy provisions in the state constitution that the Los Angeles Unified School District might have used as a basis for a challenge, particularly the release of the teacher names. I believe the district is still partly culpable for this reason.

2. The other publication that is somewhat similar to this is: *Measuring Improvements in Learning Outcomes: Best Practices to Assess the Value-Added of Schools* (Paris: Organization for Economic Cooperation and Development, 2008).

3. Public Agenda, "Teaching for a Living" survey results, http://www.publicagenda. org/pages/teaching-for-a-living-full-survey-results#q28d.

4. Jane G. Coggshall, Amber Ott, Ellen Behrstock, and Molly Lasagna "Supporting Teacher Talent: The View from Generation Y," Public Agenda, http://www.publicagenda.org/pages/supporting-teacher-talent-view-from-Generation-Y.

5. For other books and reports about value-added, see for example:

   Henry Braun, *Using Student Progress To Evaluate Teachers: A Primer on Value-Added Models* (Princeton, NJ: Educational Testing Service, 2005). This primer introduces the concept of value-added and intended for nonacademics, but it is fairly short (twenty pages) and does not provide examples or llustrations.

   Robert L. Linn, "Validation of the Uses and Interpretations of Results of State Assessment and Accountability Systems," in *Large-Scale Assessment Programs for All Students: Development, Implementation, and Analysis*, eds. Gerald Tindal and Thomas M. Haladyna (Mahwah, NJ: Lawrence Erlbaum Associates, 2001), 27–48.

   Daniel McCaffrey, Daniel Koretz, J. R. Lockwood, and Laura S. Hamilton, *Evaluating Value-Added Models for Teacher Accountability* (Santa Monica, CA: Rand, 2003). This report is intended primarily for researchers.

Chapter 1

1. Diane Ravitch, *The Death and Life of the Great American School System: How Testing and Choice Are Undermining Education* (New York: Basic Books, 2010).

2. I build on the excellent work done described by Richard Rothstein and his colleagues, showing that effective accountability is a challenge in all organizations, even businesses with apparently simple and narrow goals; see Richard Rothstein, Rebecca Jacobsen, and Tamara Wilder, *Grading Education: Getting Accountability Right*

(Washington, DC: Economic Policy Institute; New York: Teachers College Press, 2008).

3. Some of my colleagues will disagree with me on this point, but students will actually write quite a bit, and often constructively, when instructors make clear that the evaluations will be taken seriously.

4. The effective schools literature has long pointed toward mission as a key factor (see Ronald Edmonds, "Effective Schools for the Urban Poor," *Educational Leadership* 37 [1979]:15–24); Peter Drucker, while known for his work in the business sector, also has written on nonprofit agencies and mission (Peter F. Drucker, *Managing the Non-Profit Organization* [Oxford: Butterworth-Heineman, 1990]); Covey (Stephen R. Covey, *The Leader in Me* [New York: Free Press, 2008]) also discusses mission within the context of schools; O'Gorman and Doran write that "there is an overwhelming consensus in the literature that the development and management of business missions is fundamental for the survival and growth of any business" (Colm O'Gorman and Roslyn Doran, "Mission Statements in Small and Medium-Sized Businesses," *Journal of Small Business Management* [1999]: 59–66).

5. Edward Lazear, "Performance Pay and Productivity," *American Economic Review* 90, no. 5 [2000]: 1346–1361.

6. Douglas N. Harris, Stacey A. Rutledge, William Ingle, and Cynthia Thompson, "Mix and Match: What Principals Really Look for When Hiring Teachers," *Education Finance and Policy* 5, no. 2 (2010): 228-246.

7. Caroline M. Hoxby and Andrew Leigh, "Pulled Away or Pushed out? Explaining the Decline of Teacher Aptitude in the United States," *American Economic Review: Papers and Proceedings* 94, no. 2 [May, 2004]: 236-240.

8. Jo Becker, Sheryl Gay Stolberg, and Stephen Labaton, "White House Philosophy Stoked Mortgage Bonfire," *New York Times*, December 20, 2008.

9. Michael Lewis, *The Big Short* (New York: W.W. Norton and Co., 2010).

10. Suzy Jagger, "End of the Wall Street Investment Bank", *The Times* (London), September 22, 2008, http://business.timesonline.co.uk/tol/business/industry_sectors/banking_and_finance/article4800550.ece.

11. Paul Hodgson "Pay for Success III," The Corporate Library, http://www.thecorporatelibrary.com/reports.php?reportid=299&keyword.

12. Alain Sherter, "Why Goldman Sachs Should Manage Like Apple," *Financial Folly* (blog), *BNET,* December 3, 2009, http://www.bnet.com/blog/financial-business/why-goldman-sachs-should-manage-like-apple/2683.

13. Dale Ballou and Michael Podgursky, *Teacher Pay and Teacher Quality* (Kalamazoo, MI: W.E. Upjohn Institute, 1997).

14. Douglas N. Harris and Tim R. Sass. "Teacher training, teacher quality, and student achievement," *Journal of Public Economics* (forthcoming).

15. Daniel Weisberg, Susan Sexton, Jennifer Mulhern, and David Keeling, *The Widget Effect: Our National Failure to Acknowledge and Act on Differences in Teacher Effectiveness*, (Brooklyn, NY: The New Teacher Project, 2009).

16. Mary M. Kennedy, "Recognizing Good Teaching When We See It," in *Handbook of Teacher Assessment and Teacher Quality*, ed. Mary Kennedy (San Francisco: Jossey Bass, 2010).

17. Mary Kennedy, quoted in Thomas Toch and Robert Rothman, "Rush to Judgment: Teacher Evaluation in Public Education," *Education Sector*, 2008, http://www.educationsector.org/publications/rush-judgment-teacher-evaluation-public-education.

18. Ibid.

19. Ibid.

20. Weisberg et al., *The Widget Effect*.

21. Randi Weingarten, "A New Path Forward: Four Approaches to Quality Teachjing and Better Schools," speech delivered at the National Press Club, Washington, DC, January 12, 2010, http://www.aft.org/pdfs/press/sp_weingarten011210.pdf.

22. Olivia Little, *Teacher Evaluation Systems: The Window for Opportunity and Reform* (Washington, DC: National Education Association, 2009), xi.

23. The problem with evaluating state certification is that nearly all teachers are certified, which begs the question, to whom are we comparing the certified teachers? A more useful comparison would be how effective certified teachers are relative to teachers who tried to become certified but failed. But because of the way certification policies are designed, we never get to see the performance of uncertified teachers. It is plausible that the uncertified teachers in these studies were hired because they were known—for example, through a principal's personal knowledge—to have unusually strong teaching skills. If that's the case, it may appear that the gatekeeper function of the certification process is not working—even if it really is. However, it is hard to justify relying so heavily on a credential that is not directly tied to classroom observations or student results.

24. For evidence that traditional certification does not distinguish highly effective teachers, see Dan D. Goldhaber and Dominic J. Brewer, "Does Teacher Certification Matter? High School Teacher Certification Status and Student Achievement," *Education Evaluation and Policy Analysis* 22, no 2 (2000):129–145.

   For evidence of a similar result with regard to National Board Certification, see Dan Goldhaber and Emily Anthony, "Can Teacher Quality be Effectively Assessed? National Board Certification as a Signal of Effective Teaching," *Review of Economics and Statistics* 89, no. 1 (2007): 134–150; and Douglas N. Harris and Tim R. Sass, "The Effects of NBPTS-Certified Teachers on Student Achievement," *Journal of Policy Analysis and Management* 28, no. 1 (2009): 55–80.

   For exceptions to the rule regarding state certification, the following study finds a positive association between certification and performance in high school: Charles T. Clotfelter, Helen F. Ladd, and Jacob L. Vigdor, *Teacher Credentials and Student Achievement in High School: A Cross-Subject Analysis with Student Fixed Effects*, Center for the Analysis of Longitudinal Data for Education Research (CALDER) report (Washington, DC: Urban Institute: 2007).

25. Douglas N. Harris and Stacey Rutledge, "Models and Predictors of Teacher

Effectiveness: A review of the Evidence with Lessons From (and for) Other Occupations," *Teachers College Record*, 112, no. 3 (2010): 914–960.

26. Steve Farkas, Jean Johnson, and Anne Duffett, *Stand by Me: What Teachers Really Think About Unions, Merit Pay, and Other Professional Matters* (New York: Public Agenda, 2003).

27. Weisberg et al., *The Widget Effect*.

28. Arthur Levine, *Educating School Teachers* (Washington, DC: The Education Schools Project, 2006).

29. Dale Ballou and Michael Podgursky, *Teacher Pay and Teacher Quality* (Kalamazoo, MI: W.E. Upjohn Institute, 1997).

30. Douglas N. Harris and Tim R. Sass, "What Makes for a Good Teacher and Who Can Tell?" (working paper #30, National Center for the Analysis of Longitudinal Data in Education Research (CALDER), Urban Institute, Washington, DC, 2009).

31. Robert Gordon, Thomas Kane, and Douglas Staiger, "Identifying Effective Teachers Using Performance on the Job," (Hamilton Project discussion paper, Brookings Institution, Washington, DC, 2006).

32. National Commission on Excellence in Education (NCEE), *A Nation at Risk: The Imperative for Educational Reform* (Washington, DC: US Department of Education, 1983).

33. Douglas N. Harris, Michael Handel, and Lawrence Mishel, "Education and the Economy Revisited: How Schools Matter," *Peabody Journal of Education* 19, no. 1 (2004): 36–63. I return to this issue in chapter 7 in discussing how much improved teacher quality would influence economic performance.

34. National Center for Education Statistics, *NAEP 2008 Trends in Academic Progress* NCES 2009-479 (Washington, DC: US Department of Education, 2009).

35. Chris Allen and David Plank, "School Board Election Structure and Democratic Representation," *Educational Policy* 19, no. 3 (2005): 510–527.

36. See, for example, Ravitch, *The Death and Life of the Great American School System*.

37. Jeanette. B. Coltham, "Educational Accountability: An English Experiment and Its Outcome," *School Review* 81, no. 1 (1972): 15–34. I thank Debbi Harris for pointing out this quotation to me.

38. See, for example, Flavio Cunha and James J. Heckman. "Investing in Our Young People," (NBER Working Papers 16201, National Bureau of Economic Research, Cambridge, MA, 2010).

39. Valerie Lee and David Burkam, *Inequality at the Starting Gate: Social Background Differences in Achievement as Children Begin School* (Washington, DC: Economic Policy Institute, 2002).

40. Scores are reported in normal curve equivalents (NCEs), based on the percentile ranking of each school within its respective state, because direct comparisons across states are not possible on state tests. (NCEs are described in chapter 2.) *High-performing* means being in the top third in a state. The study from which these data are

drawn is: Douglas N. Harris," High Flying Schools, Student Disadvantage and the Logic of NCLB," *American Journal of Education* 113, no. 3 (2007): 367–394.

41. Ibid.

42. Summer learning loss, however, does not appear to be related to students' gender or IQ. See two studies on this: Harris Cooper, Barbara Nye, Kelly Charlton, James Lindsay, and Scott Greathouse, "Summer Learning Loss: The Problem and Some Solutions," *Review of Educational Research* 66, no. 3 (1996): 227–268; Karl L. Alexander, Doris R. Entwisle, and Linda S. Olson Schools, "Achievement, and Inequality: A Seasonal Perspective," *Educational Evaluation and Policy Analysis* 23, no. 2 (2001): 171–191; David T. Burkam, Douglas D. Ready, Valerie E. Lee, and Laura F. LoGerfo, "Social-Class Differences in Summer Learning Between Kindergarten and First Grade: Model Specification and Estimation," *Sociology of Education* 77, no. 1 (2004): 1–31.

43. Gates also had unusual access to a high-end computer in high school, but this happened, according to Gladwell, because parents (not school staff) donated the money. It was on Gates's own initiative, and additional help from a group of parents, that he later gained access to computers at the University of Washington.

44. Thomas Toch, "Measure for Measure," *Washington Monthly*, October–November (2005).

45. Ibid. Some also argue that value-added was not feasible at the time NCLB was being adopted because there was insufficient testing and those scores were not linked to individual students. This is true to a point; however, NCLB put the testing in place and simple school-level growth measures (e.g., subtracting third-grade scores in 2009 from fourth-grade scores in 2010) could have been adopted without individual student identifiers. The snapshot focus of federal accountability measures was therefore not a necessity.

Chapter 2

1. Darling-Hammond has written extensively on this topic; see, for example, Linda Darling-Hammond and Ray Pecheone, "Developing an Internationally Comparable Balanced Assessment System That Supports High-Quality Learning," (paper presented at the National Conference on Next Generation Assessment Systems, Educational Testing Service, Princeton, NJ, 2010).

2. Daniel Koretz, *Measuring Up: What Educational Testing Really Tells Us* (Cambridge, MA: Harvard University Press, 2008); Robert L. Linn, "Assessments and Accountability," *Educational Researcher* 23, no. 9 (2000): 4–14.

3. Researchers call the true amount the *construct* of interest.

4. National Commission on Excellence in Education (NCEE), *A Nation at Risk: The Imperative for Educational Reform* (Washington, DC: US Department of Education, 1983); Richard Kahlenberg, *Tough Liberal: Albert Shanker and the Battles Over Schools, Unions, Race, and Democracy* (New York: Columbia University Press, 2007).

5. *Item response theory* (IRT) is based on the idea that the probability of getting a correct answer for each individual test item or question is determined by certain specific factors, and the estimated probabilities for each item can be used to create a scale for an entire tests. Depending on the type of test item and the particular IRT model used, the probability of a correct response depends on the respondent's ability in the domain being tested, the difficulty of the item, and probability of getting the right answer by guessing. For a more detailed discussion, see for example, Wendy M. Yen and Anne R. Fitzpatrick, "Item Response Theory" in *Educational Measurement*, 3rd edition, ed. Robert L. Linn (New York: American Council of Education/MacMillan, 1989), 111–154.

6. The information on the Colorado assessment is from Derek Briggs and Jonathon Weeks, "The Sensitivity of Value-Added Modeling to the Creation of a Vertical Scale," *Education Finance and Policy* 4, no.4 (2009): 384–414. Tests can also be *backward linked* so that questions from the fifth-grade test show up on the fourth-grade exam or *forward linked* so that the fourth-grade items show up on the fifth-grade test.

7. Specifically, researchers standardize by dividing by the standard deviation of student snapshot within each grade and year. These are sometimes called *z-scores* or *effects sizes*.

8. Richard M. Jaeger, "Certification of Student Competence," in *Educational Measurement*, 3rd edition, ed. Robert L. Linn (New York: American Council of Education/MacMillan, 1989), 485–514.

9. Deria Hall and Shana Kennedy, *Primary Progress, Secondary Challenge* (Washington, DC: Education Trust, 2006).

10. As additional steps to maintain the anonymity of these schools, I am not reporting the years of the data (though they are recent) and I have multiplied the scale scores by an arbitrary number to hide the scale (scales differ across states).

11. This problem has been largely resolved by federal policies requiring at least 95 percent of students in each subgroup to participate in regular assessments. The evidence cited in the text comes from David N. Figlio, "Testing, Crime and Punishment," *Journal of Public Economics* 90, no. 4–5, (2006): 837–851.

12. Jennifer Booher-Jennings, "Below the Bubble: 'Educational Triage' and the Texas Accountability System," *American Educational Research Journal* 42, no.2 (2005): 231–268; Julie B. Cullen, and Randall Reback, "Tinkering Toward Accolades: School Gaming Under a Performance Accountability System," (working paper W12286 , National Bureau of Economic Research, Cambridge, MA, 2006).

13. Charles T. Clotfelter, Helen F. Ladd, Jacob L. Vigdor, and Roger Aliaga Diaz, "Do School Accountability Systems Make It More Difficult for Low-Performing Schools to Attract and Retain High-Quality Teachers?" *Journal of Policy Analysis and Management* 23, no. 2 (2004): 251–271.

14. It is possible that accountability was leading low-performing teachers to leave (an arguably desirable result), which is turn would drive up the overall turnover rate.

However, the accountability system in North Carolina places pressure on all schools to improve, so the only way this would happen is if the accountability policy affected the response of teachers in low-performing schools differently than teachers in high-performing schools.

15. Frederick M. Hess, *Spinning Wheels : The Politics of Urban School Reform* (Washington, DC: Brookings Institution Press, 1999).

16. Anne Duffett, Steve Farkas, and Tom Loveless, *High-Achieving Students in the Era of No Child Left Behind* (Washington, DC: Thomas B. Fordham Institute, 2008).

17. Figlio and Lucas find that arbitrary differences in school performance measures show up in housing values, even among high-scoring schools; see David N. Figlio and Maurice E. Lucas, "What's in a Grade? School Report Cards and the Housing Market," *American Economic Review* 94, no. 3 (2004): 591–604.

18. Thomas Toch, "Measure for Measure," *Washington Monthly*, October–November 2005.

19. Steve Farkas, Jean Johnson, and Anne Duffett, *Stand by Me: What Teachers Really Think About Unions, Merit Pay, and Other Professional Matters* (New York: Public Agenda, 2003).

20. Kara S Finnigan and Betheny Gross, "Do Accountability Policy Sanctions Influence Teacher Motivation? Lessons From Chicago's Low-Performing Schools," *American Educational Research Journal* 44, no. 3 (2007): 594–629.

21. Hess, *Spinning Wheels*.

22. Richard Rothstein, Rebecca Jacobsen, and Tamara Wilder, *Grading Education : Getting Accountability Right* (Washington, DC: Economic Policy Institute; New York: Teachers College Press, 2008).

Chapter 3

1. *Value-added* and *profit* have similar meanings in for-profit businesses. Another term for value-added in this context is *gross margin*, which refers to the difference between revenue and expenses, excluding some costs such as overhead.

2. The business example is not as simple as it sounds. While economists argue that prices are good reflections of the private value to individuals making purchases, prices do not reflect social value. For example, the price of gasoline does not reflect the environmental cost from burning gasoline. The example in the text still works, however, because I focus on profit rather than social efficiency as the goal.

3. This approach to measuring hospital performance is typical. States such as Colorado (http://www.cohospitalquality.org/index.php) have systems very much like that described in the text. Also, see: Bonnie Jerome-D'Emilia and D. DeLia, "Relationship Between Hospital Report Cards & CMS Quality Measures" (poster presentation at the Academy Health Research Meeting, Chicago, 2009).

4. This example of turning away sick patients is based on real data: Rachel M. Werner and David A. Asch, "The Untended Consequences of Publicly Reporting Quality Information," *Journal of the American Medical Association* 293, no. 10 (2005): 1239–1244.

5. Some people refer to performance in terms of the practices and behaviors related to the job.

6. A case can be made for using changes in relative position. See: Dale Ballou, "Test Scaling and Value-Added Measurement," *Education Finance and Policy* 4, no. 4 (2009): 351–383.

7. The states are Alaska, Arizona, Arkansas, Colorado, Delaware, Florida, Iowa, Michigan, Minnesota, Missouri, North Carolina, Ohio, Pennsylvania, Tennessee, and Texas.

8. The careful reader will also notice that this figure implies that proficiency means the same thing across grades and years. I wrote earlier that this is not the case because proficiency is arbitrary. Michael Weiss, "Can we Project Future Proficiency? Examining the Measures Used in the Federal Growth Model Pilot Program" (paper presented at the 2008 Annual Meeting of the Society for Research on Educational Effectiveness, Washington, DC, March 3, 2008).

9. Strictly speaking, this paragraph refers only to *horizontal equating*, though this is usually what the term equating means. *Vertical equating* refers to the comparability of tests across grades and ability levels, which is similar to my definition of scaling.

10. Thomas Toch, "Measure for Measure," *Washington Monthly*, October–November 2005.

11. Daniel F. McCaffrey and Laura S. Hamilton. *Value-Added Assessment in Practice: Lessons from the Pennsylvania Value-Added Assessment System Pilot Project*" (Santa Monica, CA: Rand Corporation, 2007).

Chapter 4

1. Karl L. Alexander, Doris R. Entwisle, and Linda S. Olson, "Schools, Achievement, and Inequality: A Seasonal Perspective," *Educational Evaluation and Policy Analysis*, 23, no. 2 (2001): 171–191.

2. There are actually two ways in which student background can be taken into account. First, each student's background affects his/her own achievement. Second, the composition of the school can affect school dynamics. For example, school may hit a tipping point in terms of how many disadvantaged students attend; beyond a certain percentage, schools may become overwhelmed by the outside factors that they cannot control.

3. I thank Robert Meyer of the Value-Added Research Center for making this point.

4. Here is a second middle ground option: If the concern is about how much emphasis schools place on the achievement of different groups within the school, value-added measures can be designed to weight measures for disadvantaged students. For example, suppose that minority students in a school have growth of 10 points per year while white students in that school had growth of 20 points. If the groups are of equal size, then the average growth for this school is 15 points. However, suppose we give twice as much weight to the minority students; in that case, the school's average

drops because its minority students are not growing as fast. The weighted average for this school would be 13.3. Compared with the simpler, unweighted version, where achievement of all students counts the same, this approach judges the school more harshly (13.3 versus 15) when they do not generate large gains for minorities. This weighting approach would continue to give schools an incentive to focus on the lowest-performing students. (This type of weighting scheme might seem arbitrary; however, current accountability does the same thing in more indirect ways by requiring certain achievement levels for every sub-group.) The example also highlights the fact that the decision to build incentives into performance measures to help particular groups of students is unrelated to decision about whether or not to use value-added.

5. Another possible explanation is that value-added has more random error than snapshots (see chapter 5); however, those school value-added measures have fairly modest random error, so this is not the only explanation. This phenomenon, where student income (and race) are more closely related to snapshot than to growth, is also documented in the following study: Helen F. Ladd and Randall P. Walsh, "Implementing Value-Added Measures of School Effectiveness: Getting the Incentives Right," *Economics of Education Review* 21, no. 1 (2002): 1–17.

6. This is accomplished through a statistical technique called *regression analysis*. Using data from a whole state, this type of analysis estimates the average impact on achievement from having, say, an average class size that is one student smaller than the state average. The "bonuses" described in the text are assigned based on how much small classes appear to contribute to student achievement in the regression analysis.

7. Some of the key studies include Gene Glass and Mary Lee Smith, "Meta-Analysis of Research on Class Size and Achievement," *Educational Evaluation and Policy Analysis* 1, no. 1 (1979): 2—16; Douglas N. Harris, "Class Size and School Size: Taking the Trade-Offs Seriously," in *Brookings Papers on Education Policy*, eds. F.M. Hess and T. Loveless (Washington, DC: Brookings Institution, 2007), 137–161; Alan B. Krueger, "Economic Considerations and Class Size," *Economic Journal* 485, no. 113 (2003): 34–63. Barbara Nye, Larry V. Hedges, and Spyros Konstantopoulos, "The Long-Term Effects of Small Classes: A Five-Year Follow-Up of the Tennessee Class Size Experiment," *Educational Evaluation and Policy Analysis* 21, no. 2 (1999): 127–142.

8. All analysis of Oakville data are conducted using the statistical program STATA. The estimates in figure 4-7 are based on three years of student data. For basic value-added, this means averaging two separate growth measures together. For advanced value-added, the exact same data were used as with basic value-added. The specifics of the statistical methodology are as follows: I used *random effects* as opposed to *fixed effects* to estimate school value-added, though this choice has very little impact on the results. I accounted for differences in the test scale across years by standardizing scores to a mean of zero and standard deviation of one within each grade. Also, I continue taking into account what students bring to the classroom by accounting for prior achievement (allowing for nonlinear effects) but, based on findings from Kane

NOTES

and Staiger, I excluded student fixed effects (see Thomas Kane and Douglas Staiger, "Estimating Teacher Impacts on Student Achievement: An Experimental Evaluation," [working paper 14607, National Bureau of Economic Research, Washington, DC, 2008]).

You might notice that the basic value-added measures differ from the individual student scale score growth reported previously in figure 3-4. This is because the simple growth measures in figure 3-4 are based on only one grade and two years of student data, while the basic value-added measures are based on two grades and three years of data. There is considerable variation in performance within schools and across years, so this change in the results is not surprising. The basic value-added measures in figure 4-7 are more accurate indicators of school performance.

9. I have proposed elsewhere the idea of establishing different levels of value-added based on how much students typically need to learn in order to reach a particular standard such as proficiency. Suppose that a teacher produces 5 test score points more than the typical teacher at a given grade level (a relative comparison) and suppose that students who grow 5 points more than average generally reach proficiency. (This might sound like growth-to-proficiency but it's not. With growth-to-proficiency, every student has to be on track to proficiency, whereas in the combined absolute-relative approach I propose here, the absolute standard is set based on what the TYPICAL students have to learn to be proficient later.) Even in this case, no more than 50 percent of teachers would be above average, so this is still relative.

Chapter 5

1. A second reason for testing all students is that we want to know how each student is performing for reasons that go beyond school performance measures. Most school systems send home test results to the parents of every child.
2. The picture implies that saying two measures are different becomes twice as hard, but the situation is more complicated than this, because the example (including figure 5-1) does not tell us anything about the variance in growth within school A. It only illustrates *average* growth. If the two measures of achievement were unrelated (or independent), then the confidence intervals would roughly double, as the picture implies, but each student's test score error in a given year generally depends on the error in the prior year.
3. This terminology may be confusing because the measurement error corrections are really solving the sampling error problem, not, as I discussed earlier, measurement error in each individual student's test score. But what is relevant here is the measurement error in the school and teacher value-added measures and this is why the term *measurement error correction* is used.
4. See, for example Daniel F. McCaffrey, J. R. Lockwood, Daniel M. Koretz, and Laura S. Hamilton, *Evaluating Value-Added Models for Teacher Accountability*, (Santa Monica, CA: Rand Corporation, 2003).

5. Claude M. Steele and Joshua Aronson, "Stereotype Threat and the Intellectual Test Performance of African Americans," *Journal of Personality and Social Psychology* 69, no.5 (1995):797–811.

6. Steven J. Spencer, Claude M. Steele, and Diane M. Quinn, "Stereotype Threat and Women's Math Performance," *Journal of Experimental Social Psychology* 35 (1999): 4–28.

7. This is not quite accurate from a research standpoint. In reality, the researcher does not conclude that two numbers (for example, performance measures) are the same but just that it cannot be said with confidence that they are different. To researchers, this is an important distinction, but it is not as relevant for policy purposes, since the educational leaders have no choice but to make decisions about which teachers stay and go and which schools are punished and rewarded.

8. This is based on a "two-tailed" statistical test, which assumes we are interested only in whether a number is different from another. In this case, a "one-tailed" test would not be unreasonable since the goal is for a candidate to get to more than 50.1 percent of the vote.

Chapter 6

1. *Time on reading and math:* Jane Hannaway, "Unbounding Rationality: Politics and Policy in a Data Rich System" (Mistifer Lecture, University Council of Education Administration, November 17, 2007; *instructional practices:* Laura S. Hamilton, Brian M. Stecher, Julie A. Marsh, Jennifer S. McCombs, Abby Robyn, Jennifer L. Russell, Scott Naftel, and Heather Barney, *Implementing Standards-Based Accountability Under No Child Left Behind: Responses of Superintendents, Principals, and Teachers in Three States* (Santa Monica, CA: Rand Corporation, 2007); *increased use of test results:* Joseph J. Pedulla, Lisa M. Abrams, George F. Madaus, Michael K. Russell, Miguel A. Ramos, and Jing Miao, *Perceived Effects of State-Mandated Testing Programs on Teaching and Learning: Findings from a National Survey of Teachers* (Chestnut Hill, MA: National Board on Education Testing and Public Policy, 2003).

2. There is a provision for firing all school staff in persistently failing schools (i.e., reconstitution), but this has almost never been carried out.

3. Anthony S. Bryk and Barbara Schneider, *Trust in Schools: A Core Resource for Improvement* (New York: Russell Sage Foundation, 2002), 19. Bryk and Schneider also cite John Dewey as making a similar point.

4. Douglas N. Harris, Stacey Rutledge, William Ingle, and Cynthia Thompson, "Mix and Match: What Principals Really Look for When Hiring Teachers," *Education Finance and Policy* 5 no.2 (2010): 228-246.

5. Ben Ost, "How Do Teachers Improve? The Relative Importance of Specific and General Human Capital" (unpublished manuscript, Cornell University, Ithaca, New York).

6. The same logic applies with school value-added. We could limit comparisons within school districts in order to account for district-level inputs, but many districts especially in northern states are very small.

7. I thank Howard Nelson for drawing my attention to this point.

8. Charles T. Clotfelter, Helen F. Ladd, Jacob L. Vigdor, "Teacher Sorting, Teacher Shopping, and the Assessment of Teacher Effectiveness," *Journal of Human Resources* 41, no. 4 (2006): 778–820.

9. Just as with school value-added, teacher value-added measures were estimated using random effects. The school value-added measure is not a simple average of the teacher value-added measures for two main reasons. First, not every fifth-grade teacher in each school is listed. Second, the school value-added measures include fifth grade and fourth grade.

10. Stacey Rutledge, Douglas N. Harris, and William Ingle, "How Principals Bridge and Buffer the New Demands of Teacher Quality and Accountability: A Mixed Methods Analysis of Teacher Hiring," *American Journal of Education* 116, no. 2 (2010): 211–242.

Chapter 7

1. There is a much larger literature on tracking, but it does not examine the details of the process as Monk does; see David Monk, "Assigning Elementary Pupils to Their Teachers," *Elementary School Journal* 88, no. 2 (1987): 166–187.

2. Jesse Rothstein, "Student Sorting and Bias in Value-Added Estimation: Selection on Observables and Unobservables," *Education Finance and Policy* 4, no. 4 (2009): 537–571.

3. Cory Koedel and Julian R. Betts, "Does Student Sorting Invalidate Value-Added Models of Teacher Effectiveness? An Extended Analysis of the Rothstein Critique" (unpublished working paper, University of Missouri, July 2009).

4. Douglas N. Harris and Tim R. Sass, "Teacher Training, Teacher Quality, and Student Achievement," *Journal of Public Economics* (forthcoming).

5. Thomas Kane and Douglas Staiger, "Estimating Teacher Impacts on Student Achievement: An Experimental Evaluation," (working paper 14607, *National Bureau of Economic Research*, Washington, DC, 2008).

6. There are some limitations of this experiment. As I have pointed out elsewhere, Kane and Staiger studied only those schools where principals were willing to randomly assign students. (See Douglas N. Harris, "Would Accountability Based on Teacher Value-Added Be Smart Policy? Evidence on Statistical Properties and Comparisons with Policy Alternatives," *Education Finance and Policy* 4, no. 4 (2009): 319–350.) It is likely that the principals willing to do so are similar to the ones found in the Monk study who were randomly assigning students to teachers to start with. In that case, comparing the value-added before random assignment to value-added after random assignment is not very meaningful. The real concern is about the accuracy of value-added in schools where students and teachers are not randomly assigned. This Los Angeles experiment is also useful because it provides concrete evidence about what is necessary to account for in the value-added model to produce valid estimates. Kane and Staiger compared different models and found that one or two approaches in particular produced valid results.

7. Harris and Sass, "Teacher Training, Teacher Quality, and Student Achievement."

8. Rolf Blank, "Using Surveys of Enacted Curriculum to Advance Evaluation of Instruction in Relation to Standards," *Peabody Journal of Education* 77, no. 4 (2002): 86–121; Donald Freeman and Andrew Porter, "Do Textbooks Dictate the Content of Mathematics Instruction in Elementary Schools?" *American Educational Research Journal* 26, no. 3 (1989): 403–421.

9. J. R. Lockwood, Daniel F. McCaffrey, "Exploring Student-Teacher Interactions in Longitudinal Achievement Data," *Education Finance and Policy* 4, no. 4 (2009): 439–467.

10. Cory Koedel and Julian Betts, "Value-Added to What? How a Ceiling in the Testing Instrument Influences Value-Added Estimation." (working paper NBER 14778, National Bureau of Economic Research, Cambridge, MA, 2009).

11. Douglas N. Harris and Tim R. Sass, "What Makes for a Good Teacher and Who Can Tell?" (working paper no. 30, National Center for the Analysis of Longitudinal Data in Education Research [CALDER], Urban Institute, Washington, DC, 2009).

12. Brian Jacob and Lars Lefgren "Principals as Agents: Subjective Performance Assessment in Education," *Journal of Labor Economics* 26, no. 1 (2007):101–136.

13. Jonah E. Rockoff, Douglas O. Staiger, Thomas J. Kane, and Eric S. Taylor, "Information and Employee Evaluation: Evidence from a Randomized Intervention in Public Schools," (working paper NBER 16240, National Bureau of Economic Research, Cambridge, MA, 2010).

14. Kane and Staiger, "Estimating Teacher Impacts on Student Achievement."

15. Jacob and Lefgren, "Principals as Agents."

16. Cory Koedel and Julian R. Betts. "Re-Examining the Role of Teacher Quality In the Educational Production Function" (unpublished working paper, University of Missouri, April, 2007).

17. Thomas Kane and Douglas Staiger provide one of the most well known discussions of random errors in school value-added. They report the correlation of about +0.4 between grade-level student growth from one year to the next. This tells us that the reality is somewhere in between zero and perfect correlation. However, their analysis was conducted on cohort-to-cohort growth (see chapter 3) rather than individual student growth; Thomas Kane and Douglas Staiger, "The Promise and Pitfalls of Using Imprecise School Accountability Measures," *Journal of Economic Perspectives* 16, no. 4 (2002): 91–114.

I should emphasize that the number of categories one chooses for these instability analyses influences how much switching there is—because more categories means that every teacher is closer to "passing over the bar" and into another category. So, the combination of more categories and the focus on teachers rather than schools means that we can expect more switching in their analysis compared with the above analysis of schools by Kane and Staiger. Other studies that divided teachers into fewer categories found less switching.

18. These correlations are based on the Koedel and Betts ("Re-Examining the Role of Teacher Quality in the Educational Production Function") results estimating teacher value-added by comparing teachers across schools (see chapter 6 for an explanation about why this is advisable).

    It is not possible to precisely estimate the simple correlation in this case. I placed teachers into categories 1–5 in the same way Koedel and Betts report, using their "across school" specification, which is the one I recommend later. The correlation was 0.37. This is an underestimate because many teachers were probably quite close to the cut points. McCaffrey et al. report similar correlations; see Daniel F. McCaffrey, Tim R. Sass, J. R. Lockwood, and Kata Mihaly, "The Intertemporal Variability of Teacher Effect Estimates," *Education Finance and Policy* 4, no. 4 (2009): 572–606.

19. The instability is actually greater for teachers in the middle groups. For example, only 21 percent of teachers in the second quintile remain in that quintile in the second year. This is because, in the middle, teachers have alternative performance categories on either side whereas the top-and bottom-performers can only move in one direction.

20. McCaffrey et al., "The Intertemporal Variability of Teacher Effect Estimates."

21. Care must be used with this terminology. To say that results are based on a single cohort does not mean a single year. Recall that value-added requires at least two years of data for each student to even calculate growth, and many more years can be incorporated for each student to improve the estimates. This is important because discussions about requirements for value-added measures often focus on the number of years of data when the larger issue is really with the number of students. Focusing on the number of years adds confusion because we could have 6 years worth of data for a single eighth grader. I discuss this further in chapter 10.

22. The improvement in stability when using multiple years of data is partly driven by the fact that the study by McCaffrey and colleagues ("The Intertemporal Variability of Teacher Effect Estimates") uses rolling averages, so that the achievement of some students is included in both estimates. This is reasonable from a policy standpoint. Policymakers might reasonably specify that value-added in 2011 should be based on data from the previous three years (2008, 2009, and 2010). In the next year (2012), this policy would result in value-added based on data from 2009, 2010, and 2011, and the comparison between the 2011 and 2012 measures would constitute rolling averages, with the data from 2009 and 2010 overlapping the two calculations. (Again, note that, by the number of years, I really mean the number of cohorts of students. See note 21.)

23. The above teacher value-added results are based on comparisons of teachers across schools, which I have strongly encouraged. In addition to potentially reducing collaboration, making comparisons within schools makes the value-added measures bounce around even more because any time a teacher switches schools, this changes the basis of comparison. This provides yet another reason for making comparisons across schools.

24. McCaffrey et al. ("The Intertemporal Variability of Teacher Effect Estimates") provide a concise list of the factors: "Nonpersistent changes in performance refer to all sources of year-to-year changes in the estimated impact of a teacher on student achievement, other than sampling errors. These might include variation in the teacher's true performance, 'chemistry' between students within a class, the impact of a disruptive student, test day conditions, matches between the specific test items and the concepts emphasized by the teacher, or any other classroom-level factors that vary across years." (p.578).

25. Dale Ballou, "Test Scaling and Value-Added Measurement," *Education Finance and Policy* 4, no. 4 (2009): 351–383.

26. Because percentiles are not an interval scale, we would want to convert these to NCEs, but the general point still holds.

27. Derek Briggs and Jonathon Weeks, "The Sensitivity of Value-Added Modeling to the Creation of a Vertical Score Scale," *Education Finance and Policy* 4, no. 4 (2009): 384–414.

28. Douglas N. Harris and Tim R. Sass, "The Effects of NBPTS-Certified Teachers on Student Achievement," *Journal of Policy Analysis and Management* 28, no. 1 (2009): 55–80.

29. J. R. Lockwood, Daniel F. McCaffrey, Laura S. Hamilton, Brian Stecher, Vi-Nhuan Le, and Joseph F. Martinez, "The Sensitivity of Value-Added Teacher Effect Estimates to Different Mathematics Achievement Measures," *Journal of Educational Measurement*, 44, no.1 (2007):47–67; John Papay, "Different Tests, Different Answers: The Stability of Teacher Value-Added Estimates across Outcome Measures," *American Education Research Journal* (forthcoming).

30. Robert Gordon, Thomas Kane, and Douglas Staiger, "Identifying Effective Teachers Using Performance on the Job," discussion paper 1, Hamilton Project (Washington, DC: Brookings Institution, 2006); Eric A. Hanushek and Steven G. Rivkin, "How to Improve the Supply of High-Quality Teachers," in *Brookings Papers on Education Policy*, ed. Diane Ravitch (Washington, DC: Brookings Institution, 2004), 7–44; S. Paul Wright, Sandra P. Horn, and William L. Sanders, "Teacher and Classroom Context Effects on Student Achievement: Implications for Teacher Evaluation," *Journal of Personnel Evaluation in Education* 11, no. 1 (April 1997): 57–67.

31. In contrast, there are also some ways in which the variation in teacher value-added may actually be under-stated; specifically, studies generally compare teachers with their colleagues within schools rather than across schools. While it appears that most of the variation in teacher value-added is within schools (that is, all schools have weak teachers), the differences in performance among teachers would be larger if teachers were compared across an entire state.

32. Gordon, Kane, and Staiger, "Identifying Effective Teachers Using Performance on the Job."

33. See, for example: Douglas N. Harris, "Toward Policy-Relevant Benchmarks for Interpreting Effect Sizes: Combining Effects with Costs," *Educational Evaluation and*

Policy Analysis 31, no.1 (2009):3-29; Douglas N. Harris, "Class Size and School Size: Taking the Trade-Offs Seriously," in *Brookings Papers on Education Policy*, eds. F. M. Hess and T. Loveless (Washington, DC: Brookings Institution, 2007), 137–161.

34. For a review of this research, see: Douglas N. Harris and Stacey A. Rutledge. "Models and Predictors of Teacher Effectiveness: A Review of the Evidence with Lessons from (and for) Other Occupations," *Teachers College Record* 112, no. 3 (2010): 914–960.

35. Kane and Staiger, "Estimating Teacher Impacts on Student Achievement: An Experimental Evaluation."

Chapter 8

1. American Educational Research Association, American Psychological Association, and National Council on Measurement in Education, *Standards for Educational and Psychological Testing* (Washington, DC: American Educational Research Association, 1999).

2. Douglas N. Harris, "Point/Counterpoint: Teacher Value-Added: Don't End the Search Before It Starts," *Journal of Policy Analysis and Management* 28, no. 4 (2009): 693–699; Heather Hill, "Evaluating Value-Added Models: A Validity Argument Approach," *Journal of Policy Analysis and Management* 28, no. 4 (2009): 700–709.

3. Donald J. Freeman and Andrew C. Porter, "Do Textbooks Dictate the Content of Mathematics Instruction in Elementary Schools?" *American Educational Research Journal*, 26, no. 3 (1989):403–421.

4. Douglas N. Harris, "The Policy Uses and Policy Validity of Value-Added and Other Teacher Quality Measures," in *Measurement Issues and Assessment for Teacher Quality*, ed. Drew H. Gitomer (Thousand Oaks, CA: Sage Publications, 2008), 99–130.

5. Lorrie A. Shepard, "The Centrality of Test Use and Consequences for Test Validity," *Educational Measurement: Issues and Practice* 16, no. 2 (1997): 5–24.

6. Donald T. Campbell, "Assessing the Impact of Planned Social Change," paper written for the Public Affairs Center, Dartmouth College, Hanover New Hampshire, 1976.

7. Daniel F. McCaffrey and Laura S. Hamilton, *Value-Added Assessment in Practice: Lessons from the Pennsylvania Value-Added Assessment System Pilot Project*, (Santa Monica, CA: Rand Corporation, 2007).

8. Jonah E. Rockoff, Douglas O. Staiger, Thomas J. Kane, and Eric S. Taylor, "Information and Employees Evaluation: Evidence from a Randomized Intervention in Public Schools," (working paper NBER 16240, National Bureau of Economic Research, Cambridge, MA, 2010).

9. Sara Kraemer, Elisabeth Geraghty, Deborah Lindsey, and Cynthia Raven, "School Leadership View of Human and Organizational Factors in Performance Management: A Comparative Analysis of High- and Low-Performing Schools," in *Proceedings of the Human Factors and Ergonomics Society Annual Meeting* (Santa Monica, CA: Human Factors and Ergonomics Society, 2010).

10. Douglas N. Harris, "Are the Naysayers Right?" *Education Week*, March 31, 2010.

11. Douglas N. Harris, "First Things First: Replacing 'Status' Models with Value-Added," (Washington, DC: American Enterprise Institute, 2009).

12. Frederick M. Hess, *Spinning Wheels : The Politics of Urban School Reform* (Washington, DC: Brookings Institution Press, 1999).

13. See, for example, Thomas Dee and Brian Jacob, "The Impact of No Child Left Behind on Student Achievement," (NBER Working Paper no. 15531, National Bureau of Economic Research, Cambridge, MA, 2009); Jaekyung Lee, "Tracking Achievement Gaps and Assessing the Impact of NCLB on the Gaps: An In-depth Look into National and State Reading and Math Outcome Trends," (Cambridge, MA: The Harvard Civil Rights Project, June 2006).

14. Matthew G. Springer, Dale Ballou, Laura Hamilton, *Vi-Nhuan Le, J. R. Lockwood, Daniel McCaffrey, Matthew Pepper, and Brian Stecher, Teacher Pay for Performance: Experimental Evidence from the Project on Incentives in Teaching* (Nashville, TN: National Center on Performance Incentives at Vanderbilt University, 2010).

15. Scott Bauries, "Value-Added Evaluation and Dismissal of Teachers: Two Cents from an Employment Lawyer," *The Edujurist* (blog), http://www.edjurist.com/blog/value-added-evaluation-and-dismissal-of-teachers-two-cents-f.html.

16. Ibid.

17. Ibid.

18. Susan E. Phillips, "*GI Forum v. Texas Education Agency*: Psychometric Evidence," *Applied Measurement in Education* 13, no. 4 (2009): 343–385.

19. Jane Faggen, "Golden Rule Revisited: Introduction," *Educational Measurement: Issues and Practice* 6, no. 2 (1987): 5–8.

20. Stephen G. Sireci and Polly Parker, "Validity on Trial: Psychometric and Legal Conceptualizations of Validity," *Educational Measurement: Issues and Practice* 25, no. 3 (2006): 27–34.

21. *GI Forum et al. v. Texas Education Agency, et al.*, No. SA 97-CA-1278, 1999, U.S. District Court, W.D. of Texas, San Antonio, TX.

Chapter 9

1. For an intuitive summary of the Danielson Framework, TAP, BEST, and CLASS™, see Thomas Toch and Robert Rothman, *Rush to Judgment: Teacher Evaluation in Public Education* (Washington, DC: Education Sector, 2008) .

2. The NBPTS Task Force included Lloyd Bond, Peggy Carr, Linda Darling-Hammond, Frederick Hess, Lee Shulman, and myself, and was headed by Robert Linn.

3. The relationship between NBPTS scores and teacher value-added is based on evidence from the same Los Angeles experiment discussed earlier. See Steven Cantrell, Jon Fullerton, Thomas J. Kane, Douglas O. Staiger, "National Board Certification and Teacher Effectiveness: Evidence From a Random Assignment Experiment," (NBER working paper 14608, National Bureau of Economics Research, Cambridge, MA. 2008).

4. Douglas N. Harris and Tim R. Sass, "What Makes for a Good Teacher and Who

Can Tell?" National Center for the Analysis of Longitudinal Data in Education Research (CALDER) Working Paper #30 (Washington, DC: Urban Institute, 2009).

5. Kolen discusses the creation of composites and *effective weights*, which refer to the portion of the variance of the composite measure owed to each component. Again, even when the components appear to be equally weighted, the effective weights can vary because of unequal variances across components. Michael J. Kolen. "Scaling and Norming," in *Educational Measurement*, 4th edition, ed. Robert L. Brennan (Westport, CT: American Council on Education and Praeger Publishers, 2006).

6. Valen E. Johnson, *Grade Inflation: A Crisis in College Education* (New York: Springer, 2003); James Felton, Peter T. Koper, John Mitchell, and Michael Stinson, "Attractiveness, Easiness and Other Issues: Student Evaluations of Professors on Ratemyprofessors.com," *Assessment & Evaluation in Higher Education* 33, no. 1 (2008):45–61.

7. Leslie Santee Siskin, "Outside the Core: Accountability in Tested and Untested Subjects," in *The New Accountability: High Schools and High-Stakes Testing*, eds. Martin Carnoy, Richard Elmore, and Leslie Santee Siskin (New York: Routledge Falmer, 2003), 87–98.

8. Douglas N. Harris and Tim R. Sass, "Teacher Training, Teacher Quality, and Student Achievement," *Journal of Public Economics* (forthcoming).

9. Zeyu Xu, Jane Hannaway, and Colin Taylor, "Making a Difference? The Effects of Teach for America in High School," (working paper 17, Center for Analysis of Longitudinal Data in Education Research [CALDER], Urban Institute, Washington, DC, 2007).

10. Douglas N. Harris and Tim R. Sass. "The Effects of NBPTS-certified Teachers on Student Achievement." *Journal of Policy Analysis and Management* 28, no. 1 (2009): 55–80.

11. I thank Howard Nelson of the American Federation of Teachers for providing these examples.

12. William L. Sanders and Sandra P. Horn, "Research Findings from the Tennessee Value-Added Assessment System (TVAAS) Database: Implications for Educational Evaluation and Research," *Journal of Personnel Evaluation in Education* 12, no. 3 (1998):247–256.

13. Margaret DeLacy, "Summary and Comments on the studies produced by the Tennessee Value Added Assessment System (TVAAS)," December 11, 1999, Links for Portland Parents of Talented and Gifted Children: http://www.tagpdx.org/tvaas.htm.

14. R. Darrell Bock and Richard G. Wolfe, "A Review and Analysis of the Tennessee Value-Added Assessment System," Office of Education Accountability, State of Tennessee (1996).

15. William. J. Webster and Robert L. Mendro, "The Dallas Value-Added Accountability System," in *Grading Teachers, Grading Schools: Is Student Achievement a Valid Evaluation Measure?* ed. Jason Millman (Thousand Oaks, CA: Corwin, 1999), 81–99.

16. Center for Educator Compensation Reform, "Dallas Principal and Teacher Incentive Pay Program" (Washington, DC, 2006), http://www.cecr.ed.gov/search.cfm.

17. Helen F. Ladd, "The Dallas School Accountability and Incentive Program: An Evaluation of its Impacts on Student Outcomes," *Economics of Education Review* 18, no. 1 (1999): 1–16.

18. Edward W. Wiley, *A Practitioner's Guide to Value Added Assessment*. (Boulder, CO: University of Colorado at Boulder, 2006).

19. The Houston Independent School District provides reports on teacher value-added to school leaders and teachers and these are used for professional development, diagnostic, and school improvement purposes. Principals can provide low-scoring teachers with focused professional development, mentoring, or a change in teaching assignment.

20. Terry B. Grier, "Memorandum to the Houston School Board," May, 28, 2010, http://www.houstonisd.org/portal/site/ResearchAccountability/.

21. Claudia Wallis, "How to Make Great Teachers," *Time*, February 13, 2008, http://www.time.com/time/nation/article/0,8599,1713174-5,00.html.

22. The inspectors are based in the national Office for Standards in Education, Children's Services and Skills (Ofsted), a nonministerial government department of Her Majesty's Chief Inspector of Schools In England (HMCI). Ofsted inspects schools regularly and often intervenes in those judged to be low-performing. There are other local and national agencies responsible for other school monitoring activities, but only Ofsted intervenes in schools. The degree to which value-added is weighed has varied somewhat over time.

23. Sara Kraemer, Elisabeth Geraghty, Deborah Lindsey, and Cynthia Raven, "School Leadership View of Human and Organizational Factors in Performance Management: A Comparative Analysis of High- and Low-Performing Schools," in *Proceedings of the Human Factors and Ergonomics Society Annual Meeting* (Santa Monica, CA: Human Factors and Ergonomics Society, 2010).

Chapter 10

1. Douglas N. Harris and Tim R. Sass, "The Effects Of NBPTS-Certified Teachers on Student Achievement," *Journal of Policy Analysis and Management* 28, no. 1 (2009): 55–80.

2. Douglas N. Harris and Lori Taylor, *The Resource Costs of Standards, Assessments, and Accountability* (Washington DC: A Final Report to the National Research Council. National Research Council, 2008), http://www7.nationalacademies.org/cfe/State_Standards_Workshop_1_Agenda.html.

3. The absence of student-teacher data linkages would only preclude evaluation of programs targeted to specific teachers. If a program were implemented throughout an entire school, then the student data would only have to be linked to the school rather than to individual teachers. See Douglas N. Harris, "Breaking the Logjam on Teacher 'Value-Added,'" *Education Week*, June 16, 2008.

4. See, for example, the Data Quality Campaign, http://www.dataqualitycampaign.org/.

5. NCLB permits an exemption for students who are in their first year in the United

States. These students do not have to take the language arts/reading assessment, but they do have to take the math assessment. However, districts do not have to use their math scores when calculating AYP.

6. Amy Elledge, Kerstin Carlson Le Floch, James Taylor, and Lindsay Anderson, *State and Local Implementation of the No Child Behind Act: Volume 5-Implementation of the One Percent Rule and Two Percent Interim Policy Options* (Washington, DC: US Department of Education, 2009).

7. Furthermore, changes in NCLB now permit districts to use proficient/advanced scores of up to 2 percent of the students whose scores are based on modified achievement standards that are aligned with content standards. This alternate assessment option is not intended for students who have the most severe cognitive disabilities, but for those who nonetheless would not be expected to attain grade-level proficiency within the school year.

8. I thank Gary Cook for this observation and for much of the information in this discussion of ELL students.

9. Office of Elementary and Secondary Education, *Assessment and Accountability for Recently Arrived Former Limited English Language Proficient (LEP) Students* (Washington, DC: US Department of Education, 2007).

10. Some value-added models use all the data available even if information is missing for some students. For models that do not do so, an alternative approach is to "impute" missing data—that is, to make an estimate of what the missing scores probably were based on the information we do have.

11. Some researchers also use a second correction for measurement, which involves accounting for more than one year of prior scores, as well as scores in other subjects. See, for example, Helen F. Ladd and Randall P. Walsh, "Implementing Value-Added Measures of School Effectiveness: Getting the Incentives Right," *Economics of Education Review* 21, no. 1 (2002): 1–17.

12. Confidence intervals are more difficult to calculate after the estimates have been shrunken. To see why, note that the shrinkage process is based on the same information used to calculate the standard errors.

13. Damian W. Betebenner, "Norm- and Criterion-Referenced Student Growth," *Educational Measurement: Issues and Practice* 28, no. 4 (2009): 42–51.

Chapter 11

1. This process of placing both measures on a 0—100 scale and averaging is not as simple as it might seem. See chapter 9.

2. This is a paraphrase of a comment made to me by Robert Meyer of the University of Wisconsin Value-Added Research Center.

3. Anthony S. Bryk, Penny Bender Sebring, Elaine Allensworth, Stuart Luppescu, and John Q. Easton, *Organizing Schools for Improvement: Lessons from Chicago* (Chicago: University of Chicago Press, 2010).

4. Douglas N. Harris, *First Things First: Replacing 'Status' Models with Value-Added* (Washington, DC: American Enterprise Institute, 2009). In this brief, I talked about *attainment* or *snapshots* as being the basis for the vertical axis, rather than family income. The practical results of these two alternatives would be very similar, given what I have shown about the tight relationship between poverty and snapshots, but the logic of the argument is clearer when discussing this in terms of student income.

5. Douglas N. Harris, "High Flying Schools, Student Disadvantage and the Logic of NCLB," *American Journal of Education* 113, no. 3 (2007): 367–394.

Acknowledgments

I have been thinking, writing, and teaching about value-added for more than fifteen years, but it might never have occurred to me to write a book about it all—until Rick Hess mentioned the idea. He was quite right in arguing that there were lots of useful value-added reports for statisticians and researchers, but none for the policy makers who design accountability systems or the educators who are evaluated by those systems. I thank him for planting the seed in my mind and for suggesting Harvard Education Press (HEP). My editor, Caroline Chauncey, provided excellent guidance every step of the way, and Marcy Barnes, Jeffrey Perkins, and no doubt countless others at HEP did excellent work editing and transforming what I sent into a finished product.

My aim was to make this book accessible to educators and policy makers, but still accurate and credible to researchers. Therefore, I sought input from people of a wide variety of backgrounds and perspectives—from schoolteachers to journalists and fellow economists. Adam Gamoran, Daniel Koretz, and David Plank provided important early guidance. I particularly owe much to those who read drafts of the entire manuscript: Chris Erickson, David Figlio, Adam Gamoran, Emily Harford, Debbi Harris, Deborah Lindsey, Michael McPherson, Howard Nelson, and David Plank. Dale Ballou, Gary Cook, Helen Evans, Liam Goldrick, Sara Goldrick-Rab, Mary Kennedy, Robert Linn, Sandy Kress, Harvin Moore, Matthew Springer, and Carla Stevens provided important feedback on particular chapters. I thank Heather Hill for our lively and friendly debate about value added, which is summarized in chapter 8—a debate that continues today.

Howard Nelson not only provided valuable feedback, but also initiated discussions with his colleagues at the American Federation of Teachers (AFT). I have known and worked with many at the AFT over the years and, while we have not always agreed with each other, I always appreciate the thoughtfulness of our debates. Moreover, the AFT has shown openness to using value-added and is a formal partner in many of the programs being implemented around the country. Partly for these reasons, I asked Randi Weingarten to write the foreword for the book. We share both appreciation for the potential of value-added and concerns about its potential misuses. Also, few have grappled with the practical, political, and policy realities more than Randi has, so I knew she would add an important perspective and voice to the discussion. Many thanks to Randi and everyone at AFT.

The University of Wisconsin Value-Added Research Center (VARC) is one of the nation's leading institutions providing value-added measures, technical assistance, and professional development to state and school districts across the country. Fortunately for me, VARC is located just down the hall from my office. I would like to thank VARC's director, Robert Meyer, and Chris Thorn for many useful conversations and for facilitating meetings with VARC staff at which I presented chapter drafts and discussed key points. I would especially like to thank staff members: Sarah Archibald, Michael Christian, Lisa Geraghty, Curtis Jones, Ernie Morgan, Sara Kraemer, Sean McGlaughlin, Jeff Watson, and Peter Witham.

I have given many presentations and workshops on value-added. The feedback and questions I received have been invaluable in helping me decide what the book should include and how to discuss certain issues. I especially thank Andrea Hodge and participants in the Rice Education Entrepreneurship Program (REEP); Jon Fullerton and participants in the Harvard Strategic Data Project fellows program, David Plank and participants in a presentation sponsored by Policy Analysis for California Education (PACE), Gary Estes and the WestEd board of directors, and Angel Barrett and the Elementary Principals Organization of the Los Angeles Unified School District (LAUSD).

I have had several opportunities to participate in discussions among policy makers that have influenced my thinking on some of the policy proposals in chapters 9 and 10. I thank participants in events organized by EdVoice, the National Council of State Legislators, the National Governors Association, the New York and Rhode Island Federation of Teachers, and several of the federal regional laboratories. I worked with Linda Darling-Hammond in writing a white paper about school value-added measures for the Obama transition team. Derek Briggs, Michael

Weiss, and I wrote a policy brief at the request of the Obama Administration regarding school value-added measures in the context of the Elementary and Secondary Education (ESEA) reauthorization. Adam Gamoran, Dan McCaffrey, and I also had extensive discussions about policy recommendations, which no doubt influenced my thinking in ways not explicitly noted.

Much of my own research on value added has been in collaboration with Tim Sass. If not for Tim, I might not have engaged in value-added research in quite the same way. In 2008, I chaired the National Conferences on Value-Added, with cochairs Adam Gamoran and Stephen Raudenbush, in which we commissioned new research and facilitated a rich and lively discussion among almost all of the researchers cited in chapter 7.

Regina Figueiredo-Brown provided outstanding research assistance. In addition, her background as a school principal proved invaluable in the editing process as she read and provided useful comments on multiple versions of the entire manuscript. Drew Anderson provided important research assistance in the analysis of the Oakville data. I thank him and the district that provided the data.

My wife, Debbi Harris, is a former middle school science teacher and outstanding education scholar. She has shaped my thinking about education in general and value-added, in particular. She also served as an important sounding board for my ideas as I was developing the manuscript, some of which she persuasively argued were not so sound. She provided the most detailed edits on issues large and small throughout the entire manuscript as I neared completion (or, really, as I *thought* I was nearing completion!). Debbi and my daughters, Norah and Lyndsey, put up with my working through long hours, especially in the last two months of writing. They bring greater joy to my life than I am able to express even to them.

I owe much to my parents, brothers, and other family members. Anyone who knows me well knows that I am close to all of them. They taught me to try and leave the world a little better than the way I found it. Hopefully, this book will do that in some small way, by improving teaching and learning in our nation's schools. I especially hope that the millions of educators across the country who serve our nation's students will find the book useful. The vast majority work long hours for little pay and often even less appreciation. They deserve a better accountability system among many other things.

I apologize if I have left anyone out. Also, it goes without saying that all remaining errors and problems are solely my responsibility.

About the Author

Douglas N. Harris is Associate Professor of Educational Policy and Public Affairs at the University of Wisconsin at Madison. His more than two dozen articles about teachers and accountability have been published in economics and education journals and cited in the national media, including CNN, *Education Week*, the *New York Times*, the *Washington Post*, and the *Wall Street Journal*. He co-chaired the 2008 National Conferences on Value-Added in Madison, Wisconsin, and Washington, DC. He is a regular adviser to members of Congress, governors, school districts, and other education policymakers on value-added and other educational policy issues. In addition to his research and teaching, he is a former school board member. He and his wife, Debbi, are the parents of two daughters.

Index

absolute comparisons, 86
absolute standards of performance, 85–87
  academic skills, 23, 228
  Accelerating Student Progress,
    Increasing Results and
    Expectations. *See* ASPIRE
    (Accelerating Student Progress,
    Increasing Results and
    Expectations)
  accountability, 1, 164
  academic skills, 228
  alignment, 226
  balance, 226
  capacity, 224–226
  cardinal rule of, 4–6–7, 62
  cohort-to-cohort growth, 60
  conflict and, 2
  controllable factors, 4, 222
  credentialing as substitute for, 16–21
  criterion-referenced tests, 34
  cronyism, 227
  differentiation, 224–226
  education, 164
  failing to meet standards, 44–45
  focusing attention on schools, 172
  high-stakes responses, 227
  improving methods of, 8
  ineffective teachers, 5
  inequities in pay, 227
  lack of, 20, 22–23
  minimum competency testing, 227
  more *versus* less, 1
  NCLB (No Child Left Behind), 1
  not useful for, 219
  outside of control factors, 7
  partly within control factors, 81
  performance measures, 5–6, 11, 94, 171
  personal, 13
  policies under, 1

  politics, 227–228
  positive roles, 12–14
  principals, 1
  private sector, 12
  public sector, 12
  results, 1
  rewards and measured performance, 5
  school performance focus, 1
  school report cards, 227
  schools, 109
  school value-added measures, 9
  standardized testing, 227
  struggle to get right, 227
  student test scores, 24
  teachers, 1, 46, 110, 174
  test-based, 6, 11, 20, 31, 133
  U.S financial crisis (2008), 14–16
  value-added measures, 3, 189, 200
  well-rounded, 224–227
accountability system
  challenge, 215
  counterproductive, 2
  designing, 6, 169
  messages, 12–13
  mission, 12–13
  percentage of proficient students, 59
  personal accountability, 12–13
  point-in-time test scores, 28
  systematic errors, 90
  systemic reforms, 163–164
  undermining collaboration, 115
achievement
  actual, 73, 83
  family factors, 101–102
  growth, 54
  high-income and low-income students,
    25–26
  outside of school control factors, 26
  predicted, 73, 83

performance management, 188
performance measures, 11
  absolute scale measures, 175
  accountability, 5, 6
  averaging across students, 100
  challenge, 215
  combining value-added measures with
    other measures, 175–180
  compensation, 161
  corruption of, 161
  defining, 14
  difficulties, 21
  educationally meaningful, 104
  errors, 108
  family factors, 101–102
  formative information about
    improvement, 175
  frameworks for evaluating, 176
  free-rider problem, 12
  group, 12
  improved, 29, 161
  inaccuracy, 24
  learning after testing, 207
  measurement error, 101
  messages, 12–13
  mission, 12–13
  personal accountability, 12–13
  positive roles, 12–14
  practice and, 181–182
  practices facilitating creativity, 175
  prediction, 72
  random errors, 90, 110, 175
  snapshots, 102, 218
  stakes proportional to quality of, 161
  starting-gate inequalities, 24–27
  student growth, 67
  systematic errors, 90, 110
  tenure, 161
  uncontrollable factors, 78
performance standards, 37–40, 228
  arbitrary, 38–39, 61, 217
  bubble kids, 57
  crudeness, 39
  discarding valuable information, 39, 57
  growth, 56–59

minimum competency testing, 40
  percent proficient, 56–57
  proficiency, 37–40
  random errors, 107
  setting, 38
  state definitions of proficiency, 38–39
personal accountability, 12–13
perverse incentives, 183–184
pilot programs, 174
point-in-time test scores, 28
policy makers
  applying researcher standards to
    alternatives, 158
  decision making, 157
  initial student achievement, 51
  insufficient attention to education, 2
  outmoded rules and bureaucracy, 23
  type II errors, 157
  validity, 157–158
  value-added measures, 151, 157–158
policy validity, 161
politics and staffing, 20
populations, 93
portfolios, 91
practices, evaluating effective, 184–188
practitioners perspective, 157–158
predicted achievement, 73
predictions
  accuracy, 72
  class size, 79–80
  from comparison, 72–74
  performance measurement, 72
  race and income basis, 75
  student growth focus, 72–73
  uncontrollable resources, 78–82
  value-added measures, 73–74
principals
  accountability, 1
  evaluations, 135–138
  factors beyond control of, 5, 226
  randomly assigning teachers, 130–131
  responsibilities, 122–123
  rules and compliance, 162–163
  staffing decisions, 123
  student tracking, 129–130